The Quest for Graham Greene

W. J. WEST

PHŒNIX

A Phoenix Paperback
First published in Great Britain by Weidenfeld & Nicolson in 1997
This paperback edition published in 1998 by Phoenix,
a division of Orion Books Ltd,
Orion House, 5 Upper St Martin's Lane,
London WC2H 9EA

A CIP catalogue record for this book
is available from the British Library.

ISBN: 0 75380 136 1

Printed and bound in Great Britain by
The Guernsey Press Co. Ltd, Guernsey, Channel Islands.

W. J. West was born in 1942. He was educated at a Benedictine school in Ealing and later attended the Architectural Association School of Architecture and Brunel University. Before becoming a full-time author, he engaged in a variety of activities including a spell on the footplate as a steam fireman. He first became aware of the complexities of Graham Greene's life whilst writing *Truth Betrayed*, a study of politics and propaganda.

By the same author

Orwell: The War Broadcasts
Truth Betrayed: Radio Politics Between the Wars
The Strange Rise of Semi-Literate England

For my mother Anne West,
who also lived through
the Blitz around
the Tottenham Court Road

Contents

Acknowledgements

First I wish to thank Alan Randall of Ealing who kindly granted me access to the James Hadley Chase papers he holds, and gave me every assistance in the two years following their discovery. Next I thank my editor and publisher Rebecca Wilson who saw immediately the significance of what had been found and has given the project continued support and advice throughout. Anyone writing about Graham Greene is profoundly indebted to the ground-breaking work of Professor Norman Sherry and I add my thanks and gratitude for his comments. Of the institutions that have given help on research that followed the original discovery of new Greene material I wish particularly to thank Boston College, Boston, Massachusetts which holds the great part of Graham Greene's private papers and his annotated library, and the Harry Ransom Humanities Research Center at the University of Texas at Austin whose great range of Greene material complements the Boston College Holdings.

It is inevitable in a book such as this which comes at a subject from an entirely original angle that many people have given assistance beyond that normally requested. I should like to thank the staff at the following institutions and organisations who are not separately mentioned later: Balliol College, Oxford, Blackfriars, Oxford, Bloomsbury Book Auctions, The Cabinet Office, The Camera Press Archives, Companies House, Dominic Winter Book Auctions, The Dominican Archives, Edinburgh, Durrants Press Cutting Agency, Exeter University Library, The Hulton Getty Picture Library, The Independent Labour Party Archives at the London School of Economics, The Law Society, London University Library, The Orwell Archives at University College London, The Mervyn Peake Society,

The National Museum of Labour History, The Public Records Office, Kew, the Archives of the Religious Society of Friends in Britain, Somerset House, Sotheby's Auctioneers, *The Tablet, The Times, The Times Literary Supplement*, Westminster Library Leicester Square and Charing Cross branches, The University of the Witwatersrand, and lastly, but not least, the staff of the bookshops in Britain and America from Dillons in London's Gower Street to the Brattle Book Shop in Boston.

Personal thanks are due to Eric Ambler, Mulk Raj Anand, Mrs L. D. Arnott, Father Bede Bailey, Elizabeth Beresford, Ed Breslin, Nigel Burwood, Will Cantopher, Professor R. W. Charlton, Leon Corral, Lady Crosthwaite-Eyre, Giles de la Mare, Nicholas Dennys, Quinten Falk, Andrew Flynn, Gill Furlong, Mrs Vivien Greene, George Greenfield, Sir Alec Guinness, John Hale, Anna Haycraft, Cathy Henderson, Frank Herrmann, Jasper Humphreys, John Kirkpatrick, curator at the Harry Ransom Humanities Research Center, Richard Ingrams, George Johnson, Joseph Keith, my agent Sonia Land, Stuart Leggatt, Andrew Lycett, T. D. Mathew, Michael Meyer, Gilbert McNeill-Moss, Christina Odone, Dr Robert K. O'Neill, librarian at Boston College, Dr Richard W. Oram, Mrs N. M. Paget, Robert Peberdy, Harold Pinter, Professor Ben Pimlott, Anthony Powell, Christopher Reed, Michael Richey, Kate Robertson, Julian Rota, Amanda Saunders, Barbara Smith LaBorde, Frank Surry, Father Francis Sweeney, Geoffrey Wansell, Barry Webb, Tom West, Richard West, John Wilkins, Nigel Williams, Dominic Winter, Jon Wynne-Tyson, Rob Vickers and Philip Youren. There are many others whom I have not mentioned here; I owe them all a debt of gratitude and must also add that the opinions expressed here are entirely my own and that the responsibility for the facts and references I have used is also mine alone.

Preface

Ealing, Catholic Ealing, seems an unlikely place to embark on a quest for Graham Greene. What connection could there be? Scobie in *The Heart of the Matter* reflects on his marriage in Ealing and the atmosphere then – an almost forgotten echo of the time when Ealing was the queen of the suburbs. But the links are still there. My only meeting with Shane Leslie, to whom A. J. A. Symons dedicated *The Quest for Corvo*, was in Ealing. Leslie spoke of that book briefly, but dwelt more on the happy memories of his prep school days there which he said he far preferred to Eton where he was later to go. At the same time, René Raymond lived nearby with his family while his father worked in Calcutta establishing the Raymond Research Institute. Forty years later, with Shane Leslie and René Raymond both dead, the bulk of the family papers of that Raymond branch surfaced in Ealing, and it was my discovery of these that began this quest.

Temporarily stored in the basement of premises off Ealing's Haven Green, the papers included over 500 letters, covering a period of over sixty years, written by René Raymond, better known as James Hadley Chase, the author of *No Orchids for Miss Blandish*. Reading through them it was soon obvious that he had known Graham Greene since the last days of the Second World War and for a long time afterwards. Their paths crossed repeatedly over the next forty years, particularly in the 1960s, when both fell foul of a Mafia scam. Quite by chance both men were living in the same small Swiss village of Corseaux-sur-Vevey when they died, Chase in 1985, Greene in 1991.

At first the material seemed worth an article. A letter to the authorised biographer Professor Norman Sherry revealed that the friendship of the two men had hitherto been unknown. More importantly the role played by the Mafia problem in Greene's life, which had led to his exile, was also entirely unknown. Chase had been much closer to the frontman for the operation, another Calcutta man Tom Roe, a solicitor honoured with a CBE for his services to charity. The revelations about who was behind Greene's loss and about the damage done to other friends of Greene, particularly Charlie Chaplin and Noël Coward, who had also been clients of Roe, suggested that there was more to be discovered. The quest for Greene had begun, and this book is the first result.

Memories of Shane Leslie and A. J. A. Symons' earlier book, which he subtitled *An Experiment in Biography*, crowded in and filled that basement room with the papers and books of this forgotten branch of a great family. Greene himself was a Raymond through his mother, and his brother Raymond, who played a significant part in Greene's own life and fiction, was named after her family. And, like Corvo, Greene was a Catholic convert. But the parallels were soon exhausted. Even so, the two quests had curious similarities, with information emerging from entirely unexpected sources at least as often as it came from more obvious paths.

When Symons began his quest, Corvo was a forgotten figure except amongst a few literary admirers of his novels. Greene, however, had been one of the most talked-of English novelists for most of his life. After his death there had been a brief lull as the collective consciousness of readers and literati tested whether his reputation was of the more evanescent kind which springs from the living personality of the author. That period safely over, his name once more assumed cult status. How could there be more to find out about the man? Greene had written two volumes of autobiography, and an authorised biographer had been appointed who had spent more than twenty years following Greene's extensive travels and combing the archives of institutions around the world that held Greene material.

But the answer to this obvious question was found in the basement in Ealing. Here was a friendship extending across nearly half a century which had been kept from the biographer and had not been known to anyone else interested in Greene. It was not the only link of that kind which emerged quite soon after my quest had begun.

Perhaps the most interesting of these was discovered through a Catholic priest, Father Denys Lucas, whom I had known in the 1950s. It seemed that the Catholic world which Greene had inhabited, largely in Spain for the last quarter of his life had its parallels in England.

In the preface to the Folio Society edition of *The Quest for Corvo* Shane Leslie, himself an author and bibliophile, called Symons a dilettante. That was also a word used by a colleague of Greene's in his secret work for the Foreign Office, who remarked in retrospect that Greene 'was inclined to adopt a somewhat "dilettante" approach to intelligence requirements, a cheerful, enterprising and unconventional traveller.'[1] But the casual exterior often gave Greene an advantage over more conventional cloak-and-dagger operatives. His colleague also candidly remarked: 'His visits to Indo-China proved of assistance to the local station.'[2] And that laconic understatement, which included in its embrace personal interviews with Ho Chi Minh and other leaders, in South Vietnam as well as North, reveals a central reason why much still remained to be discovered about Greene. He was bound by secrecy in many of the matters about which he wrote for the press or which he transmuted into his fiction. Corvo's secrets were personal ones, and the difficulties A. J. A. Symons encountered in his quest were simply caused by the embarrassment which people felt about their association with so strange a man. Greene's secrets were important politically as well as personally. What he knew related to some of the most dangerous episodes in a century during which espionage turned from a dilettante affair into a deadly earnest one.

The very fact that Greene had associations with the intelligence services might well have damaged his standing with people to whom, as an author, he genuinely wished to talk, particularly behind the Iron Curtain or in South America. And it is important to understand that Greene did not work for MI6 beyond his full-time service in that organisation during the war. He simply liaised through his old colleagues, and was sometimes regarded as more than a little difficult to control.

In much the same way as Greene's intelligence life often coincided with his literary and personal activities, before the war his writing was closely linked to authors, well known at the time, who had been forgotten when fame really claimed him. The name J. D. Beresford means little or nothing to today's readers, but he was Greene's idol as a teenager, an author on whom he consciously modelled himself. Greene did not disown Beresford and mentioned him in passing in his autobiography, referring for example to the effect Beresford's novel *Revolution* had on him as a youth. But no biographer had followed this trail, and amongst the more pleasurable bypaths in my quest for Greene was a visit to Alderney, where Beresford's daughter now lives.

Before the war Greene was himself a great admirer of A. J. A. Symons and his biography of Corvo. His collected essays, which he chose with some care, contained three essays on Corvo, grouped together in one section. Only Henry James, whose story of another literary quest, 'The Figure in the Carpet', was the true predecessor of Symons' book, received a greater accolade from Greene. There is no essay by him on Corvo more recent than 1935 and no sign that Greene thought of his own life as presenting a quarry for a future biographer. But Professor Sherry found, as I did, that his life was just that. More importantly, the normal distinction between fiction and reality repeatedly broke down in Greene's work. In the second volume of his biography Sherry remarked:

> Novels declare themselves as fictions not as personal histories, though they mine the personal terrain. Greene always felt that so long as he presented his intimate experiences as fictions his secrets would remain unrecognised, and this appealed to his guarded nature.[3]

Sherry went on to discuss the consequences of this for Greene's novel *The Heart of the Matter*. In this novel and others Greene relied on the loyalty of friends and on the secrecy essential in his professional life to maintain the illusion that his fiction was simply fiction and nothing more.

This book will for the first time draw together many facets of the life of this secret man, his Catholic background as well as his political espionage and his literary activity, and will show how they stemmed directly from his life. The figure that emerges from the pattern in the carpet is a profoundly human one, and a living answer to the challenges of the terrible century which undid so many.

In looking at Greene's entire life the appearance of new material and the discovery of new perspectives were not uniformly spread over every decade, nor did they touch every one of his many books. There is a focus in this book on hitherto unknown areas which have resisted previous biographers' enquiries. The influence of Zoe Richmond, the serious political background to some of Greene's earlier 'entertainments' – a term Greene put on the title-pages of his more popular books – his involvement with the communist cell at Oxford as an undergraduate – a shock for those who thought all that sort of thing began at Cambridge a decade later – the life of his cousin Ben Greene, the influence of the forgotten novelist J. D. Beresford: themes such as these are examined as fresh evidence appeared on the quest. In other areas, such as those involving travel and travel books, with Greene's journeys to Mexico and Liberia, Kenya or Cuba full investigation has been carried out over two decades by Norman Sherry. There are similar insights into Greene's personal life. A great deal is uncovered here about Dorothy Glover and Greene's relationship to her, about Greene's friendship with James Hadley Chase and his connection to *The Third Man* and most importantly about Greene's involvement with Kim Philby.

CHAPTER ONE

Psychoanalysis and the Birth of an Author

My quest for Graham Greene often resembled one of his own favourite detective stories, as I came upon tantalising clues that he had himself planted. After a while it was possible to recognise them, a hint, a passing off of something as unimportant which in reality yielded vital insights. Not the least significant of them related to the early days of his life. In the volume of his autobiography called *A Sort of Life* Greene mentioned that a novel by J. D. Beresford, *Revolution*, had influenced him as a teenager. Quite by chance I had a copy of this book, which was filled with echoes of the preoccupations evident in Greene's fiction. How well had he known Beresford? Where were Beresford's papers?

A quick check on the chronology of the main events in Greene's life showed that he had known Beresford when the older man was actually writing the book, a brilliant success in its time that attracted reviews from figures now far more famous than he, amongst them Virginia Woolf. It seemed essential to trace Beresford's family and friends. But all enquiries at literary agents and publishers were fruitless; all his books, over sixty of them, were out of print and he was as forgotten as it is possible for an author to be. The key that allowed entry into his world came from looking at the list of his books in the British Library Catalogue. Some of these had been written in collaboration with Esme Wynne-Tyson, an early friend of Noël Coward's. But there were entries also for her son Jon Wynne-Tyson, his books published by the small press that he still ran, Centaur Press. He was able to provide much vital information, for J. D. Beresford had effectively been his step-father and he possessed many of the late author's surviving papers, most usefully for the later stages of the quest his small appointment books. He was also a fount of information about the family and gave an introduction to Beresford's daughter Elizabeth, who had become famous in her own right as the author of a long and successful series of children's television programmes, *The Wombles*.

The flight to Alderney where Elizabeth Beresford lives was almost an adventure in itself. With four other passengers in a very small plane whose body was no wider than a canoe, it seemed that the clouds were there to be reached out for and touched. From the air the island looked scarcely large enough for a plane to land. In the Beresford home were copies of all his books and of those written by others in his circle, including complete sets of those by Walter de la Mare, his lifelong friend, and ecstatically inscribed copies of Henry Williamson books. Elizabeth Beresford and her daughter provided more memories about someone whom they thought had been absurdly and unjustly neglected. There was also a collection of photographs, including that of Zoe Richmond illustrated here. The quest for Greene had begun in earnest.

Graham Greene was born on 2 October 1904 in Berkhamsted, where his father Charles was headmaster of the public school. He was part of the last generation in England to regard large families as the norm, as they had been for countless generations. He had two elder brothers, Herbert and Raymond, an elder sister Molly, a younger brother Hugh and a younger sister Elizabeth. But the family connection with Berkhamsted did not end there; on the other side of the town lived his uncle Edward and his family. They were known as the rich Greenes and the house had no fewer than twenty-four servants. The wealth came from South America, mainly Brazilian coffee. Edward Greene had got married in Brazil to a German girl whose family, like himself, were economic migrants. He had been brilliantly successful and the family he established was as numerous as the intellectual Greenes – as Charles Greene's family was known.

Three of Greene's cousins became involved in his life at varying times: Ben Greene, a giant at six foot eight inches, whose religious and political views were to have a great effect on Greene in the early 1920s and later in the war; Barbara Greene, with whom Greene travelled to Liberia in 1935, but who spent the war in Germany with her husband Count Strachwitz; and 'Tooter', Edward Greene, with whom he also travelled.

But the Greene family was not confined to Berkhamsted. Its money originally came from brewing, and their family firm Greene King still thrives. The West Indian plantations, which mainly grew sugar, an early source of their wealth, were still remembered in Greene's childhood. When Greene visited St Kitts in the Leeward Islands he was always on the look-out for people bearing his name, for one of his forebears was said to have fathered eleven children on the island from local families before dying at the age of nineteen. Links of this kind were a commonplace amongst old colonial families. The fortune of George Orwell's family also derived from the West Indies, and there were similar stories of concupiscent forebears.

It is unlikely that Greene's literary interests came from his father's side of the family. On his mother's side, by contrast, there was wide literary culture, the most famous literary relative being her cousin Robert Louis Stevenson. Greene was named partly after his namesake, his uncle Sir Graham Greene, one of the founders of Naval Intelligence and a great friend of Churchill's, but also partly after a Stevenson cousin, Graham Balfour.

But by far the most significant feature of Greene's childhood was that he was brought up in a school environment with the ubiquitous green-baize door, then to be found in every household of any size, in his case separating him from the school rather than from the servants' quarters. In later life he used to talk a great deal about the plight of a headmaster's son. In 1968 the television producer Christopher Burstall asked him about those days. Greene said: 'I wasn't beaten or bullied physically. But I was in a hopeless position of divided loyalties. I was Quisling's son.'[1] But many others have been in a similar situation without ill effect, not least Greene's own brothers – his elder brother Raymond became head boy – and even his cousins, who attended the same school.

It is possible that these worries, that he was seen as a spy for his father, that nobody trusted him, were artificially exaggerated when Greene underwent a course of treatment at the hands of a man mistakenly believed to be a psychoanalyst after a breakdown of some kind when he was sixteen. Greene was undoubtedly a sensitive boy with a vivid and creative imagination, as those around him soon realised, but there may have been other, extraneous reasons for these problems. Most boys going to a boarding school would first have attended a prep school and have learned to live in close proximity to people of their own age and background. Gangs, bullying, team rivalry and other trials are all gone through harmlessly and with great rapidity. Although Greene did attend a prep school, after education at home, it was one set up at Berkhamsted by his father and he was not a boarder there. Charles Greene thus shielded his son from a crucial part of the growing-up process experienced by the boys with whom Greene mixed. A sense of isolation resulted which remained with him for the rest of his life. However, had it not been for his psychoanalysis the passage of a few years would probably have seen these difficulties completely forgotten.

Greene's conversion to Catholicism has naturally drawn some attention to his early religious life. Although it has been widely said that he became a convert simply because his wife Vivien was a Catholic and he had to do so in order to marry her – untrue in fact as the Church had no such rule – others have tried to look further back to find a reason. Vivien Greene had gone over to Rome under the influence of her mother's family and that of a saintly Dominican, Father Bede Jarrett. Nothing like that can be found in Greene's family: Berkhamsted School was an Anglican foundation and there was instruction in divinity, and school chapel with the usual Victorian hymns such as 'Abide with Me' no doubt sung lustily. But there were nonetheless signs of definite early Catholic influence. Greene recalled in later life that even as a child he had been critical of relatives who found scandal in tales of priests in Spain living with a housekeeper or said to have indulged in an affair. Their failings should not be confused with the office they held, he thought – a mature observation in such a young mind which was almost certainly learned from Robert Louis Stevenson.

Throughout his life Greene talked about the books which had influenced him as a child. During his school holidays he had the run of the school library and, for those long summer days the school was like a large country house with a particularly well chosen library of its own. Many of the books he refers to were typical children's adventure novels like Rider Haggard's *King Solomon's Mines*. But he made an unexplained reference to more serious matters: 'The influence of early books is profound. So much of the future lies on the shelves: early reading has more influence on conduct that any religious teaching.'[2] The impact of Robert Louis Stevenson, whom Green's mother was proud to say was her first cousin, and what was then one of his best-known controversial 'open letters', on Father Damien, can be traced in Greene's later life; it affected both his view of Catholicism and the interest which finally led him to the Congo and the writing of *A Burnt-Out Case*.

The letter was written to a Dr Hyde, a missionary in Honolulu. It is a brilliant defence of the Catholic priest, who died among the lepers he was serving, against terrible defamation by Hyde, whom Stevenson repeatedly refers to as his co-religionist. The facts were well known to everyone in Graham Greene's youth, though they are now largely forgotten. Dr Hyde had written a letter in ruthless terms to one of his colleagues, H. B. Gage, attacking Father Damien shortly after the priest's death from leprosy. Stevenson came across the letter because Gage had sent it to the *Sydney Presbyterian*, where it had been published on 26 October 1889. He was profoundly upset by it and published his open letter in *The Times* in response. The crudest example of the malice in Hyde's letter was his statement that 'The leprosy of which he died should be attributed to his vices and carelessness.'[3] Stevenson explained that Hyde was alluding to rumours that Damien had had a liaison with one or more of the lepers. His rebuttal of this story, even if it were true, echoes Greene's later objections to stories about priests which he heard in his own family.

When Greene mentioned Damien in *A Burnt-Out Case* he was not unconscious of the reference to Stevenson that this implied, although today it might have needed explaining. In fact his interest went further: he had several times thought of writing a biography of Father Damien and also one of Stevenson; biography, however, was not something that came easily to him. His own life was so complex that he despaired of ever finding enough material to write the life of anyone else. The one exception in his work, his life of the Earl of

Rochester, was of an historical figure about whom all there was to be known could be found with some certainty.

Stevenson also made a pointed comment which may well have affected the way Greene saw the world, besides the obvious fact that Stevenson too travelled vastly. He said to Gage:

I imagine you to be one of those persons who talk with cheerfulness of that place which oxen and wainropes could not drag you to behold. You, who do not even known its situation on the map, probably denounce sensational descriptions, stretching your limbs the while in your pleasant parlour.[4]

Earlier Stevenson had attacked Hyde, as a Presbyterian missionary, for the sumptuous way he lived in contrast to the severe monastic economy practised by Damien in the leper colony.

There is one other striking example of a nascent Catholic sympathy in Greene's time at Berkhamsted. The school had formal debates on topics of the moment and in one of these, in February 1921, Greene made an impassioned contribution on the situation in Ireland. Anyone going against the Black and Tans, the quasi-military British police force named after their uniforms, would naturally be assumed to have sympathy for the Catholic cause, albeit sympathy of a political kind. Very much later in his life Greene revealed to Pierre Joannon in an interview published in 1981 in *Etudes Irlandaises* that his hero had been Michael Collins, who was assassinated in August 1922, more than a year after the debate. Did Greene see Collins as a hero because he had stood up to the British? Or did he admire the newly emerging statesman who had struck a deal with the British, and eventually was to be killed for it? When he spoke to Joannon Greene's own memories had perhaps faded, but in another interview he said something which seems to place the matter in a clearer light: 'I think that many people still have the same picture of the old-style IRA which existed during and after the First World War. I do admire that IRA, but the provos have turned into out-and-out gangsters, devoid of ideals ... They terrorise the Catholics.'[5] Across fifty years his view has not changed, in his own eyes. And his evident sympathy with the Catholic population is equally clear, long before his conversion. His reaction at the time and after is of a piece with Stevenson's condemnation of his co-religionist and his support for the Catholic Damien.

Two schoolfellows of Greene's played some part in his later career. Claud Cockburn, a cousin of Evelyn Waugh, and Peter Quennell. Quennell was a friend with whom Greene had occasional contact over the years, particularly in London literary life before and after the war. Cockburn on the other hand was a close friend at Oxford, though politics came between them in the 1930s and arguments over financial matters in the 1960s. Greene found him companionable because of his natural tendency to revolt against authority, his cosmopolitan background – he had been born in China and his father lived in Belgrade – and his attractive personality. If Cockburn is to be believed, his own interests had already taken a political turn when he was at school. He claimed to have been much involved in an incident on Armistice Day in 1918 when drunken troops and revellers were let into the school, taking part in what he later called his first experience of revolution. Cockburn recalled with amusement Charles Greene's stern warnings to the school in the aftermath of these happenings about the spread of bolshevism.

Since both boys were barely fourteen when this incident occurred, and since Greene never refers to it, Cockburn may well have embroidered it, as he was to do with other stories in later years. His reporting of the Spanish Civil War included many incidents which were complete fiction, as he was to admit. No less problematic were his writings in the *Daily Worker* during the Second World War in support of Hitler and the Nazi–Soviet pact. More typical of his escapades with Greene was an idea they carried through during their first vacation at Oxford. They disguised themselves as travelling musicians and, armed with a barrel organ, begged their way around the home counties. Their disguise was good enough to fool the people of Berkhamsted when they passed through. It was this saga that Greene chose to refer to when Cockburn asked him to write a preface to his memoirs, published in 1981, by which time they had drifted far apart.

Whether Charles Greene actually did warn the school and his impressionable literary-minded son about the dangers of bolshevism, the mark left on Greene's mind was insignificant; Greene never once referred to it or anything like it. But there is no doubt that his father influenced him in his admiration for the work of Browning – as will be noted at several points in this book. For the moment it is enough to recall Greene's comment in his first volume of autobiography *A Sort of Life*, published in 1971:

> If I were to choose an epigraph for all the novels I have written it would be from 'Bishop Blougram's Apology':
>> Our interest's on the dangerous edge of things.
>> The honest thief, the tender murderer,
>> The Superstitious atheist, demi-rep
>> That loves and saves her soul in new french books -
>> We watch while these in equilibrium keep
>> The giddy line midway.[6]

This interest of his father's, with frequent reading aloud of Browning's poems in classic Victorian style, perhaps played some part in his becoming a writer. But there was another quite extraordinary development which affected him directly and profoundly as a result of the breakdown he suffered at sixteen. He had left home under some domestic stress with the idea of running away for good but was soon discovered and brought back. His parents decided to send him to stay with one of the new breed of psychoanalysts that had sprung up during the war. It was a decision which had entirely unforeseen results which they did not understand for many years.

To the end of his days Graham Greene said that the happiest time of his life was the six months he spent when he was sixteen in the household of Kenneth Richmond and his wife Zoe. It was also to set Greene on his path as a writer with real ambitions and real idols in the contemporary literary world.

Richmond practised as a psychoanalyst, and somehow Greene's parents had got to hear of him. The most likely introduction was through Greene's elder brother Raymond, who was studying medicine at Oxford. Richmond was the joint author with the novelist J. D. Beresford of a book on educational and psychological theory written in the unusual form of a biography of a person who was an exponent of their views, W. E. Ford, but who did not actually exist. The book had a cult following, and Raymond could well have heard of it at the time. But when Greene's wife Vivien asked her mother-in-law about it just after the war at a crucial period in the break-up of her marriage Greene's mother said she had destroyed Richmond's letter and forgotten the details.

Psychiatry had experienced a boom during and after the First World War, in large part prompted by a new interest in industrial psychology as a means of increasing munitions output and also of dealing with the breakdown of workers who were being driven beyond endurance, many of them women working in factories for the first time in their lives to replace men who had gone to the front. The troops themselves were also found to be in urgent need of treatment as a result of their experiences. Indeed J. D. Beresford's novel *Revolution* has as its hero an officer who has been under acute psychological stress and has become incapable of involving himself in normal life. Also fashionable in the 1920s was psychoanalysis, usually focusing on the work of Freud and his interpretation of dreams in largely sexual terms. Freud's theories were never taken seriously in the mainstream of English life in the way that they were in America, and it would still today be considered unusual to place a young man like Greene in the hands of someone such as Richmond for residential care, particularly when there was nothing the matter with him in behavioural terms. The whole field was reviewed by a well-known practitioner, H. D. Harrison, in 1925 in his book *Industrial Psychology and the Production of Wealth*, which mentioned the objections of literary men to many of these ideas, including passing reference to Walter de la Mare.

Kenneth Richmond fell squarely into the 'society' category of psychoanalyst, but he had no qualifications at all and owed his reputation to the backing of J. D. Beresford, who was highly regarded as a novelist at the time, and also worked as a general editor in London for the publisher William Collins. Greene's parents seem to have been unaware of Richmond's true status. Richmond's practice was based loosely on some variation of Freudian dream analysis, but in modern terms he was quite simply a quack. Greene's biographers have all regarded this interlude in their subject's life as important; they could hardly avoid doing so since Greene never once forgot the experience and there are references to it throughout his work. But the reality of what happened in 15 Devonshire Terrace has never been understood.

Greene's description of his days at the Richmonds' mentions his regular morning excursions to Kensington Gardens, where he would read books on subjects he was studying at school. His account implies that Devonshire Terrace enjoyed a very desirable location on the park. In fact the Richmonds lived behind Paddington station in a relatively small house in a section of Devonshire Terrace that overlooked one of the smallest London squares, Queens Gardens. It was typical of the numerous stucco terrace houses in the neighbourhood, with two columns either side of the front entrance supporting a balcony above. The houses were then small hotels and rooming houses, much as they are now. Today the hotels have been upgraded, but in Greene's day the entire area behind Paddington station held an ambiguous social position. The closer the hotels were to the station the more likely they were to offer rooms for rent by the hour. This was a world Greene described in his later novels, most notably in *The Confidential Agent*, and it was also a world in which he himself lived for much of his life. The streets around which Greene must have walked were a red-light district of the kind which flourished around the great stations in London, particularly during and after the war. The Richmonds' house itself was on the very edge of the district and they kept strictly within the pattern of respectable life in the neighbourhood. Every Sunday they went to church, leaving their two daughters in Greene's care. The church they visited was a spiritualist church of a very unusual kind, whose preacher used often to ask the congregation whether they wished to hear a sermon or engage in discussion on psychoanalytic or other themes.

The Richmonds lived in a highly avante-garde world in which people like Ouspensky and Gurdjieff, cult Theosophists and mystics, represented the more intellectually rigorous figures. J. D. Beresford and his wife and the Richmonds ran a joint literary salon visited by many whose names are remembered when theirs have been completely forgotten. When Katherine Mansfield became interested in Ouspensky it was Beresford who took her along to meet him. Other frequent visitors to the Richmonds' house were the poet Walter de la

Mare and his close friend Naomi Royde-Smith, who was then literary editor of an influential paper, the *Weekly Westminster Gazette*. Greene kept for the rest of his life the copy of de la Mare's poems *The Veil*, which the poet inscribed for him at the Richmonds', and it is now with his remaining papers and books at Boston College in Boston, Massachusetts. Few books of Greene's survive from those days, and his keeping it points to the profound effect which this strange world had upon the gauche young man. The psychoanalysis he had seems to have been a trivial matter in comparison. For an hour each morning he had to call on Richmond in his rooms and describe the dreams he had had the previous night. Often Greene could not remember any, and when he invented them Richmond seems not to have noticed the difference. For the rest of the day he was free to walk about London and do as he pleased. It was then that he began his lifelong hobby of frequenting second-hand book shops. He remembered buying a copy of one of Ezra Pound's book of poems from a shop near the Thames, and the influence it had – immediately moving him away from his idol de la Mare.

In his autobiography Greene makes clear the effect that meeting these visitors had on him:

> Naomi Royde-Smith, the editor of the *Weekly Westminster* who had published Rupert Brooke's early poems [visited the Richmonds]. She was too kind to me, so that a year later I began to bombard her with sentimental fantasies in poetic prose (she even published some of them). J. D. Beresford came too – a novelist crippled by infantile paralysis. *The Hampdenshire Wonder* remains one of the finest and most neglected novels of the period between the wars, although it was an inferior novel *Revolution* which appealed to me more then.[7]

By chance Greene had fallen into the centre of one of the most influential literary coteries in London in the 1920s. Although he dismisses *Revolution* as an inferior novel (and wrongly suggests that *The Hampdenshire Wonder* appeared between the wars – it was published in 1911), if one reads the book now one can see why it had the impact on Greene to which he candidly admits. The hero Paul Leaming has come back from the trenches suffering from some acute psychological problem. He simply stays at home while his father attends to the family business in the City and his family carry on their life around him, keeping as quiet as possible so as not to disturb him.

The novel begins with Leaming's father becoming angry when his son defends a socialist leader who is causing much upset in the chaotic social conditions that trade problems after the war have caused. A general strike is talked of and the action of the novel develops as the strike is called. When the socialist leader is shot by a sniper, revolution breaks out. Instead of joining the officers' reserve to fight against the workers, Paul Leaming remains neutral or, if anything, sides with the men whom he has known in the trenches. One of these former soldiers does not know whether to trust him and thinks for a moment that he might be a government agent tasked with finding out what the workers are doing. Paul convinces him that he is not, and sticks to his work. The revolution is not bloodless, and leaders and men on both sides are killed in the cities and the countryside.

The foreshadowing of the themes which run through Greene's novels for the rest of his life is striking. But it was the influence of Beresford's personality and the ambition which he fired in Greene which were more important. Beresford visited the Richmonds frequently while he was writing his book, during the period when Greene was staying with them. It is scarcely any wonder that Greene was later to say, in a television programme in the 1970s, that he idolised Beresford. In a letter to his family at the time Greene recounted one incident which proves this beyond doubt.

Shortly before he went to the Richmonds Greene had had a short story published in the *Star*, having sent it in on impulse after it had appeared in the school magazine. He showed the story clipped from the paper to the Richmonds and asked them who they thought it was by. They said that surely it was J. D. Beresford. Greene reported this with relish and pride in his letter. In later life he was to talk of the influence of Conrad and Henry James, and later still of Ford Madox Ford. But these were men whom he admired for literary reasons after university. He did not conceive his ambition in terms of their actual lives; they were not real people to him as Beresford was.

Despite his admiration for Walter de la Mare, it was fiction that he

12

wanted to write, not poetry. While there is a full account of the relationship between the Beresfords, Walter de la Mare and Naomi Royde-Smith in Theresa Whistler's definitive biography of de la Mare, *Imagination of the Heart*, nowhere is Greene's early contact with him mentioned, nor did any member of the family know of it.

Those who took a particular interest in Greene seem to have been the women who gathered around Zoe Richmond, Kenneth Richmond's extremely beautiful wife. They included not only Naomi Royde-Smith but also Clemence Dane, then emerging as a successful playwright, and Mrs Belloc-Lowndes. Others that the Beresford family remember in the Richmond–Beresford circle in 1921 were John Galsworthy, who, like D. H. Lawrence, stayed at the Beresfords' farm in Cornwall, St John Ervine, H. G. Wells, Hugh Walpole, Arnold Bennett, Sir John Squire and Katherine Mansfield. As the reader and editor of Collins' London list it was obvious that Beresford had a wide literary friendship. As co-author of his most controversial book at the time it is obvious that Kenneth Richmond was also a key figure here.

It is equally certain that if Greene did not actually meet all the people in this circle he was fully aware of who they all were and felt able to relate to them directly, almost as an adult. When he went to Oxford two years later he kept in touch with those he had felt closest to, although they may not always have been able to place him as the tall blond-haired youth who had been a patient at Devonshire Terrace.

The one person whom Greene did not see after leaving the Richmonds was Zoe Richmond herself. Yet it was she who exerted the most lasting influence of all. The classic reference to her is in Greene's volume of autobiography *A Sort of Life*. He describes how his 'analysis' had reached a point 'when the emotion of the patient is due to be transferred ...'.[8] He then relates how Richmond introduced him to someone else at the time to whom this emotion might be transferred instead of to Richmond himself. But this ploy failed, and Greene instead fell in love with Zoe. He began having erotic dreams about her which he then felt duty bound to recount to her husband. He describes struggling against the normal impulse not to reveal such dreams, but his commitment to the analytic process instilled in him by Richmond steeled him against any embarrassment. He told the dream:

> 'I was in bed,' I said.
> 'Where?'
> 'Here.'
> He made a note on his pad. I took a breath and plunged.
> 'There was a knock at the door and Zoe came in. She was naked. She leant over me. One of her breasts nearly touched my mouth. I woke up.'
> 'What is your association to breasts?' Richmond asked setting his stopwatch.
> 'Tube train,' I said after a long pause.
> 'Five seconds,' Richmond said.[9]

It is probable that Greene was adding in the idea of transference from his own later knowledge of psychoanalysis. This account seems like a simple dream, but it is even more likely that it was an actual event. This is not simply a deduction from scenes in Greene's later books: in *The Comedians*, for example, where a character, a young man still at school, is seduced by an older woman, or at the end of his second unpublished novel where another youth is seduced by a married woman. And there are numerous scenes where a man is making love to a woman when her husband is in the same house, or even in one instance, in the same room. Despite the weight which conventional literary criticism would place on such coincidences, let alone any one of a dozen schools of psychoanalysis, this is not proof or even circumstantial evidence. But there is direct evidence.

In November 1961 Zoe wrote to Greene out of the blue. He had not heard from her for forty years. She wrote to tell him that her son had just had his first book published and she wondered if Greene might take an interest in it. *Christ's Drama: The Nature of Spiritual Growth* may have appealed to Greene, but he had not been able to find a copy when he replied in a candid letter that raised interesting questions.

He commented tactfully that he had been surprised by the letter, but not unpleasantly since his memories of those days were still with him, and still happy ones. He went on to reveal that not only did he not know about Zoe's son's book, but he did not know that she had had a son. He inferred that he must have been born shortly after Greene had returned home. Despite the passage of over forty years, Greene recalled Zoe's two daughters perfectly and his being entrusted with their care on Sundays, while the Richmonds were at their spiritualist church in Lancaster Gate, when he was himself little more than a schoolboy.[10]

The remarkable thing about this letter is that Greene should not have known that Zoe had given birth to a son shortly after Greene had returned to his school at Berkhamsted. Greene had not heard from Zoe, and the connection between them was broken as a result of the obvious attraction, but he had gone on seeing and meeting Kenneth Richmond. Richmond had never mentioned that he had a son either, which would have been very unusual since Greene had grown close to all of them. The most obvious interpretation of this, that Greene had had an affair with Zoe, is not the only one. Richmond's family have pointed out to the author that Kenneth was already an alcoholic, and had been one for ten years before his wife found out. It might be that Greene did have a strong attraction towards Zoe and even that he did enjoy with her the sexual relationship which echoes through his work. There is an entry in one of his diaries at the University of Texas at Austin which seems to refer to this: he comments that at the time he had thought he was using her, although later he realised she was using him but she had been very loyal. However none of this goes anywhere near suggesting that he was the father of Zoe's son. Indeed it may have been thought best not to tell Greene of the son's birth for the very reason that he might conclude that it was his child.

There was another incident which occurred during Greene's brief stay which Richmond kept from him. He had written to his parents to say that he thought Greene might have epilepsy. His sole ground for this diagnosis was Greene's fainting at a dinner party when someone gave a lurid account of an accident. Richmond claimed to have consulted a doctor, who did not examine Greene and was later found to be as doubtfully qualified as Richmond himself.

Bearing in mind that Richmond was totally unqualified and had almost no experience in analysis, which in Greene's case had gone so far as transference of emotion, it is at least possible that he had lost control of himself completely when he realised that Greene had become attracted to his wife. His letter to the Greene family may have been the result of subconscious antagonism or plain malice. He must surely have known that he had little or no experience in such matters, and there was the overall question of the responsibility he had assumed for 'treating' Greene. Perhaps he believed that the best form of defence was attack, and his letter was a first line of defence in case anything went seriously wrong as a result of his and Zoe's involvement with Greene.

When Greene returned to school the effects of his time away was immediately obvious. Like anyone who has been away from a small town and spent six months in the metropolis he had acquired an abruptness, a harshness, which people did not like. Superficially it might have seemed like self-confidence and a sign, to those who knew why he had been away, of a successful overcoming of his problems. Those closest to him saw more than that. His cousin Ben was to make one of the shrewdest comments, years later, when talking to Greene's authorised biographer: 'Graham was not a man gifted with intimacy but the one I remember and like best was Graham before the psychiatrist ... If you are a perfectly ordinary diffident boy [you could be] corrupted by, twisted by, a psychiatrist, so that dangerous fantasies are put into your head.'[11] This was the opinion of someone whose life had run in parallel with Greene's, with even more chaos and upset, and even agony. It is a measured conclusion and very accurate. Had he realised that the 'psychiatrist' was nothing of the kind, but at best a well-meaning amateur, at worst a fraud? It seems unlikely. When he made this statement in 1977, Greene's first volume of autobiography had been published and Ben Greene must surely have read it and have noted Greene's praise of his father and brother for choosing Richmond. He had perceived that when the book appeared in 1971 Greene still seemed not to have understood what had happened to him.

There are two possible explanations, first that Greene preferred to stay with the illusions which had run through his life and books – just how much will become obvious in the following chapters. The second is that Greene, having received Zoe's letter breaking a forty-year silence, realised that he had to be extremely circumspect in what he wrote. He always said that people were entitled to their privacy or, as he sometimes put it, they had the copyright in their own lives.

Charles Greene and his wife would have noticed a more direct literary influence resulting from his stay in London. Greene persuaded Walter de la Mare to come to Berkhamsted and visit his parents at one of their garden parties. One of the few detailed recommendations Richmond made at the end of his analysis was that it was important for Greene to continue writing – hardly necessary advice in view of his mother's ambition for him as a writer and given his early success. He had had pieces published in the press and even wrote regularly to the literary editor of the *Weekly Westminster*. But Greene's parents must have concluded that the appearance of de la Mare in their house showed that they had done the right thing in sending their son to Richmond.

The only direct near-contemporary evidence of the kind of treatment that Greene received at Richmond's house appears in a letter written to his fiancée Vivien. He describes coming back from his analysis with what he called a competition complex. He said he felt the need to compete with his brother Raymond, who had been head boy, and that he strove to do better than him. When Raymond became a mountaineer abroad, Greene claimed that he began his travels in emulation; another of Raymond's successes led him to an interest in politics. It is noteworthy that he had already written out of the script the one person with whom he really did compete, not his brother Raymond so much as his cousin Ben Greene, who was just ending his university career at Oxford when Greene went up to Balliol in the autumn of 1922. Ben had created a stir by becoming a Quaker at Oxford, and it would be difficult to see what Greene could find to compete with in this gentle giant of a cousin. But Ben Greene was a very untypical pacifist.

CHAPTER TWO

An Oxford Political Odyssey

The next stage in my quest for Graham Greene was sparked off by a small lot I noticed in an auction in Swindon, Wiltshire. It was an item of ephemera, a dinner menu that had been signed by Greene using the earliest form of his signature, H. Graham Greene. It was for an Oxford undergraduate dining society, based in Balliol, the Mulla Mulgars. It is a reflection on how literary taste changes that neither I nor any of the wide range of people I have contacted knew who the Mulla Mulgars were. The Beresfords and others of their generation would have known who they were, of course: the Royal Monkeys, characters in Walter de la Mare's book of the same title. The copy of the book which de la Mare inscribed to J. D. Beresford is still in the family library on Alderney.

The club was a window on a forgotten world. Even the de la Mare family knew nothing of the club, founded in his honour by Greene and his friends. The signatures include those of Sir Robert Scott, later to become High Commissioner in East Africa, as well as the initials of the man who so fortunately kept the card, Henry Brooke. But most significant of all was the man invited as guest of honour to the dinner – John Buchan.

Buchan had come to live in Oxford with some hopes of representing the university in parliament – the universities then counted as parliamentary constituencies – and this dinner was perhaps a discreet form of lobbying. As far as Greene and the others were concerned they were meeting one of the most famous authors of the day, whose *Thirty-Nine Steps* already had a hold over people's imaginations which it was never to lose. The different courses on the menu are all given names from Buchan's novels, but sadly no record has been found of what the dishes were, or of what Greene experienced when eating 'The Thirty-Nine Steps'. Indeed had the menu not survived we would never have learned that Greene had known Buchan, to whom he refers frequently later, as we shall see. He never once gave even a hint that he had met him.

Almost as interesting are the names that do not appear on the menu. Evelyn Waugh and others of the 'Brideshead' generation are absent. Were he and Peter Quennell, Tom Driberg, Harold Acton, Roger Hollis or even Claud Cockburn not invited? Evelyn Waugh surely provided the answer when he remarked that Greene did not share the revelry of the generation to which he inadvertently gave the name for later commentators thanks to his book *Brideshead Revisited*. Greene responded by saying that he was part of a boisterous group of Balliol heterosexuals and that 'I was not suffering from any adult superiority.'[1]

The sly mention of adult superiority in Greene's letter to Waugh and his reference to boisterous heterosexuals points to a basic fact of Greene's time at Oxford: he did not get involved in the homosexual sub-world which plagued the university in the inter-war years. Tom Driberg has described this world and the homosexual debauchery common in some of the more 'exclusive' undergraduate societies. A lifelong homosexual, Driberg did not mention any of the more conventional clubs to which Greene and innumerable other under-graduates belonged, such as the Mulla Mulgars. Almost certainly Waugh, Driberg and the others were not at the dinner because they were not invited; they were many things, but boisterous heterosexuals they were not.

There is a legend perpetuated by some of Greene's biographers that he was somehow an outsider at Oxford, a legend which possibly has its origin in his shunning of many of those now thought to have been at the heart of Brideshead Oxford. A key quotation might be that from Peter Quennell's autobiography *The Marble Foot*: 'Why Graham at Oxford should have so carefully avoided notice is a question I cannot answer.'[2] Quennell's remark is curious, possibly driven by some annoyance at Greene's later success, which in fact echoed his very high profile at Oxford. However famous the Brideshead generation became later, if anyone had a high profile at the time it was Greene. To take the most obvious example, Greene was editor of the magazine *Oxford Outlook* for much of the time he was an undergraduate. He had started out as deputy editor to C. H. O. Scaife and took over as editor when Scaife went on to become President of the Oxford Union.

It would be difficult to be more at the heart of things. *Oxford Outlook* had been founded five years before by Beverley Nichols, who knew the Beresfords and Naomi Royde-Smith. Greene's contributors included Peter Quennell, who was no doubt grateful at the time, and Edmund Blunden, whom Greene got to know well later when he returned to Oxford in the 1930s. But Greene was not content to leave things there. The confidence he gained from friendship with people at this level led him to aim higher still. He wrote to Edith Sitwell with a detailed defence of her poetry, asking her for a contribution to his magazine, which she duly provided. A few years later, in 1926, Edith Sitwell became known for her experiments reading poetry through a megaphone to the accompaniment of music by William Walton. Greene was ahead of her; the year before in January 1925 he had led a group of undergraduate poets in a pioneering live poetry reading for the BBC. The others were A. L. Rowse, Harold Acton, Brian Howard, Joseph Macleod and Patrick Monkhouse, and the entire event stemmed directly from Greene's editing of *Oxford Outlook*. The origins of his very skilful dealing with the latest medium can readily be found in the appearance of the poem he read two days later in Naomi Royde-Smith's magazine the *Weekly Westminster Gazette*: clearly it had all been prearranged with her.

The avant-garde literary world in London was echoed in Oxford by the Contemporary Poetry and Drama Society, which Greene ran. Again, this was a high-profile activity which is scarcely ever mentioned by later writers on the period. Its most practical purpose was to invite leading figures from the London scene to meet undergraduates who were interested in the latest movements. At the time the best known of these was Clemence Dane, whose plays, produced by Basil Dean and published by Heinemann, were extremely popular. Her introductions proved invaluable to Greene throughout his career. Unlike Quennell he did not forget what he owed to those who helped him, and was not above giving her work a favourable mention, even in one of his novels, years later: the expatriate community in Sierra Leone in Greene's *The Heart of the Matter* is shown welcoming the arrival of Clemence Dane's new novel.

Another friend of Clemence Dane's, now forgotten, but then a power in the theatre, was Clifford Bax. He was well acquainted with the literary underworld and the newly emerging caste of literary agents; he was happy to introduce Greene to the best of them, A. D. Peters, and he in turn readily took on the novel which Greene somehow found time to write amongst all his other undergraduate activities. This book was one of Peters' few failures, for he could not place the book and Greene later went elsewhere.

All these activities, conducted alongside the reading necessary for his degree, pale into insignificance as far as his future life is concerned beside the extraordinary adventures he pursued during his vacations abroad, first in Ireland in 1923, and then in French-occupied German territory in 1924. These excursions began an involvement with politics and espionage which left a legacy of isolation and often despair that he shared with countless others in a century cursed by wars and political strife.

Visiting Ireland was his own idea, but it was one of many for which he was to seek support outside his family. He obtained an immediate response from Naomi Royde-Smith at the *Weekly Westminster*, who agreed to fund his trip on the condition that he wrote something for her paper in return. His journey was so successful that he tried to set up another excursion for his next vacation, this time writing to the Irish government offering to go to the six counties in the North on an espionage assignment. They declined his offer, unsurprisingly, and must have wondered what was behind it. Greene never really explained, but his later excursion into French-occupied Germany around Trier perhaps provides an answer – an inexhaustible appetite for fresh adventure.

On Greene's earliest trips he rarely travelled alone. In Ireland he tramped around with his cousin Edward Greene, 'Tooter', carrying heavy rucksacks and talking continuously. Greene's report, 'Impressions of Dublin', published as agreed in the *Weekly Westminster*, is already recognisably his, with its mixture of realistic descriptions and acute observation of character. He describes the thirteen

women hunger strikers then 'contending for the heavenly crown'[3] –
he was not then a Catholic. This slightly ironic reference to martyrdom
indicates the tone he adopted in his first open remarks about Catholicism. A comment in a similar vein in the *Oxford Outlook* brought
an unexpected response some months later, as we shall see. When
Greene's article was republished in 1990, in his *Reflections*, it still
stood as a piece of genuinely revealing reporting, despite all that had
befallen Ireland in the intervening years.

In their journeys through Ireland Greene and his cousin must have
talked of the exploits of Ben Greene, Tooter's brother. Although
Greene's biographer Norman Sherry mentions Ben, he gives no
indication of his extraordinary personality, or of the inspiration he
must have been to both his brother Tooter and his cousin Graham.
My discovery of Ben Greene's travels came quite unexpectedly. I had
seen a reference to Ben Greene having stood for Parliament as a
Labour candidate. The Labour Party was unable to help but referred
me to the Museum of Labour History. The Museum was able to
supply some coverage of his campaigns from its press-cuttings file,
but little else. It was enough. One newspaper article from Hull, where
Ben Greene was a parliamentary candidate in the 1930s, referred to
his having served with the Quaker famine-relief effort in the great
Russian famine of 1922–3. And this brief reference led me to the
Quaker archives in England, held at Friends House in London's Euston
Road.

When I visited Friends House in August 1996 I had no idea that
I was actually following in Greene's footsteps; later I was to read in
his diaries in Texas that he had once attended a reception there. It
was one of many occasions when I found I had unknowingly followed
him, walking through the same doors, standing in the same rooms,
perhaps even asking the same questions.

The archives yielded up a rich store of information about the
famine and about Ben Greene's part in the desperate attempts to save
lives. Sadly the Friends' own biographical entry for Ben Greene was
scant for someone who had been a member and keen supporter for
most of his adult life. He had joined the Society of Friends when he
was at Oxford, an unusual thing to do – there were not many
Quakers in Oxford and even fewer at Wadham, Ben Greene's college.

He is shown in the records for the first time in the List of Members and Attenders at the Berks and Oxon Quarterly Meeting, 1923. The general feeling at the time might have been that his joining a pacifist organisation implied cowardice. But Ben Greene, a giant of a man, was not like that. He was possessed of determined courage that took him almost immediately to one of the most dangerous places that could be imagined – Russia in the aftermath of the revolution.

The Russian famine of 1922–3 was described by those from the West who saw it as the most awful human suffering that they had witnessed and this was within a few years of the First World War, the most destructive conflict Europe had ever seen. As always in such circumstances there was no shortage of famine-relief volunteers and the Quaker movement was in the forefront of work in the most severely distressed areas. Over the winter of 1922–3 they were feeding 80,000 people and could have done a great deal more if the Soviet authorities had allowed people and supplies into the country. Ben Greene was amongst a group of ten British volunteers who finally got permission to enter Russia at the beginning of 1923. By March he was in Buzuluk. He worked next in Alexievka and in June moved to Moscow, where he remained until September. The body he had joined was the Friends War Victims Relief Committee, whose General Secretary was Ruth Fry.

Writing about the Quaker relief work, Ruth Fry said, 'The district of Buzuluk was one of the very worst in the famine area and we found ourselves in an area where death seemed more real than life.'[4] Sir Benjamin Robertson, Commissioner of the British Relief Societies, had visited the area and reported that the suffering was worse than anything he had seen in the Indian famines. Television has inured us to starvation in a way we often fail to realise; in 1923 there was no such softening of what was a terrible catastrophe. When Ben Greene arrived in Buzuluk, between 60 and 70 per cent of the district's entire population were suffering from cholera. A Quaker doctor, Dr Melville Mackenzie, set up a hospital and began training staff, but with milder weather the Soviet authorities became ever more restrictive and he eventually ceased work. The head of the delegation in Moscow wrote to Ruth Fry in London on 21 September: 'Just before leaving Buzuluk things had got to such a state with the local authorities that we were all beginning to drop back to the feeling ... that we were not wanted.'⁵ Shortly afterwards Ben Greene and the others returned to England.

Within a few months Ben Greene had plunged into political activity in Swindon, where he stood as the Labour candidate in the second election of 1924. He was defeated but his influence was not diminished, for he became personal private secretary to Ramsay MacDonald, leader of the Labour Party. Over the period 1923–4 his cousin Graham had swung around from being an ardent Conservative campaigner to giving his whole-hearted support to the Liberal candidate for Oxford, Frank Gray.

The influence of Ben Greene's extraordinary travels on his cousin Graham was direct, for it is difficult to imagine that Greene would have had the nerve to embark on his next trip without Ben's example. But, whereas Ben had gone to Russia inspired by Quaker feelings of compassion for the starving, Greene embarked on his trip to French-occupied Germany near Trier, known as the Palatinate, without the slightest trace of pacifist intention – quite the reverse. Kenneth Richmond would have attributed Greene's desire to travel to rivalry with Ben of a complex psychological kind. There may have been something to this, but if so it was a rivalry that others in their family would have found most gratifying, not least Sir Graham Greene.

Soviet Russia, and the Palatinate, were both places where British intelligence services were thin on the ground. The information Ben Greene was able to bring back from Russia would have been invaluable to them, even if he was a genuine Quaker and not a spy – or what would later be termed an unconscious source. This was equally true in the Palatinate. Papers in the Public Record Office reveal extensive efforts by MI3 – an organisation now almost entirely forgotten, unlike the more famous MI5 and MI6 – to obtain detailed information about a supposed separatist movement in the Palatinate. MI3 wanted to know if the movement was genuine or simply being fomented by the French. It is difficult now to recall the perspective of those days, but many thought that there was a possibility that the next war would be fought by the British against France, and intelligence from that country was regarded as particularly suspect.

Greene states in his autobiography that it was the reading of

'Defeat', a short story by Geoffrey Moss in a collection published under the same title, that prompted him to go to the Palatinate in his long vacation in 1924. Successive biographers have enquired no further, but, like the novels of J. D. Beresford, Moss's book and his world were of great importance for Greene's later life. Geoffrey Moss was cast very much in the mould of a Buchan hero. A Grenadier Guards officer, he served with Osbert Sitwell and remained friends with him for the rest of his life. It was a literary connection to a world that Greene also knew, and he could well have heard of the book through the Sitwells. Moss wrote other remarkable books and showed acute political insight throughout the period between the wars. His novel *I Face the Stars* was dedicated with remarkable prescience:

> To those who have stood for the Polish corridor and for the war guilt clause in the Treaty of Versailles and to the Sons of the reader of this book who will in consequence lose their lives in the next great war.[6]

His last important work, *The Epic of the Alcazar*, a gripping account of one of the most heroic actions in the Spanish Civil War, lost him the sympathy of the popular-left audience, although his final books written before the Second World War established precisely the danger the country faced from Germany. Once when stopped at a border by a Nazi official he claimed to be on intelligence duties, although his family knew nothing of this. If he was working for anyone at the time he wrote 'Defeat', it would have been MI3, which dealt with intelligence in defeated Germany.

Greene's next move before setting off was so unusual that it needs to be examined to see if there was something else behind it. He wrote to the German Embassy to ask if he could spy on their behalf in the Palatinate, in exchange for funding for his trip. Far from this astonishing proposal being ignored, Greene records how he came back one day to find Count Bernstorff, an attaché at the German Embassy, sitting in his rooms. He had already drunk most of Greene's brandy and was keen to talk about his project. It all seems like an adolescent fantasy. How could it have happened?

To begin with it was surprising that Count Bernstorff was able to install himself in Greene's rooms at Balliol with such aplomb. The explanation was that, although German, he was an Oxford man, one of the first Rhodes scholars from Germany in 1909. Since the war he had become known as an Anglophile and had secured a post at the Embassy in London; Oxford was a second home to him in England, and his tutors and those administering the Rhodes scholarships were still there – no doubt he visited them, as he did Greene. His name was well known because his uncle, also a Count Bernstorff, had been German Ambassador to Washington and had been caught running espionage rings there before America came into the war. Later he too became an Anglophile and an ardent supporter of the idea of England being welcomed into a United States of Europe – a union of course to be run by Germany. Greene describes the Count's daughter once visiting his rooms and leaving a scented glove behind. Albrecht, Count Bernstorff, who visited Greene, was not quite so high-powered, but he was senior enough to be given the task of handling this unlikely recruit into the German espionage system. He happily agreed to Greene's request for funds and in due course provided enough cash to cover the expenses Greene and his chosen companion Claud Cockburn incurred.

Greene's family knew about these developments, and it is difficult to believe that there was not some deeper game afoot. Before looking further into this question and what happened, it is necessary to emphasise the political situation at the time. A glance at any history book would have established for any biographer, if a reading of 'Defeat' did not, that Britain had every sympathy with Germany's difficulties in the Palatinate. The French had attempted to set up their separatist movement in the German lands they occupied. Known as the Revolver Republic, it was precisely that, and the first President Herr Heinz had been assassinated. Significantly he had been refused the last rites although he was a Catholic, and this was seized on by the French as showing that the Catholic clergy in the Palatinate took their orders from Munich. Greene was to learn more about the religious side to the affair when he visited Trier and other places in the Palatinate.

The Foreign Office files for 1924 reveal a difficult intelligence situation. The Office had obtained a special report which established that there was no support amongst the local population for the

French separatist activity. This was the position which Moss's story 'Defeat' expressed in the form of a Buchanesque tale. However, the army in particular wanted further information, which was proving very hard to get since the forces involved were those of Britain's ally of only a few years before in the supposed war-to-end-war of 1914–18.

With this perspective it is clear that Greene's trip might well serve a purpose useful to the British. He would be obtaining information of a kind that was extremely difficult to get, and he was doing it without in any way compromising the British government should he get into trouble. It would be the German authorities who would speak for him as a journalist sympathetic to their cause. Similar ploys were used in the Spanish Civil War when Kim Philby acted as a journalist on Franco's staff. Cockburn, Greene's travelling companion, later played the same game for the Comintern. However that may be, the central point being made here is that, far from betraying his own country and treacherously acting for the Germans, he could well have been working very closely with the British authorities. He would not have acted very much differently if he had. Even if he were an independent operator, British intelligence could have sat back and let him run, feeding on the information he eventually produced either as gossip to his ever fascinated uncle Sir Graham, or even as journalism.

This immersion in espionage and intrigue, the great game so beguiling to generations of readers of John Buchan's books, was the way Greene was to live his life, with only a brief respite in his early married life. But there was a closer link to his later personal life, as a reading of his second novel *The Name of Action* rapidly shows.

The report of the separatist movement already referred to, makes a point of saying that, on the separatist question, there was no difference to be found between those of Protestant and Catholic backgrounds. Greene's version in his novel shows that on the contrary he had come across a distinct Catholic group in the Palatinate. He repeatedly stresses the presence of a Catholic movement in a community which was largely born Catholic. Encountering it so soon after his travels in Ireland, the homeland of his hero Collins, Greene must have found many similarities. Anyone born a Catholic in

England will find in reading these pages of his book an immediate explanation of why Greene seems a born Catholic as opposed to, say, his old friend Evelyn Waugh, who was always evidently a convert.

The explanation is that he formed a romantic attachment to a Catholic community on his visit to Trier and the Palatinate. Some extracts from the novel will make this quite plain. Discussing where to store the arms needed for an insurrection against the dictator Demassener the hero Oliver Chant expresses his anxiety that there might be consequences for the family of the man whose house is to be used:

> 'The Risk?' Chant said. 'Is there no one without a wife and family who would store the arms?' His protest was half-hearted for the man's sacrifice seemed in part to hallow the cause that had once been selfless, but had become so confusing a mixture of his own love and hate.
>
> 'They are all good Catholics,' the man said quietly. He apparently referred to his family. It was the first time in Trier that Chant had heard a hint of religious antagonism.[7]

There followed a fierce discussion, which ended with a repetition of the same sentiment from the man storing the arms:

> Only when the discussion had subsided, except for an occasional excited word from the wizened man, he repeated his original assertion – 'They are all good Catholics' – as though he held some standard that had nothing to do with elementary school or priests or even attendance at Mass.[8]

Later Chant talks to the man's wife and comes to realise what a good wife and a good Catholic is. He decides that he will try and persuade the wife of the dictator to come away with him and even marry him after her present marriage – never consummated – has been annulled: 'In Trier he was to see Anne-Marie Demassener and persuade her to marry him ... He wanted, yes, more than food, the sight of a "good wife and good Catholic".'[9] There are other extensive passages of a similar kind, including an exchange where one revolutionary who, responding to the objection that Demassener goes to Mass, declares that he too goes to Mass – and he is an atheist.

This Catholic world was one Greene was to play games with

throughout his life. It certainly lies at the heart of the differences between Evelyn Waugh and Greene in their view of the Church. Waugh could never have followed Greene in his continental views of Catholicism; Greene lived by them to the end of his life. There were even direct links to some of his later work, particularly *The Honorary Consul*, in the world he found about him in Trier. He became involved, very lightheartedly, with a group of men who specialised in kidnapping people and taking them across the border to exact ransom. Greene never went into detail about these adventures, but they were serious and left their mark, which he was later to regret.

An important theme running through his experiences in the Palatinate which recurred throughout his life was the role of America in politics. There is a substantial vignette in *The Name of Action* featuring an arms dealer who produces a thousand revolvers and five machine-guns for Chant for cash down and a profit of 50 per cent. He is an American who can square anything for cash: 'In a bierhaus with an open door occasional glimpses of Mr. Crane could be caught leaning across a table towards a bribed and amiable customs officer and telling tales of prohibition in bad German.'[10] Crane, who bears more than a passing resemblance to Harry Lime of *The Third Man*, boasts of his business skills – 'Oh, boy, until you've seen me hustle you don't know what hustling is'[11] – and freely admits to selling arms to Demassener as well. Greene greatly admired American writers such as Dos Passos and Edmund Wilson, but here is the first appearance of his hatred of another side of American life.

Greene and Cockburn returned to England in early October 1924 in time for the new term at Oxford. They had planned to write a novel together based on one of John Buchan's, but this came to nothing. Whether Greene ever reported to Bernstorff on how the money he provided was spent is unknown. But the results must have been satisfactory, for Greene embarked on plans for a trip during the next vacation of even greater complexity, intending to get backing from a pro-French group and see the other side of the situation in the Palatinate. But this came to nothing when the separatist question was solved by international negotiation. Greene did go to France, early in the following year, 1925, but it was as a member of the Communist Party of Great Britain. This extraordinary event, which seemed to cap even accepting money from the German Embassy, stemmed from Greene and Cockburn's involvement in Oxford politics in 1923.

The general election in the autumn of 1923 was unique in Oxford's history. Not only was the campaign fought with bitter intensity, but there was evidence of corruption in the Liberal Party. So widespread were the rumours that when the election expenses of the successful candidate Frank Gray were being scrutinised it was thought best to investigate what at first seemed a trivial error of a few pounds. To the horror of the authorities it was discovered that this small discrepancy resulted from the failure of much larger sums to cancel each other out as had been planned so that everything would look above board. A typical ruse was uncovered immediately: a printer had made a bogus allowance for the return of allegedly undelivered handbills, thus reducing the bill he had to charge. It was decided to petition for the election result to be overturned, and a full enquiry was launched.

Greene had somehow or other got himself involved in the thick of this affair through his editorship of *Oxford Outlook*, with Cockburn in the wings. On becoming editor he had immediately set about improving the magazine's finances. His London experiences in the literary world, and his friendship with Naomi Royde-Smith, literary editor of one of the best-known papers, set him apart from other Oxford undergraduates, who knew next to nothing about running a magazine. By paying attention to advertising revenue he succeeded in making the magazine profitable for several issues. However, in the autumn of that year, 1923, he found he needed a fresh draft of funds if he was to balance the books. Someone, it is not known who, took the fatal step of introducing Greene to Frank Gray. He solved the problem immediately by offering a subsidy of about £200. There was a price he asked in return, and from that moment on the *Oxford Outlook* became an outspoken supporter of the Liberal Party. Immediately before the election Claud Cockburn wrote an article extravagantly praising Gray and the party.

Gray's efforts to persuade the voters of Oxford to vote for him, by corrupt methods also used by the leader of the party Lloyd George – such as the sale of honours through an agent, Maundy Gregory – were ruthlessly exposed. He was unseated. His autobiography *Confessions of a Candidate* gives his side of the story, but there is no mention of the activities into which he had drawn Greene. Nor is there any record of what happened within *Oxford Outlook* as a result of the small part it played in the scandal.

At about this time Basil Blackwell agreed to take the magazine over and become its publisher. Blackwell discussed the future of the magazine with Greene, but he also drew the young editor out on his literary ambitions. It was an unforeseen by-product of the political scandal, and it was to have important consequences for Greene. Blackwell agreed to publish a volume of his poems, which appeared in due course as *Babbling April*, Greene's first published book. He also asked to see some chapters of Greene's novel 'Anthony Sant' and was impressed enough to ask to see the book when it was finished, making this a condition of his publishing the poems. Blackwell had had wide experience of publishing undergraduates' verse, only to find them going on to fame elsewhere.

The following year Greene steered clear of politics in the accepted sense; he did not join a mainstream party with a view to a parliamentary career. Ben Greene had begun his search for a seat, standing for Swindon in 1924, but Greene did not follow him. For most of the year politics to him meant the great game fought out in Europe, however small the part he played. But when he and Cockburn returned to Oxford that autumn they took the momentous step of joining the Communist Party, turning their back on parliamentary politics. It was the world of J. D. Beresford's *Revolution*, but in deadly earnest. Exactly when they joined is uncertain, but Greene's membership card showed that he paid four weekly subscriptions and he visited France as a member of the party in early 1925.

After the war Greene said frequently, in his autobiography and in interviews, that he and Cockburn had joined as an undergraduate prank, hoping to get free transport to Moscow for a holiday along the lines of their trip to French-occupied Germany. The Communist Party of Great Britain did indeed offer special travel scholarships to students from Britain, setting up a special propaganda school for them in Moscow. But this scheme did not start until 1926, and recruitment did not begin until the summer of 1925, by which time Greene had already left Oxford. However, this was completely forgotten by the time he came to suggest this seemingly innocent reason. Another well-known member of the Communist Party at Oxford, the historian and television personality A. J. P. Taylor, made just such a trip, and others followed. The most famous group travelled in 1935, when Anthony Blunt went with his brother Wilfrid, though by then everyone paid a reduced excursion fare rather than the free trips offered in 1925.

When A. J. P. Taylor joined the party he was recruited in a most casual way by Ieuan Thomas, leader of the Oxford branch. In his memoirs Taylor states that Thomas had a very difficult time as a result of his political activities, which he claims precipitated a nervous breakdown and forced Thomas to leave Oxford. But that story, followed with slight elaboration by others, for example by Francis Wheen in his biography of Tom Driberg (who succeeded Thomas as leader of the party in Oxford), is substantially wrong.

It is still not known exactly how Thomas' branch of the CPGB was set up, but Greene was later to say that his membership card bears the number 1, although he could not remember how this came about. The only logical conclusion is that the branch to which Greene and Cockburn belonged was set up when they joined the party, with Thomas taking the lead. Since both men had wide experience of continental politics it might be wondered what qualities of leadership Thomas possessed and how they and A. J. P. Taylor came to be convinced by him. He was indeed a remarkable man.

Ieuan Glyn Thomas was born in 1906 in Llanelli, South Wales. He was a native Welsh-speaker who had matriculated from grammar school early and spent three years working in the library of the Mechanics Institute in Llanelli before going to Oxford at the age of seventeen. He had won a scholarship to Merton and read modern history specialising in the Art of War under Professor Major-General Sir Ernest Swinton, the inventor of the tank. He was later to remark:

> Llanelli was a working class town in a region of steel works and coal mines and it was at that time ranked as a very depressed area. Consequently I arrived in Oxford as a convinced and ardent radical socialist. In my reading of history I had observed how firmly the ruling classes have ever sought to retain for themselves and their hirelings a

monopoly of military knowledge and a monopoly of education in the Art of War. It seemed to me that this was a monopoly which ought to be breached – and who better to make the attempt than myself!'[12]

He found that all his fellow students spent their time riding to hounds and at the Bullingdon club, while awaiting their commissions in smart Guards regiments. He was almost the only serious student of the Art of War in his class: 'I won the favour and friendship of Professor Sir Ernest Swinton. This warm association between the retired Major-General and the Bolshie teenager is perhaps of that kind of unique phenomenon which can occur only in a place like Oxford.'[13]

And the word 'Bolshie' is the only allusion he made to the events which nearly destroyed his life and, but for the intervention of Swinton, surely would have done, for in 1926 Thomas became involved in one of the most intense political battles in this century. It was this that A. J. P. Taylor remembered in such vague terms. Although Greene had left Oxford when the storm finally broke he had been at the centre of things with Thomas as they evolved and the shadows cast affected Greene directly or indirectly for the rest of his life.

The main events were precipitated by a police raid on the CPGB headquarters in London designed to obtain evidence to support a prosecution of the leaders of the party for subversion of the armed forces. They succeeded and five senior officials were sent to prison after trial in November 1925. But the police and the security services also found out about the Communist branch at Oxford of which Greene had been a founding member. They were particularly angry to discover that a central purpose in setting up an Oxford branch had been to attract Indian undergraduates.

Within days the evidence of Communist activity in Oxford was placed before the Vice-Chancellor of the University by the Home Secretary Joynson-Hicks with the instruction that Thomas and the other members be sent down forthwith. This the Vice-Chancellor bravely declined to do; but he had to do something, so he drew up an oath which Thomas and his main assistant, a Rhodes scholar called Stephenson from Australia, were asked to sign, obliging them to take no further part in political activity while they were at Oxford. These events became public knowledge and a special motion was tabled at a meeting of the Oxford Union on 8 February 1926 which was passed with one of the largest majorities ever recorded. The motion fully supported Thomas and deplored the influence of national political figures on the intellectual life of the university.

Thomas may have had a nervous breakdown, but he did not go down without a degree. He was given an aegrotat in 1926 – a form of degree given to those prevented from taking their exams – and shortly afterwards left for South Africa, where Swinton and friends from his college seem to have arranged a teaching post for him. Thomas' ability and energy were soon recognised and he moved to Witwatersrand University. There he began a life in exile during which he reached the highest levels in the university, an association of forty-six years which saw him become Vice-Principal in 1954, before he finally retired in 1974 as Academic Adviser to the Office of the Vice-Chancellor. He was perhaps one of the most important anti-Apartheid figures in South Africa. It is astonishing that to this day his role in early life in the CPGB remains unknown there, but the explanation for A. J. P. Taylor's silence during the rest of his life and that of so many others, not least Greene himself, has its origins in a wish not to destroy by any further scandal the life of this heroic leader in the struggle against the despotic regime in South Africa.

Greene never made the slightest allusion to these events and his success in making light of his membership when asked about it even in talking to the biographer he himself appointed, is striking. His choice of South Africa as the setting of his novel about a communist double agent in *The Human Factor*, published in 1978, is the closest he gets even to hinting at these crucial events. The mystery which still remains is how Greene's membership of the party was dealt with by the police and security services in 1925 and later when he joined MI6. As will become obvious later, MI6 was unaware of Greene's membership at Oxford until he volunteered the information himself after the war. The only plausible explanation is that Sir Graham Greene arranged for the slate to be wiped clean. He was close to Churchill at the time, whose kick-out-the-reds campaign was in full swing, and also to the heads of two branches of the security services,

Naval Intelligence and MI6. Over seventy years later, with records either lost, closed or unindexed, and therefore inaccessible, the truth may be unattainable.

Claud Cockburn went on to become a fully-fledged member of the party, soon to work for the Comintern, later run by the GRU (Soviet Military Intelligence), a far more serious and dangerous organisation than its better-known civilian counterpart, the KGB. Why did not Greene follow him? There were many who later thought that he had done so, even including wartime colleagues in MI6, but that he had gone underground. Even his official biographer Norman Sherry went halfway along this path when he suggested in a television programme in December 1996 that Greene had known Philby was a spy and done nothing about it.

All these speculations were groundless. They were wrong, although Greene's struggle to find the human face of communism and reconcile it with the Catholic faith was to dominate his life. He had already found the revolutionary face of Catholicism in Ireland and the Palatinate, but that had been speedily replaced by the need to find a good Catholic woman to marry. Greene's steering away from the disasters which were to beset Cockburn, and which he chronicled extensively in a series of autobiographies, was due to his success in finding her.

Vivien Greene – she was born Vivienne Dayrell-Browning, and later shortened her christian name – was the single most important person in Greene's life in his last days at Oxford and for many years afterwards. A devout Catholic, she had been received into the Church by Father Bede Jarrett, whom she saw daily at the Dominican Priory in Hampstead when staying with her mother's family. Her mother, a Green-Armytage, had taken her daughter to live with her family when she separated from her husband during the First World War. Her family had likewise gone over to Rome under the influence of Bede Jarrett, a saintly man who was the first Dominican to study at Oxford since the Reformation and later went on to found Blackfriars, the Dominican House in Oxford that survives today.

In Hampstead Vivien's mother felt that her daughter should learn useful skills to prepare her for life, so she learned shorthand and typing and took pottery lessons. She began to write poems when quite young, and her mother arranged for the publication of some of these when she was fifteen, without her knowledge. Basil Blackwell agreed to put them out, with an introduction written by G. K. Chesterton, possibly through the assistance of her uncle R. N. Green-Armytage, a bibliophile and philanthropist who later helped fund the Ditchling Press for Eric Gill. At the time Vivien was embarrassed by the publication, but not long afterwards she went to Oxford to work for Basil Blackwell. She soon became responsible for sections of Blackwell's children's books list and also dealt with some of the poetry list, which was shortly to include Greene.

Although the Dominican House at Oxford had yet to open, there were already strong Dominican links to Oxford, which Vivien knew of through her work for Blackwells. In 1922 Basil Blackwell had been approached by Bede Jarrett over the future of the Dominican magazine *Blackfriars* and he had agreed to publish it, just as he agreed to publish *Oxford Outlook* the following year. It had been thought at first that it might have to close, but the return of the Dominicans to Oxford must have caused second thoughts. The proposal to bring the Dominicans back had been seriously considered in 1911, when the authoress Baroness de Paravicini had agreed an endowment of £1,000 towards the purchase of a house, and had altered her will to that effect. When Vivien was at Oxford the Baroness lived next door to the Dominican nuns in Headington. In 1891 she had published a history of Greene's college, Balliol, and had been working for many years on another book, *Do We Remember? A Story of Oxford under the Tudors*, which finally appeared in 1928. This was the essential background to Vivien's Catholic Oxford.

Vivien first wrote to Greene about a review in *Oxford Outlook* in which he made a disparaging reference to Catholics who worshipped the Virgin Mary. She saw the magazine frequently as it went through Blackwell's offices and no doubt typed out many of the letters which went back and forth, but this time she wrote for herself. She corrected Greene, telling him that the correct term for Catholic devotion to the Virgin Mary was hyperdulia, and it was not a matter of worship. Greene responded immediately and they began a hectic courtship, with Greene sending her literally thousands of letters in the few years before they were married in 1927. One of the more astonishing of these mentioned Greene's political escapades, and shows the extraordinary state of mind he was in:

> The only thing worth doing at the moment seems to be to go and get killed somehow in an exciting manner ... Don't take any notice of all this morbidity ... I am getting to know these moods. I have had them almost as long as I can remember and have found different cures ... later I got out of it by my Irish tour for the W[eekly] W[estminster] and then there was that trip to the Ruhr [the Palatinate] in the hope of getting into trouble with the French, Cockburn (that's why I like him) being much of the same temperament as myself. And then there were the Paris Communists in January...[14]

It is hardly surprising that she was at first taken aback by what she had started and that she felt a little wary of him. At least one biographer, Anthony Mockler, has said that the entire relationship was ill-fated and that the marriage which came two years later was 'a disaster'. This was emphatically not the case – as we shall see, they were extremely happy for twelve years and had two children. The first shadow was not cast until the coming of war in 1939. More importantly, Greene's view of Catholicism changed through the Catholic circle he discovered around Vivien. In the chaotic months of their courtship it was to have a profound effect on him, and here again the influence of Bede Jarrett, to whom Vivien was devoted, becomes apparent.

Bede Jarrett had published several books which bear considerably on Greene's view of the Church in later years, most obviously *Medieval Socialism*, published before the war. Another book, written after an approach by Harold Laski in October 1923, *Social Theories in the Middle Ages*, appeared in 1926 while Greene was in the midst of his courting of Vivien. Jarrett expressed views Greene could speedily come to terms with, but set them in a broader historical context than that of the hectic battles taking place in Ireland and on the continent. At the very end of his life Greene argued for the compatibility of Catholicism with Marxism by citing Marx's condemnation of the suppression of the monasteries. This was a theme he had come to through Jarrett, and the connection had been provided by the good Catholic woman he had been seeking.

CHAPTER THREE

Journalism with a Little Help from his Friends

Having handled his introduction to Oxford life with such masterly aplomb, courtesy of his preview of the adult world at the Richmonds', Greene almost made a serious mess of things when he left in 1925. The problem was not simply his flirtation with communism, however beguiling that might have been. He soon got over that, avoiding the breakdown that Thomas suffered, and went on to get a reasonable second-class degree. The question then arose of a career, and Greene embarked on the usual succession of interviews. He was offered a job in China with the British American Tobacco company, but he was very far from sure that this was what he wanted to do. The complication was his growing involvement with Vivien.

Over the summer and into the early autumn Greene pursued an increasingly erratic path. He started with BAT on 4 August 1925, but after a few days he left in confusion. He later said he could not face the life ahead of him, or endure those future colleagues whom he met in his initial briefings in London. But the main reason was that a posting to China would mean parting from Vivien. She was extremely attractive, with many admirers, and, although she favoured him most, matters were still far from certain. They had not even reached the stage of an unofficial engagement.

Turning down a business opportunity in those days of formal introductions and references, all taken up from his college tutors downward, was a grave matter. The Greenes had already known that their third son was liable to behave unpredictably, but this time there was no question of a breakdown and no need to think of a more professional version of the Richmonds' treatment. Greene had simply changed his mind. An important element in his decision not to pursue a literary career stemmed from a decision by Blackwells not to publish his novel 'Anthony Sant'. A. D. Peters had had no better luck and decided not even to try with Greene's second novel 'The Episode'. Neither book was published, although the manuscripts survive. When he left Oxford Greene actually sold his library to pay not very burdensome debts, keeping only a few treasured volumes, such as his inscribed book of Walter de la Mare poems, *The Veil*. Shortly after rejecting the job at BAT Greene realised he had to get some sort of employment; like countless graduates before him at a loose end he obtained a teaching job through the scholastic agents Gabbitas and Thring. He had only one pupil for a brief period but he soon began writing again, between the continual flow of letters to Vivien.

During this crucial period Greene swung slowly back to the idea of writing for a living. He dreaded the idea of teaching full time, thus following in his father's footsteps. Instead he remembered some advice given to him by his Balliol tutor Sligger Urquhart, who had responded to one of Greene's essays with the remark that he might make a good journalist. Here was an obvious way to earn his living, which meant he would be able to marry if Vivien would have him, and at the same time he could carry on with his next novel. There was nothing very original in this idea; had he not seen that world of journalism and letters close-to at the Richmonds'? It must have seemed almost like a world he was born into. However, Greene did not make the mistake of going directly to one of the great national newspapers. Instead he decided to serve what was effectively an apprenticeship at a provincial paper, even without pay if it meant earning a larger salary a few months later when he had learned the ropes. The question was to which paper should he apply?

After several false starts Greene once again fell back on the contacts he had made at the Richmonds'. Naomi Royde-Smith arranged for him to meet Sir Charles Starmer, who owned the *Westminster Gazette* and the *Weekly Westminster Gazette*. Then a newspaper magnate of some importance, but now a forgotten figure, he also owned a string of provincial papers including the *Birmingham Gazette* and the *Nottingham Journal*. Exactly what she said to get Greene the interview is a mystery, for Sir Charles appeared for some time to think that the young man was a friend of a nephew of his. After the direct intervention of Sir Charles, the Birmingham paper offered Greene a post as leader writer, with a salary, to start immediately, in October 1925. Sir Charles had no doubt been influenced by his literary editor's enthusiasm, and by Greene's experience in editing the *Oxford Outlook*. Greene did not share this optimistic view of his abilities, perhaps realising how little he knew of the technicalities of editing and sub-editing. He asked instead for a post at the *Nottingham Journal* as a trainee sub-editor without salary.

This decision seems illogical given that his main purpose was to earn a living so that he could marry Vivien, but Greene had made a shrewd calculation. He realised that if he began in Birmingham with a salary he was simply on the bottom rung of a very steep ladder. If he went to Nottingham and learned the ropes there he could then try for a proper job, with a good salary, on one of the great papers. He did not wait long after starting in Nottingham that November before taking the opportunity of a few days in London to visit Sir Charles Starmer again and ask for a leader writer's job on the *Westminster Gazette*. It seemed at first that he would actually succeed, with Naomi Royde-Smith's influence still carrying him, but then disaster struck. Financial difficulties forced Starmer to close the *Westminster Gazette* almost without warning, and there was no job for Greene to have. Naomi Royde-Smith herself lost her post. She decided to leave the newspaper world altogether and lead a more settled life. She married the actor Ernest Milton and went on to write many novels which enjoyed considerable success. This was Greene's first brush with the turbulence of London literary life. He seems to have lost contact with Naomi in the years that followed, and her influence has been largely forgotten.

Fortunately Sir Charles managed to keep his provincial enterprises afloat and Greene settled down to the winter months in Nottingham learning how to sub-edit a paper. Although he lived in Nottingham for only four months, less time than he spent in Devonshire Terrace, it made a profound impression on him. He felt himself to be not just away from home and on his own, as he had when a youth of seventeen, but almost in another country. The contrast with those days in London when he had been served tea in bed in the mornings by a maid in uniform could not have been greater. In Nottingham he lived in a succession of lodging houses which he immortalised in his novels – with Nottingham itself transformed into 'Nottwich'. As his biographer Norman Sherry has demonstrated, for the rest of his life Greene followed the same pattern: explorations in the real world beyond Oxford and Cambridge would store up images which he would later use in his fiction, with the circumstances and characters transformed. This reality, the world of ordinary people at all levels of society, was at the very root of his view of life, and when he was said by supercilious young critics later in his life to have created a world that might be called Greeneland he became angry. In what world did these critics live? he asked.

Vigorous lobbying of everyone he could think of, even asking Richmond for a letter of recommendation to the *Daily Telegraph*, finally produced a result. He was offered a post as a sub-editor on *The Times* to start on 10 March 1926. He had achieved a remarkable turnaround, recovering from his rejection of a neo-colonial career as a box-wallah in China to land one of the most sought after jobs in London, on a salary which made marriage possible. The entire project, indeed, had been driven forward by his continuing fascination with Vivien. This had assumed a more intense quality during his stay in Nottingham, for it was there that he went through the formal process of instruction needed to become a Catholic in adult life. The priest from whom he received his instruction was a retired actor called Father Trollope, as far removed from the Catholic Oxford of Bede Jarrett and the Dominicans as could be imagined. Greene later described their conversations on the tops of buses in Nottingham and other unlikely places for his instruction.

When Greene first decided to become a Catholic Vivien was overjoyed, and it must have played a major part in her decision to marry him. The change implied in his character ran right through his letters to her and one in particular, where he refers to his political views as an undergraduate, is in stark contrast to the tormented letter of only a few months before in which he spoke of going off and getting killed:

I think some of my shady political past – is it Irish republicans, German

separatists or French Communists? – has found me out. Two villainous
individuals have been patrolling in front of the house ... and have been
joined by an official in a blue uniform ... I heard him say 'This must
be the house.' I feel like a character in John Buchan. And I haven't got
my revolver, darling. What shall I do?[1]

The men turn out to be from the gas board. Greene's shift away from
youthful undergraduate political radicalism to indifference in the face
of life's struggles seems almost a parody of what countless students
later in the century went through. But his allusion to Buchan, and
his literary background, shows that there was still an imaginative
involvement with the politics he knew. Seen in literary terms Greene
was still living in the world of J. D. Beresford's *Revolution*, lightened
in his last days in Oxford in 1925 by Buchan's romanticism. Then,
in the space of a year, he found himself living through one of the
episodes in *Revolution* in real life and acting entirely differently from
his earlier hero in the book, Paul Leaming. When a special officers'
reserve is set up in *Revolution* to act as a police force if violence
should break out Leaming refuses to join it. When the General Strike
of 1926 was declared shortly after Greene had started with *The Times*,
he not only joined the strike-breakers but went further and sided
against the strikers in the politically emphatic form of becoming a
special constable.

In his series of interviews with Marie-Françoise Allain published in
1983 Greene was taxed with this decision and its contrast with his
left-wing principles. He replied that at the beginning of the strike
someone had tried to set fire to *The Times* building in London and he
had helped douse the flames; he felt loyal to the paper and his
colleagues. They all saw it was important to keep the paper going,
he said, particularly as Churchill had set up a rival government paper,
the *British Gazette*, which would otherwise have had a monopoly. As
we shall see, he confided a different story to his diary in 1933, but
there were two other determining factors which he did not mention.
First, his brother Raymond also became a special constable, so there
was almost certainly family pressure; and, secondly, if he had joined
the strikers he would have lost both his job and his future wife. It is
an interesting question what Greene would have done if he had been

in a country where the working men were largely Catholic and there was a religious element to the strike. Joining the Black and Tans would have been too much for him no matter what personal happiness was at stake.

With the strike over, Greene carried on as before, working on his novel in the morning and then going in to work for *The Times* through the evening, counting the days until his marriage, which had been formally announced just before he left Nottingham. The wedding was not to take place until October the following year, a conventional enough delay in those days. In the meantime he found somewhere for them to live, a self-contained flat in Hampstead, after asking for a rise in time-honoured fashion. But there were also problems.

Shortly after he had told his parents that he and Vivien were to become engaged, they wrote to suggest that he visit Kenneth Richmond. Greene went on 15 November 1925. There Richmond told him for the first time that he had detected signs of epilepsy during his stay at Devonshire Terrace and that he had told his parents of this. Greene's parents had kept this from him and apparently could not even bring themselves to discuss it with him, preferring Richmond to do it for them. What is astonishing to us now is that Greene's family should have taken the word of such a man and even have sent Greene back to him. They seem not to have known that Richmond had meanwhile abandoned psychoanalysis and was attempting to make a living selling a proprietary system of shorthand which he hoped would oust Pitman's from the field.

At their interview Richmond went on to say that as epilepsy could be inherited Greene should think carefully before getting married and having children. He purported to sweeten this bitter pill by pointing out that Dostoevsky had also had epilepsy and had still become a brilliant novelist. That Richmond knew perfectly well when he uttered these savage remarks that he was totally unqualified to make them, and indeed was no longer even pretending to be a medical man of any kind, suggests that he was deliberately wounding Greene. The one possible reason was the connection which had sprung up between Greene and Zoe. In showing him around his new house, Richmond remarked on its being larger than Devonshire Terrace, but he did not even then tell him that he had had a son since Greene had stayed with them five years before.

Greene was stunned and totally unprepared for such news. In *A Sort of Life* he recalled standing on an Underground platform trying to summon up the courage to kill himself:

> It was not my new Catholicism which restrained me. There was no theological despair in what I felt. I was simply tired out by the thought of starting a completely different future than the one I planned. But suicide requires greater courage than Russian roulette. The trains came and went and soon I took the moving staircase to the upper world.[2]

Greene's reference to Russian roulette relates to an episode in his late teens after his return from the Richmonds' when, he claimed, he had played the game with a revolver he had found in his brother Raymond's cupboard. In a later telling of the story to V. S. Pritchett in 1978 Greene implies that he knew it was loaded only with blanks – dangerous enough if fired directly at the head. But nobody has remarked on the point that Greene played this game after he had been through his supposed analysis. Was Greene saying in his autobiography that his games of Russian roulette were prompted by his last dealings with the Richmonds, by his parting from Zoe? It is not a comfortable reflection that thoughts of suicide had also been the result of this later encounter with Richmond.

Luckily for Greene he experienced another fainting fit, this time at work. *The Times'* medical correspondent was present and was able to state there was no sign of an epileptic attack. His brother Raymond, now fully qualified as a doctor, arranged to have tests conducted which established that there was no sign of the affliction. Greene wrote candidly to Vivien about all this, and the marriage went ahead as planned, without any of the fear and doubt which Kenneth Richmond had sought to instil.

The marriage took place at St Mary's Catholic Church, Hampstead, on 15 October 1927. Greene and Vivien were extremely happy, conscious that their marriage was an act of faith in themselves and their world. Greene described their honeymoon in the South of France as the most idyllic anyone had ever spent. They returned three weeks later to their new flat, which Vivien's mother had filled with flowers.

It was the beginning of a delightful marriage. Vivien's parents' marriage had failed under the stress of war and, tragically, her marriage was likewise to founder under the pressures created by the next war. But this was more than a decade off, and no hint of foreboding bothered them. By far the best evidence for their contentment is Greene's poem 'First Love', which won the *New Statesman* sonnet prize in September 1926. The paper was then at the height of its inter-war success and a myriad of aspiring poets must have attempted to win the prize. Poems on such a subject would have led many to outpourings of hope showing little knowledge of the real world. Greene's description of the replacement of the ineptness of first attempts by

> Perfect control of voice, lips, hands and eyes
> And comfortable ease in Paradise

was obviously the result of his great happiness. Towards the end of his life, in 1983, Greene included the poem in a very small edition of his poems privately published in Los Angeles. He gave the original manuscript of the poem to Vivien in a book which he specially created for her – only she knew he wrote the poem – now in the Harry Ransome Humanities Research Centre at Texas University. His publication of the poem under his own name so many years later shows clearly that the memories of those happy early days of his marriage stayed with him.

Greene was soon back at work on his third novel, his first published, *The Man Within*, an historical tale set on the south coast of England a century before. For complex reasons involving his hatred of his father, a young smuggler Francis Andrews has betrayed to the Revenue the men with whom he has been sailing for three years. He gains the courage to give evidence against them in court after a chance meeting with a young woman who lives alone in a cottage, where he finds refuge. Parallels with Greene's betrayal of the workers in the General Strike and his being given the courage to do so by Vivien's love can easily be found, but one should not perhaps read too much into them. The story ends on an appropriate note of tragedy with Andrews and his girl both dead.

Greene had approached Charles Evans at the publishers William

Heinemann directly, without an agent. This had long been the normal way of proceeding, but times were changing. By the end of the century it would be almost impossible for a book to find a publisher that did not have an agent behind it; in 1928, however, the new agents were only just beginning to realise their power. Evans was more than happy to take Greene's book, both on its merits, which he did not doubt, and because he knew that Greene had very good connections already, besides working on *The Times*. It was a bonus, no doubt, that he did not have to deal through A. D. Peters. *He* had faith in Greene, while Peters had dropped him.

Clemence Dane, a supporter from the first, was not the only Heinemann author who saw *The Man Within* in proof and felt able to give it a push. In Nottingham, Greene had briefly met the popular Heinemann author Cecil Roberts, later to have immense success with such books as *Havana Bound*. Roberts learned of Evans' enthusiasm and began to spread the word himself. There were more newspapers and literary magazines in London than there are today and many hundreds of influential people got to hear that an important new book from a very young author of exceptional promise was about to appear on Heinemann's list – itself a recommendation. Over a hundred advance copies of the book were sent out to the main booksellers with personal letters to the fiction buyers. But these efforts could not guarantee a success, nor could the stream of flattering reviews which appeared after the book's publication in June 1929. What mattered were the sales and which section of the market they reached.

There was an immediate reprint in the month of publication, which augured well, and a second reprint the following month. This meant that it had started to sell outside the usual circle of those who sampled first novels as part of their day-to-day literary lives to keep up to date with the latest names. It would also include first-edition collectors, a market which experienced a boom until the stock-market crash later that year. But Evans would still have been waiting for the final confirmation that his launch had been a success, the wave of orders that would follow from the lending libraries as the reputation of the book took a hold. The August holidays were crucial. In the event, orders flooded in. A further reprint had to be made in September and Evans knew he had a real success on his hands. The novel had sold nearly 10,000 copies in hardback in the first six months. The myriad of small lending libraries had taken the book; even such a small chain as the Ray Smith libraries based in Farringdon Street, which charged two pence a week for people to borrow, sent in an order.

Greene could scarcely believe what was happening, but he had a sense of the true origins of his success. He attended a garden party held by Evans at his home and wrote a full account of it to his wife, ending with a wry comment: 'I felt very seniorish as the last two [novelists Barbara Noble and Gillian Oliver] knew nobody and their books had not been a success.'[4] Greene, by implication had known people there, and of course had had a success. The interesting point was that the two people he had known longest had also invited him to visit: 'Oh my dear, I've been and gone and promised to Clemence Dane – "all butter" for a weekend; Old Lowndes and his wife were there [Mrs Belloc-Lowndes]. Mrs said she wanted to invite us to dinner ...'[5] It is not clear what the phrase 'all butter' means; perhaps he expected to have to 'butter her up'. Clemence Dane was already known as a feminist writer, the author of *Regiment of Women*, but she had also written some brilliantly successful plays, *A Bill of Divorcement* and *Will Shakespeare*, produced by Basil Dean, which had made Heinemann a great deal of money. She would soon be of great importance to Greene.

The impact of *The Man Within* had an immediate effect on Greene's life, for both he and Evans realised that he was wasted at *The Times*. With such a success behind him Greene had only to write more and he would become one of the great names. It was agreed that he should receive a salary of £650 a year from Heinemann and write full time. *The Times* failed to dissuade him, and later declined to take him back when he urgently needed to return to some regular employment.

In 1930 a salary of £650 a year was very substantial, and Greene was able to supplement it with a flow of review work. By contrast a library assistant with some years' service would then have received about £120 a year, and income tax was not levied on the first £300 (thus, as is so often forgotten, working men and women did not pay the income tax before the war). Greene had moved dramatically into a world where life in a country cottage became not a dream but a reality. In March 1931 Graham and Vivien told their friends that they were moving from their London flat to Chipping Camden in the Cotswolds, not far from Oxford.

Little Orchard was a thatched cottage of great age with the thatch almost reaching the ground. But they soon discovered that there were drawbacks to the picturesque life. Plumbing was difficult, and cooking, which Vivien had never done before, was certainly a challenge on an old-fashioned range. In those days farmworkers' cottages were often in their native state, without ceilings – that is there was nothing between the ground-floor rooms and the floorboards and joists of the rooms above. This meant that dust was forever coming down into the rooms below and that draughts were endemic. But it was an idyll nonetheless, with Greene writing every day.

Greene's two suppressed books, *The Name of Action* and *Rumour at Nightfall*, were both published while he was at Chipping Camden. The decision to suppress these books, a determined action by Greene which he made binding on his heirs, is not easily explained. When interviewed in 1979 by Marie-Françoise Allain he remarked, in a conversation about psychoanalysis and the danger of an author projecting himself directly into one of his novels, 'I realised later, for instance, that my two books *Rumour at Nightfall* and *The Name of Action* were bad because I had left too little distance between them and myself. The umbilical cord was left unbroken, you might say.'[6] In his first volume of autobiography, *A Sort of Life*, published in 1971, Greene had said almost completely the reverse:

> A writer's knowledge of himself, realistic and unromantic, is like a store of energy on which he must draw for a lifetime: one volt of it properly directed will bring a character to life. There is no spark of life in *The Name of Action* or *Rumour at Nightfall* because there was nothing of me in them. I had been determined not to write the typical autobiographical novels of a beginner, but I had gone too far in the other direction. I had removed myself altogether.[7]

These two accounts cannot both be true, nor is it a case of him changing his mind. In his autobiography he refers to *Rumour at Nightfall* as having been written under the influence of Conrad, and states that it was no more than 'the distorted ghost of Conrad'.[8] Anyone reading the book, if they can find a copy, would agree. About *The Name of Action* he says nothing. But *The Name of Action* is based so clearly on his time in Trier and the Palatinate that his vivid description when talking to Marie-Françoise Allain, of the umbilical cord not having been cut, has the ring of truth. Literary inspiration must have been provided by Geoffrey Moss's 'Defeat', which, although it is only a short story, contains the essence of the subject. The book as a whole is much in the genre of *Revolution*, though set in a different country, with religion adding a new dimension to the plot.

From the first, Clemence Dane enthusiastically supported *The Name of Action*. An extract from her review of *The Man Within* for *Book Society News* appeared on the dustwrapper, and Greene later said that she had provided the title for the book. Evans at Heinemann was equally keen, which was to the good, for he knew, as Greene perhaps did not, that second novels were the most severe test for a promising author. Sales might be very good for a first novel, but it was not until the success was carried through that a publisher could be sure that he had a best-selling author on his hands. In the event sales of the book were disappointing; the committee of the Book Society, the first large book club, no doubt discounted Clemence Dane's enthusiasm for the book as special pleading. If the news was conveyed to Greene he did not let it disturb him as he carried on with *Rumour at Nightfall*. For this book he returned to an historical setting, but in Spain rather than England. It was a fatal mistake, as Greene had never been to Spain other than for a few hours as a boy.

As soon as he received the book Evans realised there was something wrong, although he expressed his usual supportive enthusiasm. Greene was also given hope by a report from his brother Raymond that the senior member of the committee on the Book Society panel, Professor Gordon, had liked *Rumour at Nightfall* better than either of his previous books and was going to recommend it to his fellow committee members J. B. Priestley, Hugh Walpole and Sylvia Lynd. All to no avail; if the sales of *The Name of Action* were disappointing, those of *Rumour at Nightfall* were a disaster. When the book was published in America, Doubleday pulled out all the stops, openly referring to Greene on the dustwrapper as the brilliant young nephew of Robert Louis Stevenson, a ploy which Greene would never have agreed to in England. He was becoming used to bad news, but this was gloomier than he had expected. To make matters worse another project on which he had invested a great deal of time, many hopes and a lot of research, *Lord Rochester's Monkey*, a biography of the poet and rake, was refused by Heinemann by return of post.

For the first time in his adult life Greene seems to have begun to realise the crisis that ordinary people in the country were going through. His own financial predicament brought home to him that this was the reality of life for nearly everyone. Even the girl who came daily to do the housework was affected, and Greene made a full note of her day in his diary entry for 28 July 1932. It began at four in the morning picking peas before doing Greene and Vivien's more difficult housework. She then went on to their neighbours for more cleaning. But this was not the end of her day. She finished by picking currants and finally went home to make jam with what were called 'gleanings' – a part of what she had harvested that she was allowed to keep for her and her family. And the need for all this was simple: her father's unemployment pay had ended and there was no money or food in her house.[9] A short while before, on 13 June, Greene had no doubt shocked Raymond, who was visiting with friends, by arguing vigorously over lunch for a capital levy and a Marxist state. He was not following a party line left over from his days in the CPGB in Oxford but was attempting to think out his own views and theories. He admitted in his diary that his economic ideas were very vague. Shortly afterwards he started reading some of the leading texts. He began with Trotsky's *History of the Russian Revolution*, at first being annoyed by the book's style, in his diary entry for 2 August finding it difficult to read either because the translator was American or because of the language itself, but then he rapidly changed his mind. He went on to praise the book unreservedly but regretting that he did not have the time to transcribe extracts which seemed to him particularly important. He was struck by the way Trotsky made his hero not an individual but the crowd itself – workers, soldiers and others at the time of the first mutiny.[10]

There was a further unsettling incident when Kenneth and Zoe Richmond paid a surprise visit to Chipping Camden. Vivien was not

51

at home and the day may have been a painful one, as Greene makes no comment at all in his usually voluminous diary.

When the sales figures for *Rumour at Nightfall* came in, it was obvious that the regular payments which the publishers, on the basis of the early success, were still making to Greene would soon be reduced, prior to suspending them altogether and demanding something from him that would clear the unearned balance on his account. Today this seems a harsh line to take. The publishers had knowingly taken a risk; they would hardly have regarded the salaries paid to their staff as a debt which had to be repaid in the wake of disappointing sales of a book they had worked on.

Greene was determined not to fall back on his family, particularly because his branch of it was not as wealthy as his cousins at Berkhamsted, let alone the brewing side of the family or his uncle Sir Graham Greene. Nor would his wife have heard of it. Instead Greene simply carried on, looking for fresh ideas for a new book. Almost immediately after he finished *Rumour at Nightfall* he began working on what was to become *Stamboul Train*.

The success of a book creates an identity for it which may not have existed when it was being written. *Stamboul Train* is a case in point. It is true that Greene wrote it under intense pressure to come up with a success which would at least match his first book, and the style in which he wrote it was a change from what had gone before. But the content was a logical development from some of his earlier material, notably in *The Name of Action*. It is simplistic to say that both books began and ended on a train, but it is true nonetheless. European politics with a revolutionary edge is again at the centre of the plot, and there is a streak of violence which can be found in *The Name of Action* and in his later novels. Any book dealing with politics in the Europe of that day which did not refer to violence would not have been honest. The difficulty was that the mass market was escapist and could only take violence dressed up as a detective story.

Stamboul Train succeeded because it had a new range of characters, sharper writing and a great deal more creative effort expended on it. It is possible that Greene had been dissipating his energies in writing about Lord Rochester, not just in the time he spent on him, but in the draining effect of the intense intellectual effort necessary for writing historical literary biography. Even though Greene called some of his later books 'entertainments', *Stamboul Train* being the first of them, they required intensive work. The book contains some extremely shrewd comments on Greene's own religious position, on his political views and even on the literary life with which he was beginning to come to terms as an adult after his precocious introduction to it as an adolescent. There are also two portraits of leading literary figures, considerably disguised in what was to become Greene's classic manner, sometimes hidden even from himself. They were a popular novelist, Quin Savory, and a lesbian female journalist, Mabel Warren. If the journalist owed something to Clemence Dane, she was vastly amused by it and an enthusiastic supporter of the book, to good effect. The same could not be said for the original of the popular novelist, J. B. Priestley. One exchange between Mabel Warren and Quin Savory explains why:

> 'Your opinion of modern literature?' she asked. 'Joyce, Lawrence, all that?'
>
> 'It will pass,' Mr. Savory said promptly with the effect of an epigram.
>
> 'You believe in Shakespeare, Chaucer, Charles Reade, that sort of thing?'
>
> 'They will live,' Mr. Savory declared with a touch of solemnity.

And Savory later continues:

> 'You do follow these views ... they're important. They seem to me the touchstone of lit'ry integrity. One can 'ave that you know and yet sell one hundred thousand copies'...
>
> 'Very interesting,' she said. 'The public will be interested. Now what do you consider your contribution to English literature?' She grinned at him encouragingly and poised her pencil.
>
> 'Surely that's for someone else to state,' said Mr. Savory. 'But one 'opes, one 'opes, that it's something of this sort, to bring back cheerfulness and 'ealth to modern fiction. There's been too much of this introspection, too much gloom. After all the world's a fine adventurous place...'[11]

Clemence Dane was on the committee for the Book Society which considered *Stamboul Train*. The other members were as before, except

53

that Edmund Blunden had replaced J. B. Priestley. When the vote was taken it appears that Hugh Walpole, Clemence Dane and Sylvia Lynd were strongly in favour of the book and that Edmund Blunden gave it guarded support. Blunden had recently met Greene on a visit to Chipping Camden, introduced to him by his younger brother Hugh, later to become Director-General of the BBC, who was at Oxford and had caught Blunden's eye as a promising undergraduate. With this support the opposition from Professor Gordon made no headway, though he was right in saying, as Greene's biographer Professor Sherry records, that many members would object to the controversial content, not least the lesbian interludes. *Stamboul Train* received the committee's nomination as their choice for the Book Society members.

The good news for Greene, desperately needed, was tempered by the less than happy reaction to the book of the other person portrayed, J. B. Priestley. Had he been on the committee he would almost certainly have blocked the book, as he had managed to do with Greene's previous submission. This time he threatened legal action, saying that Quin Savory was an instantly recognisable portrait of himself. Later critics, and Greene himself, have said the resemblance was tenuous, relying almost entirely on references Greene made to Dickens – Priestley was known as an authority on the great Victorian writer – but it is very likely that the portrait was deliberate. Priestley was adamant. He wanted all the passages removed or altered in an agreed manner. The publishers concurred and Greene was forced to pay the cost of having pages reset, the existing pages physically removed from the books already printed and bound and new pages substituted. It was a tribute to the printers' and binders' skills that this complex work was carried out without undue delay to the publishing schedule.

Looking at the text now it is impossible to understand what the fuss was about. One of the more serious deletions was the removal of Dickens from the list of names that Mabel Warren suggests as being classics in English literature. Greene's note of humour including Charles Reade with Shakespeare and Chaucer – but not Dickens – was well judged. One of Reade's best-known titles at the time was *Hard Cash*. Although Greene was mocking Priestley and his literary aspirations, which the Yorkshireman attempted to reconcile with massive sales, he was soon to find a large boost to his income from pursuing a similar path. But, whereas Mr Savory aimed at hundreds of thousands, Greene's target was the millions who watched the cinema screen. He had written the book in cinematic style, hoping to catch a film company's eye, and he succeeded.

In May 1933 Greene's agent in America secured a sale of the film rights in *Stamboul Train* to Twentieth Century-Fox for $7,500. At the prevailing exchange rate this was nearly £2,000, which, after agent's commission, left Greene with the precisely recorded sum of £1,783 3s 8d. The money came none too soon, although the sales of the book itself were by far the best he had so far enjoyed.

CHAPTER FOUR

Politics and Religion: The ILP
and Father Bede Jarrett

In the first volume of the authorised biography of Graham Greene, Professor Sherry observed in passing that Greene had joined the Independent Labour Party. I decided to follow this up by going to the party's archives, which are now deposited at the London School of Economics. The holdings there include a run of the ILP paper the *New Leader*, its back pages listing meetings and clubs, alongside poems and the cartoons of Claud Flight, the pioneering print-maker. It was immediately obvious that Greene's novels of the mid-1930s had a specific political view behind them, something he had successfully concealed from biographers and interviewers.

In one of the few direct comments on his work Greene described *It's a Battlefield* as his first overtly political novel. This is a broad clue that has not been followed up by any of the host of commentators who have followed Graham Greene's life. The statement is precise and refers to actual political purpose and political origins. The facts can be established once the focus pulls back from a close-up on Greene and takes in the surrounding political activity with which Greene was closely involved, although the search for them is made more difficult by the deliberate disinformation inserted in Greene's second volume of autobiography, *Ways of Escape*. It is evidently deliberate because he states that he has re-read his diaries in order to bring back the day-to-day struggles, and yet ignores much detailed information in those diaries which he must have known contradicted what he then wrote in his autobiography.

A good example is his statement that the police commissioner in the book was based partly on his uncle: 'My uncle Graham Greene, who had been Secretary of the Admiralty under Mr. Churchill during the First World War, lent a little of his stiff inhibited bachelor integrity to the character of the Assistant Commissioner.'[1] Yet he does not mention that by far the most likely original of the character was, on the evidence of his diary, a man who had been a close friend when he was living in Chipping Camden. He had indeed been an Assistant Commissioner in the prison service and held exactly the opinions Greene gives to the policeman in the book. It is interesting to compare his diary description of this man with that of his uncle. Colonel Turner, despite having been a prison governor before rising to Assistant Commissioner, was a humanitarian who believed in the individual above movements and even the English legal system. Greene compared him favourably as a humanitarian with Galsworthy whom he had known since the Beresford days. In Greene's eyes commitment to the individual was the highest form of humanism.[2]

Turner was married to an American, the novelist Margaret Wilson, whom he had met in India where she had been a missionary. She was a pacifist, and Greene describes a visit to one of her pacifist parties, as well as frequent social occasions when and Vivien went out with her and her husband. It is possible that it was Margaret Wilson who introduced him to American authors such as Edmund Wilson, whose *Devil Take the Hindmost* he records reading, and even more John Dos Passos. The most striking resemblance between Turner and the Assistant Commissioner in the novel comes when the fictional character remembers how a rich businessman had produced medical certificates at a trial in mitigation, avoiding incarceration, while a thief who had taken some worthless jewels was imprisoned:

> He knew quite well the cause of the discrepancy: the laws were made by property owners in defence of their property; that was why a fascist could talk treason without prosecution; that was why a man who defrauded the State in defence of his private wealth did not even lose the money he had gained; that was why the burglar went to jail for five years; that was why Drover could not so easily be reprieved – he was a communist.[3]

Conrad Drover's plight is at the heart of the novel. He has killed a policeman who attacked his wife during a demonstration, and there was strong political pressure for the death sentence to be reduced to life imprisonment. Greene has his character comment: 'The Assistant Commissioner was more than ever thankful that justice was not his business.'[4] The resemblance to his comment on Colonel Turner is so close that one wonders what the Turners and their friends made of it when *It's a Battlefield* appeared.

The wider role of the book in Greene's own political life arose from his involvement with politics after his success with *Stamboul Train*. The Hollywood sale enabled him and Vivien to move back into Oxford and take a modern flat, as stark a contrast as possible from their cottage at Chipping Camden. It was newly built, the paint barely dry, and they were to have congenial neighbours. Shortly before they moved in they learned that Hugh, Greene's younger brother, had mentioned the flats to Edmund Blunden and his new wife and that they too had decided to live there.

Greene's political interest as it now developed may have reflected his cousin Ben's continuing involvement with the Labour Party, in which he was making a name for himself with campaigns for the reorganisation of constituency representation in the party. But he did not follow Ben's example; instead he decided to join the Independent Labour Party and set up a branch in Oxford. In 1932 the ILP, as it was known, had split away from the official Labour Party after the financial crisis of 1931 and the creation of a coalition administration. A key question was to what extent the ILP should be co-operating with the Communist Party in day-to-day tactics. The ILP worked with the CPGB in 1932, and a debate on the question was continuing. But in 1933 there had been a new development: the movement's newspaper the *New Leader* had begun printing letters from Trotsky and had already gone some distance along the path that saw it back the POUM in the Spanish Civil War. George Orwell was a member of the ILP and this was why he fought with the POUM (or the United Marxist Workers Party, which had its own militia and was referred to as 'Trotskyite' by the Communist Party). From reading Greene's diaries, for example the entries referred to in Chapter Three above, it is obvious that Greene joined the ILP because of his sympathy with Trotsky's views.

In 1933 there was a serious split in the ILP between one faction led by John Middleton Murry, an intellectual who had edited the magazine *Rhythm* with his wife Katherine Mansfield before the war, and another led by the Labour MP for Glasgow, James Maxton. Greene hoped that he could set up an Oxford branch of the ILP, with Maxton giving an inaugural speech: this demonstrates that he was a member of Maxton's faction and was opposed to Middleton Murry. And it is here that the direct political origins of *It's a Battlefield* appear. In his autobiography *Ways of Escape* Greene says that the politician Mr Surrogate in the novel owes something to Middleton Murry. Oddly he also says that he did not know Murry. This is another of Greene's enigmatic clues – how could Greene have modelled a character on someone he had never met, and why should he? The answer is now plain: he knew Murry very well in political terms and he disagreed with him. When it is understood who the subject is, his portrait can be seen to be an especially savage one. In purely literary terms *It's a Battlefield* relates directly to Beresford's *Revolution*, and is further informed by Greene's own experiences of actual political conflict in Europe and his own rapidly developing political views.

There is some mystery about Greene's proposed branch of the ILP in Oxford. The surviving papers of the ILP make no mention of any branch there, and a 1933 edition of the *New Leader* with full branch listings does not show one for Oxford. However, the newspaper did run an advertisement the following year, 1934, asking for anyone interested in setting up an Oxford branch to get in touch. But there is no doubt that Greene joined the party. He records his joining on 11 August 1933 and then adds a fascinating account of his previous history. He began by saying that he had supported the Conservatives when he first came to Oxford, reflecting no doubt his attachment to Buchan. He then admitted that he had taken money from Frank Gray and his membership of the Communist Party. He revealed that he was ashamed of the part he played in the General Strike, not just that he had helped break it but had accepted a silver matchbox, an album of photographs and additional pay. The salient fact here is that, if he thought his early political activity was not entirely serious, he must have believed that he had joined the ILP in earnest; by the same token he took membership of the CPGB to be on a par with his other political activity at the time, and certainly did not regard it as an undergraduate joke, as he maintained after the Second World War.

Serious though his decision to join the ILP may have been, it did not survive long. In a letter written to John Lehmann, famous as the editor of the Penguin 'New Writing' series, to thank him for a favourable mention in his New Writing and Europe in 1940, Greene said that he was not as far to the right as Lehmann supposed, although he had allowed his membership of the ILP to lapse three or four years earlier, that is in 1936 or 1937. It seems most likely that the process of drifting away from the views he had developed living in poverty and isolation at Chipping Camden began as soon as he returned to Oxford. And here again the influence of Vivien and the religious life in Oxford were paramount factors.

When their daughter Lucy Caroline was born in December 1933, Bede Jarrett became her godfather. Sadly he died very shortly afterwards and the task was taken over by David Mathew, a priest whose brother Gervase, a Dominican, was close to Greene. Bede Jarrett's death at the age of fifty-three came as a shock to everyone, not least the Greenes, for Raymond Greene was one of his doctors. He had seemed very much alive and was engaged once again in Oxford life, having reached the end of his term as Provincial of the Order in England.

Now that he was back in Oxford Jarrett had taken over the editorship of Blackfriars helped by an assistant, Thomas Gilby. It was a time of literary and religious controversy. The Tablet, a leading Catholic intellectual magazine, had condemned Evelyn Waugh's book Black Mischief in very severe terms and a letter of protest against the editor had been fired off, signed by many of the leading Catholic clergy and laymen of the day. The letter was significant, for it brought together a group who were to exert great influence over the Church and, incidentally, over Greene. Bede Jarrett had been one of the signatories.

The letter had been organised by Tom Burns, a young publisher who was also to become a close friend of Greene's. The editor against whom their rage was directed, Ernest Oldmeadow, was dismissed shortly afterwards when his protector Cardinal Bourne died. The Tablet, previously the property of the Church, was sold to a group of three laymen, including Tom Burns, who later established a trust which now owns the paper. Greene was a trustee until he died.

Curiously Waugh, whose book had caused all the fuss, veered over to the right, whereas Burns and Greene maintained a liberal view to the end. Other signatories included Father Martindale, for whom Greene had the highest regard, and Eric Gill. But the central figure as far as Greene was concerned was Bede Jarrett. His death was a double tragedy, for, had he lived, much of the confusion on religious questions into which Greene fell, and which have caused his readers and critics such confusion, would surely have been resolved.

The importance of Bede Jarrett in Greene's life at the time can be seen in a letter Greene wrote to his brother Hugh, who had now left Oxford and gone to work for the *Daily Telegraph* in Germany. Hugh had wanted some information and introductions, which Graham happily supplied:

> I don't know any of the Jesuits, but I saw Bede Jarrett who has just
> come to an end of his term as Provincial of the Dominicans. He's going
> to ring me up with introductions to Jesuits and to some of the leading
> lay Catholics in Munich ... I don't have to give him any reason. Tell
> me if you become a Catholic.[6]

Greene clearly hoped that contact with German Catholicism would have the same effect on his younger brother as it had had on him. In the years to come anyone who had normal left-wing views but was not a Catholic would find this position very difficult to understand. Indeed an Englishman who was anti-Nazi and left of centre was assumed to be anti-Catholic, and this was largely as a result of the Spanish Civil War. The position of Evelyn Waugh was made even more complicated in this context by the publication of his biography of Edmund Campion in 1935, which Greene praised and was influenced by. It took a pronounced recusant position, attacked the Protestants vigorously, and found strong parallels between the English priests who suffered for their faith and the Mexican priests who had died under a Marxist government. So difficult was this problem for Greene that he could resolve it only by actually going to Mexico, largely through Tom Burns' efforts.

England Made Me (1935), Greene's sequel to *It's a Battlefield*, also had its beginnings in his fraught later days at the cottage at Chipping

Camden. Just as the crash of 1929 and the slump that followed took time to reach the publishing world – the curtailing of Greene's income stemmed in part from that – so it took time to reach the greatest fortunes. The Swede Ivar Kreuger controlled virtually all the world's match business, a near-monopoly which business analysts and politicians alike thought would be immune from a slump no matter how severe, because as things got worse people would smoke more and use more matches. Kreuger did not disillusion the stream of banks and governments that came to him for loans. Even the finance ministers of Europe were not too proud to take loans from his corporation, Kreuger and Toll. But in 1932 the inevitable happened, and Kreuger committed suicide when it was found that he had pledged forged securities on a massive scale. Greene wrote a review of one of the instant biographies that appeared in March 1933. He saw this as yet another instance of the coming collapse of capitalism and was sure he had found the subject of his next book. By now he had learned his lesson about writing a book without visiting the place depicted, and over the last months in the cottage he looked for someone to go with him – solitary voyages were still an unusual event for him. In the end his brother Hugh tagged along.

The original title of the book had been *Brothers and Sisters*, and although the title was dropped the book did deal with a brother and sister who were very close, an almost forbidden theme at the time. When Leonhard Frank's *Brother and Sister* appeared in an English translation in 1930 it had to be in a limited edition of only 500 copies to avoid possible legal action. Indeed it is possible, from the closely similar title, that Greene took his theme from Frank.

To this Greene added the Kreuger theme – his book was a portrait of a wealthy Swedish businessman – and it followed the precedent of *It's a Battlefield* by using a member of his family, his eldest brother Herbert, as a lay model for the anti-hero Anthony Farrant. Greene in his autobiography describes how one of the characters whom he thought of as being a bit-player developed while the book was being written and became a central character, the journalist Minty. Greene is wryly admitting that he found his own personality intruding into the book without his realising it.

Buried in the text of *England Made Me* is a typically Greene hint, tantalisingly suggesting that he had visited Russia. The passage is brief but suggestive. Fred Hall, assistant to the Swedish businessman, travels frequently on the continent and Greene describes his journeys, which are clearly based on his own visits, comparing them to life on the Brighton Pullman:

> He knew the airports of Europe as well as he had once known the stations on the Brighton line – shabby Le Bourget; the great scarlet rectangle of the Tempelhof as one came in from London in the dark, the headlamp lighting up the asphalt way; the white sand blowing up around the shed at Tallinn; Riga where the Berlin to Leningrad plane came down and bright pink mineral waters were sold in a tin-roofed shed; the huge aerodrome at Moscow with machines parked half-a-dozen deep, the pilots taxiing here and there, trying to find room, bouncing back and forth, beckoned by one official with his hat askew. It was a comfortable dull way of travelling but sometimes Fred Hall missed the racing tips from strangers in the Brighton Pullman.[7]

Most of these places were well known to any seasoned traveller, but Tallinn and Moscow were not. Greene had been to Tallinn early in 1934, and his description of Moscow seems to be Greene at his most observant. Some commentators have made much of the possibility that Greene visited Moscow at this time, but if he did so he kept it from everyone, including MI6 and his family and friends. However, the circumstantial political evidence established here suggests that it is highly unlikely that he would have taken the risk. Anyone with an ILP background, a Trotsky supporter in Moscow's eyes, would have been committing suicide by going to the Soviet Union, certainly with any political purpose.

When he describes in his autobiography *Ways of Escape* the journey he made, to Tallinn in Estonia, he makes a great mystery of why he went, claiming that it was 'for no reason except escape to somewhere new'.[8] Rarely did Greene go somewhere to escape simply because it was new. The tourist instinct was never strongly developed in him and seems to have been extinguished with a Swan-Hellenic cruise he took with his wife in the 1930s, and a round-the-world trip on which he embarked after the war with the author and playwright Michael Meyer. Elsewhere he talks of his real reason for the trip to Estonia; it involved Nordahl Grieg, the Norwegian poet and brother of Greene's publisher in Norway, who had once visited Greene in Chipping Camden:

> I sometimes wonder whether he didn't also leave spells in far off places which drew me there long afterwards. Why did I take a solitary holiday in Estonia in the thirties? Was it because I was following in his footsteps? And Moscow in the fifties? It was no longer any use then going to Room 313 in the hotel Novo Moscowskaja, the address he had given me in case 'you one day suddenly find yourself in Moscow', his ghost had moved a long way on.[9]

There were no tourists on that trip.

J. F. Leslie, a British diplomat, was the only other passenger on the plane which took Greene from Riga to Tallinn, and the author noticed that they were both reading books by Henry James. Leslie was also a convert to Roman Catholicism and they got on very well. When he died he left Greene his collection of James first editions but there is little else known about their friendship, which started in such strange circumstances, other than an allusion to spying in Tallinn in the first drafts of what became *Our Man in Havana*. This was originally to be set before the war in Tallinn, and the recruitment of Wormald as a spy for MI6 was a classic example of bungling by the authorities. Was Greene that man? Or was Greene saying that Leslie, who had earlier been in the armaments business, was an MI6 man, the model for Wormald? The answers will almost certainly be found in MI6 archives, if a search can ever be authorised. At the moment it appears from the Cabinet Office briefing that Greene did not visit Russia at this time and he was not known to have worked for MI6 before the war. It has been suggested that Felix Greene might have visited Russia at this time, following his brother Ben's initiative, but for entirely different motives.

A final note of mystery was added on Greene's return. He was supposed to pass through Riga and, on the very night that he should have been there, a revolution broke out. His brother Hugh was due to meet him the next day in Germany and he hoped for a scoop – eyewitness accounts from Western observers were almost non-existent. He was astonished when Graham said he knew nothing of any revolution, although he had passed through Riga when it was supposed to be taking place. Was this simply classic bad luck – or had there been nothing to see? (A similar thing happened to him in Prague during the revolution in 1948, when there was little to see and less to report, though Greene tried his best.) Or had Greene indeed gone on to Moscow, and returned by a different route?

When Greene returned to Oxford he soon became absorbed in domestic affairs with a very young daughter. Financial matters had improved, but he knew well enough that he could not rest on his laurels. Many of his friends had travelled abroad and written about their adventures afterwards in a way which he had in effect pioneered when they had been at Oxford with him; at first sight Greene's trip to Liberia and the book that followed, *Journey without Maps*, seems cut from the same cloth.

He later gave the impression that his journey was made almost on impulse, and certainly the decision to take his cousin Barbara, Ben's sister, does seem to have been reached over an extra glass of champagne or two at Hugh Greene's wedding. But the underlying purpose was not casual at all.

In his diary entry for 19 November 1932 Greene made a note of some current reading and the thoughts it inspired. A book that particularly influenced him was a biography of H. M. Stanley, the African explorer, by Carl Jacob Wassermann, translated by Eden and Cedar Paul. The romantic view of Stanley and Central Africa had had added to it in Greene's mind the literary world of Conrad's *The Heart of Darkness*. He had also read Gide's *Voyage au Congo* but it was Wassermann's book that left the lasting impression reflecting the literary symbolism established by Conrad and Gide.[10] This entry is the precise origin of the very unusual travel book which Greene was to write, as much a journey of self-exploration as a travel book, as Clemence Dane was to remark in her review, faithfully reprinted on the dust-jacket of the American edition. But Greene did not make the journey until 1935, nor get down to planning it seriously until after his daughter had been born.

Journeys around Europe, however risky politically, were completely different from travel in areas where there were no maps which cost a great deal more money. Travel by plane from city to city was not cheap, but having to employ large teams of bearers with equipment to cross country where there had never been roads and where, literally, no white man had been seen before, involved outlay of a different order. Greene knew this and began searching for backers. This time it was his uncle Sir Graham Greene who came to the rescue. He still lived in his large country house in the grounds of which Graham had played as a child, and was still a bachelor much involved in espionage matters. He had visited Graham and Vivien in Chipping Camden and Oxford and was keen to help.

Sir Graham was also a member of one of the great Victorian philanthropic institutions that still played a part in British life at that time, the Anti-Slavery and Aboriginal Protection Society. The Society was very keen to see Greene go on an expedition to Liberia, where there was a very unstable political situation and worrying reports which its members were enquiring about. A condition of its support was that Greene would have to address the members afterwards and make a report. For his part Greene obtained the backing of a publisher. He then went to the Foreign Office for an interview and to get general advice on the type of assistance that might be available. Understandably they tried to dissuade him, particularly when they discovered that he intended taking a young cousin along with him. Liberia was not society territory. Greene's initial letter to the man at the Liberia desk, Mr Thompson, makes it quite clear who the driving force behind the operation was for his very first words referred to Sir Graham Greene as the person who had smoothed his path.[11] Sir Graham had found the right person at the right desk for his young nephew to see and there can be no doubt at all that the entire venture was in his hands from the start. It was soon obvious to G. H. Thompson that all arrangements had been made by Sir Graham and that there was little else to do but warn his nephew of the dangers, especially those of illness – a final telling thrust that might yet dissuade him. Greene replied that he had access to all the necessary medical advice with a knowledgeable reference to hyperdermic syringes and other medical accoutrements.[12]

The expedition, which set off at the start of 1935, proved to be a success. Greene did become ill in the hinterland, but the syringes and serums, no doubt provided by Raymond, had been left on the coast and so were of no use. For a while his life seemed in danger, but he threw his fever off, and he and Barbara performed better than anyone might have expected. Both were to write books of their journey, but the first serious report came from the Embassy in Liberia. A. E. Yapp wrote to the Foreign Secretary Sir Samuel Hoare giving an account of the opinions expressed by visitors during the year, beginning with the Greenes:

> Graham Greene and Miss Barbara Greene. These people trekked last spring through from Pendenbu to Bassa and lived with me for 12 days. They were charmed by the President and the members of the Cabinet they met, but complained against one District Commissioner. I think they found conditions in Liberia so normal they were disappointed! Miss B.G. has, as far as I know, written only one article for the *Daily Chronicle* which she ended up by a stupid and unnecessary reference to the President's clothes being aired on the balcony of the Mansion House (we are all obliged to do this here).[13]

It was a suitably prosaic note on which to end his report. If Sir Graham Greene had arranged for them to obtain more serious information for his friends in MI6, it never became known to the men on the ground. But the trip was important for Greene in establishing the pattern which he followed in later life of going to a country and naturally expecting to visit the President and senior political figures. It never seemed to occur to him how unusual this was; he absorbed Sir Graham Greene's patrician, colonial view of the world, held unconsciously no doubt, and it remained with him for the rest of his life.

Soon after his return Graham decided, with Vivien, that they would have to return to London. He had become involved with the circle around the *Spectator* and its literary editor Derek Verschoyle was able to recommend a property which his sister had just refurbished on Clapham Common. It had a grand staircase and an enticing Georgian atmosphere – this was the day of the Georgian Society, founded by Douglas Goldring and his friends, and A. J. A. Symons' First Edition Club in Bedford Square – and it had space for a growing family. It is interesting to compare the homes Greene chose for himself and those which others found for him, particularly after Chipping Camden. The Oxford flat was as complete a contrast with their cottage or the house at Clapham as might be imagined. Much later when he came to settle in Antibes he chose a similar flat of modest dimensions. Was it the memory of the slavery to which large houses condemned the girls who had to keep them up, like his daily at Chipping Camden, that affected his choice? Certainly it was not a world he knew from the example of his uncle Sir Graham or anyone else in his family.

The first practical use he made of his being in London was a prosaic one. He attended a Royal Commission on armaments.

CHAPTER FIVE

The Chaco Wars: Arms and the Guilty Men

By now the clues that Greene seems to have left for anyone on a determined quest for the origins of his work were becoming easier to spot. When he talked of his novel *A Gun for Sale*, published in 1936, and said that he had attended an armaments conference but could not remember whether this was before or after he had begun the book, adding that anyway it made little difference, this was a clear signal that there was something worth exploring.

Checking through the indexes for *The Times* I soon identified the conference. The paper's coverage was good and the origins of Greene's plot and characters, and even his likely political perspective, were soon established.

In its detailed, if laconic, accounts of one of the meetings of the 1935 Royal Commission on Armaments, *The Times* commented that the meetings were held in public but that attendance was meagre. One of those settled in the public seats in the Middlesex Guildhall, where most of the sittings took place, was Graham Greene. In his autobiography he said that he could not remember whether he went to the meetings to gather material for *A Gun for Sale* or whether they gave him the idea. He made light of the proceedings and spoke of his book as a thriller. In fact it was an acutely political book, at least as much as *It's a Battlefield*. Was Greene drawing a veil over his views at the time; or was he leaving clues, if he was indeed making a detective story out of his life?

Nineteen-thirty-five was a crucial year in the political shadow-boxing that led up to the Second World War. The previous year had seen a public ballot in Britain on the question of peace and war, and on the key question of whether the public thought that armaments manufacture should be taken out of the hands of private companies and turned into state enterprises; 6,500,000 had voted for a ban on arms sales and 490,000 had voted against. This represented an enormous demonstration of public concern and the Prime Minister, Ramsay MacDonald, deciding to do something about it, set up the Royal Commission. There was a similar enquiry in the United States organised by Roosevelt, and the results were to be considered by the League of Nations disarmament conference in Geneva which was then in session.

The terms of the Commission showed clearly why it was set up. Its main task was:

> To consider and report on the practicability and desirability of the adoption by the United Kingdom (alone or with other countries) of a prohibition of private manufacture or trade in arms and munitions of war and in the institution of a State monopoly of such manufacture and trade.[1]

Amongst those on the committee was J. A. Spender, who had been editor of the *Westminster Gazette* for many years, and the redoubtable figure of Dame Rachel Crowdy, who had recently held the post of Chief of the Social Affairs and Opium Section of the League of Nations. Sir John Eldon Bankes, a retired lord justice of appeal, presided. It was the evidence to this committee which gave Greene much of the background to his book and about which he is more than usually misleading. He commented in *Ways of Escape* in 1980:

> My chief memory of the hearings is of the politeness and feebleness of the cross-examination. Some great firms were concerned and over and over again counsel found that essential papers were missing or had not been brought to court. A search of course would be made ... there was a relaxed air of *mañana*.[2]

Greene's reference to great firms is almost certainly to the armaments manufacturers Vickers Armstrong and the allegations made against them in public by Fenner Brockway, author of a well-known book on the trade in armaments, *The Bloody Traffic*, but in this instance speaking on behalf of his party, the ILP. Brockway dwelt on the fact that six retired senior government officials had taken up directorships of Vickers, and the first name he gave was the then chairman of the company, General Sir Herbert Lawrence. He added salt to his charges by alleging that *Times* reporters had habitually acted as agents for Vickers and submitted reports likely to increase fear of war so that the company's shares would rise in price. *The Times*, in commenting on the allegation, admitted that it had been true but stated that there had been only two reporters involved who had resigned in 1925 and 1927, adding that they had held only minor posts reporting from capitals in the Balkans. But the Balkans of course were not so minor: it was the assassination of Archduke Franz Ferdinand in Sarajevo in 1914 which sparked the First World War.

Greene was still with the ILP, and it may have been to listen to this evidence that he attended the hearings. But there was other evidence, given by Lord Cecil, which bore even more closely on his theme in *A Gun for Sale*. Cecil had been at the Disarmament Conference at Geneva in 1927 and had seen documents showing the disreputable attempts by armaments companies to ensure that they were not harmed by the proposed arms reductions:

> The influence of armament firms tends to dampen the actual effort for peace. There had been cases in which active steps had been taken by great armament interests to prevent the conclusion of disarmament negotiations. The most startling case was that of Mr. Shearer who was employed by certain great firms in America to prevent the conclusion of the disarmament conference in Geneva in 1927.[3]

But it was not only American firms that were involved. Dame Rachel Crowdy asked Lord Cecil about the war in South America between Bolivia and Paraguay, known as the Chaco Wars, and he confirmed that British armaments manufacturers had been supplying both sides and, effectively, fomenting the war.

Sir William Jowitt, in submitting evidence on behalf of the Union for Democratic Control, suggested that the committee should call Sir Basil Zaharoff, perhaps the most notorious private arms dealer of the inter-war years, though in reality a relatively minor player that larger principals – American, British, German and others – used as an intermediary. He did not appear, but, as Greene explains, he did help form the central character in his book:

About the same time somebody had written a biography of Sir Basil Zaharoff, a more plausible villain for those days than the man in Buchan's *The Thirty-Nine Steps* who could 'hood his eyes like a hawk'. Sir Marcus in *A Gun for Sale* is, of course, not Sir Basil, but the family resemblance is plain.[4]

The reference to Buchan is crucial and is the key to an understanding of what Greene was about in writing these books, which he so guilefully characterised as 'entertainments'. He went on to make one of his fullest statements; it is essential to reproduce it in full here:

> An early hero of mine was John Buchan, but when I reopened his books I could no longer get the same pleasure from the adventures of Richard Hannay. More than the dialogue and the situation had dated: the moral climate was no longer that of my boyhood. Patriotism had lost its appeal, even for a schoolboy, at Passchendaele, and the Empire brought first to mind the Beaverbrook Crusader, while it was difficult, during the years of the Depression, to believe in the high purposes of the City of London or of the British Constitution. The hunger marchers seemed more real than the politicians. It was no longer a Buchan world. The hunted man of *A Gun for Sale*, which I now began to write, was Raven, not Hannay: a man out to revenge himself for all the dirty tricks of life, not to save his country.[5]

It is absolutely clear from this that Greene was consciously following in Buchan's footsteps – and it is interesting that he never mentions that he met Buchan at Oxford. But rather than admiring him in a simple schoolboy fashion, he admires him in an entirely contemporary way, with anti-hero substituted for hero. Far from being trivial entertainment *A Gun for Sale* is extremely serious. This paradox goes to the heart of the quest for the real Graham Greene – when he says he is 'entertaining,' he may be at his most earnest.

The central plot of *A Gun for Sale* is taken directly from the cold reality Greene had discovered in the almost empty Middlesex Guildhall as he and a few others took their notes. Sir Marcus, who runs Midland Steel, has arranged for the assassination of an old friend of his who is now a senior minister in a Balkan country. He knows that someone with a letter from himself will be able to get in to see the minister. He sends Raven, who is desperate for money and agrees to turn into a killer for £200. The murder works exactly as Sir Marcus hopes. Although the government suspends all export licences for arms – a detail which Greene got from the Royal Commission hearings – the trade in metals needed for guns goes on and he makes over half a million pounds in profit when armaments and metal-company share prices soar. But the greed of his agents destroys him. They pay Raven in forged money which is immediately detected, and he finds his dreams of marrying a girl in his Soho world gone. Instead he hunts down the man who paid him, who in turn leads him to Sir Marcus in his midlands steel town; eventually he kills them both.

The midlands town Nottwich is once again Nottingham, for which Greene had a lasting affection. But there was one detail in the final scene, when arrangements are being made for a public meeting, which could have caused his publishers difficulty, and which could still do so today. On the wall above the speakers' platform is a photograph of the Grand Master of the Masonic lodge in whose hall the meeting is being held, and it is of course Sir Marcus.

If the book was taken as having a political message, it would be that working men who find themselves caught up in the schemes of armaments manufacturers manipulating war and fears of war for their own gain should take their courage in their hands and go and kill the men manipulating them. Greene's view of Raven quoted above is not far off that interpretation. But, bearing in mind the likely audience for his books, it could equally well be read as a warning to the armaments men of what might happen if they went on playing these odious games.

Greene was developing themes which were to stay with him for years to come. The hero Raven is involved in gang warfare around Brighton race-course and with a razor has actually killed someone called Kite taken up later in *Brighton Rock*. It is possible that Greene was having doubts about creating an anti-hero to replace Hannay. He and countless others had taken Hannay as their hero – what would happen to those who took Raven as theirs?

If today the book lacks the force it would have had in 1936, that is surely because the facts of the international armaments industry are now accepted as normal and governments have taken over the trade which used to be co-ordinated by Sir Basil Zaharoff and his fictional counterpart Sir Marcus. Governments are all armaments speculators now and the millions who suffer in Africa and South America, and in many other third world countries, as a result of their arms-sales programmes are then helped by humanitarian campaigns launched from the same sophisticated societies that created the weapons. Such is the miraculous symmetry of late twentieth-century industrial civilisation. The only difference between the present-day situation and the one that Greene attacked in 1936 is that the millions no longer die on the Somme or Passchendaele but in some obscure place in Africa where the violence is always black on black.

A Gun for Sale is written in graphic cinematic terms, and Greene again had hopes that the film rights would be sold. They were, but to an American company, Paramount, which produced a film in 1942 whose script was so altered that its origins and message were completely lost. Had the film been made in England in 1936, strictly in accordance with the text with a realistic setting and good casting, it might have had a political impact. Fortunately the film is forgotten, but given a knowledge of the background the book can be read today with undiminished effect. The point is important because the distortions in the film prompted Greene to go beyond simply writing books that he hoped would be turned into films and to become involved in film itself. It was a path that was to lead to *The Third Man*, one of the best films of the twentieth century.

Not surprisingly a feature of Greene's extensive film reviews at this time, collected in *Mornings in the Dark* (published with an introduction by David Parkinson in 1993), was his severe criticism of the output of the major American studios, and this extended to the few producers in England who were turning out films on a similar scale with mass appeal. The man most often in the centre of his sights was Alexander Korda. Korda asked to meet the man who was so ruthlessly attacking him. Greene says that it was H. G. Wells who built the first bridge between them, but there may have been others willing to lend a hand or, more importantly to tell Korda that there was a human side to Greene.

Clemence Dane was the most likely intermediary. She was working for Korda at this time producing a string of film scripts, sometimes adaptations, sometimes original work. Her original screenplays, such as that for *St Martin's Lane*, which appeared in 1938 and starred Charles Laughton, had some success. It was her great skills at writing for the medium that Greene was eager to learn. The likelihood that the introduction came indirectly from Clemence Dane is strengthened by the fact that once Korda had accepted him as a screenwriter Greene worked with Basil Dean, her collaborator on all her plays.

When the two men finally met Korda plunged right in: had Greene anything he was working on that might be of use to him? Greene immediately started describing the scene from *A Gun for Sale* in which Kite is standing on a railway station with blood from a razor cut streaming to the ground – the scene has shifted from Brighton to Paddington station, but the germ of the idea is the same. When Korda eagerly asked what happened next, Greene said he was working on it. This pitch was enough to get him a job writing what was to be his first, and worst, film script, *The Green Cockatoo*. Its greatest importance, perhaps, was that it enabled Greene to incubate a story which finally emerged as *Brighton Rock*, to be filmed in its turn after the war.

The stern impartiality with which Greene lambasted his next project for Korda, with Dean directing – an adaptation of Galsworthy's story 'The First and the Last' – shows how objective he could be about his own work when he knew it was bad:

> Perhaps I may be forgiven for noticing a picture in which I had some hand, for I have no good word to say of it. The brilliant acting of Mr. Hay Petrie as a decayed and outcast curate cannot conquer the overpowering flavour of cooked ham ... I wish I could tell the extraordinary story that lies behind this shelved and resurrected picture, a story involving a theme song, and a bottle of whisky, and camels in Wales ... Meanwhile let one guilty man, at any rate, stand in the dock swearing never, never to do it again...[6]

Greene added a sideswipe at the censor who would not allow a suicide to appear on screen in those days – the film finally appeared in 1940. As Greene remarked, this was a difficulty in a story which hinges on a suicide. But Greene stuck to screenwriting despite the setbacks, because he hoped that he would soon be able to stop writing novels altogether and simply write for the films and perhaps even get into production himself. The astonishing fees were what finally turned his head, as they did with almost everyone who got involved in film in those days. In the end it also led to him revising his opinion of Korda and becoming a very close friend.

Korda had Greene on his doorstep and was able to draw his sting. The American moguls could not get near him, and the reviews Greene wrote grew worse when he became editor of a new London weekly, *Night and Day*, which was intended to rival the *New Yorker*. Even Korda had difficulty in restraining Greene from putting violence and sexual innuendo in some of his scripts and actually rejected material from him for this reason. The trouble was that Greene saw film in those terms, particularly sexual. When Shirley Temple, the child star, appeared in *Wee Willie Winkie*, a film freely adapted from Kipling's book with what seemed to him sexual overtones, Greene could not restrain himself and, as editor of the magazine, had nobody to restrain him. In the issue of 28 October 1937 he launched an outright attack on the film-makers Twentieth Century-Fox for their use of the young girl. It proved too much even for Hollywood to stomach, and the film company sued Greene and the publishers of the magazine on Shirley Temple's behalf, and won.

Wee Willie Winkie was directed by John Ford and, as Greene put it in his 350-word review, was horrifyingly competent. It is difficult now to see exactly what provoked the fierce condemnation with which the judge concluded his remarks in the High Court. His words so angered Greene that he reproduced them verbatim, with choice excerpts from the transcript, in his volume of autobiography *Ways of Escape* in 1980. The judge referred to the review Greene had written in the bluntest terms: 'This libel is simply a gross outrage,'[7] and he awarded damages accordingly against both the magazine and Greene. Today in a world which nods in passing at Jodie Foster in *Taxi Driver*, a modern critic may miss Greene's underlying point, that the makers of the film had pandered to the unnatural lust of elderly and respected members of the community – in other words, that Shirley Temple was being abused by her employers. His interpretation of the film may well have genuinely disturbed many of the readers of that issue of *Night and Day* who had not had an injection of pseudo-Freudian analysis at the age of sixteen. They *were* outraged. And there is some evidence that the reason for the seemingly oppressive response from the court was not simply because the content of Greene's review was objectionable.

By the time the 28 October 1937 issue of the magazine appeared, *Night and Day* was already in financial difficulties. The poster for that issue cited the Shirley Temple review and did so in such terms that W. H. Smith and other distributors refused to touch the magazine, despite having happily sold previous editions. The poster has never been published, although it was produced in court, and it has not been possible to find a copy. However, when the ban by Smith's was announced Greene and the magazine's sales department immediately trumpeted the news and began an intense sales effort on the back of this welcome free advertisement. Shirley Temple had a mass following at the time, and it was not composed of elderly vicars with a prurient interest in her emerging virginal sexuality, as Greene had suggested. Had he been in England when he was identified as the perpetrator of the outrage he would have found the fine of £500 the least of his worries. But he had left the country and was in Mexico on an assignment which he was later to say began his emotional rather than intellectual attachment to the Catholic Church.

It has often been repeated that *Night and Day* closed because of the court case, but the last issue had already appeared on 23 December 1937, long before the court judgement on 22 March 1938. The sales ploy had failed and nobody else could be found to supply the capital needed to keep going on a day-to-day basis – that is, to provide Greene's salary and pay the printers. There is a similar slip in chronology in Greene's own account of the affair, for he concludes, 'From film reviewing it was only a step to script-writing. That also was a danger, but a necessary one as I now had a wife and two children to support and I remained in debt to my publishers until the war came.'[8] In fact Greene's active film work had already ended by the time he went to Mexico.

Before he set off Greene pulled together a novel, *Brighton Rock*, set in

Brighton, which in the late 1930s was becoming violent, a centre for criminal activity of every kind from protection rackets to the sale of stolen antiques. Much of the violence was found at the race-course. Brighton was easily accessible from London, and Greene began making frequent visits, picking up background material for the book, which was finally published in 1938. He had come to the idea through his work for Korda, as we have seen, and initially he intended the book to be another detective story with film-rights sales as the first consideration. But then the young gang leader whom he had chosen as his anti-hero took over. Although he is only seventeen, Pinkie has already killed one man, Kite, and kills another shortly after the book begins. Greene decided to make him a Catholic, born into the faith, and to look at his behaviour from a theological point of view. It was a decision which turned the direction of the book, as Greene explained years later in his 1968 interview with television producer Christopher Burstall:

> I wanted to make people believe that he was a sufficiently evil person almost to justify the notion of Hell. I wanted to introduce a doubt of Pinkie's future in the words of the priest, who speaks of the appalling strangeness of the mercy of God, a doubt whether even a man like that could possibly merit eternal punishment.[9]

Greene's later books, notably *The Power and the Glory* and *The Heart of the Matter*, developed his theological interest in people and their relationship to God. All are exhaustively examined by Professor Roger Sharrock in his book on Greene's novels, *Saints, Sinners and Comedians*, published in 1984. However there is one aspect of *Brighton Rock* which could be said to have a religious dimension but which was until recently entirely ignored, and that is its supposed anti-semitism.

Those who knew of Greene's long friendship with Alexander Korda, which lasted until the end of the film producer's life, found the suggestion that Greene was an anti-semite difficult to understand, particularly in view of his hatred of Nazism. The charge was made public by an unauthorised biographer, Michael Shelden, in his book *Graham Greene: The Man Within*, which appeared in 1994. It is necessary to give a brief extract from the book, if only to give an idea of the nature of the attack, which was widely reported and featured in a public debate between Shelden and Professor Sherry:

> There is no point in trying to minimise Greene's contempt for Jews which is reflected in several works ... and which provoked his most vicious insults ... *Brighton Rock* is the best-known example ... the rich gangster who controls most of the criminal action in Brighton has an Italian name – Colleoni – but for no obvious reason Greene makes him Jewish, and does his best to imply that Jews have a natural talent for shady dealing.[10]

The reason why Greene made Colleoni Jewish – and there are many Italian Jewish families in England – was that his book was based on Brighton in the 1930s where such gangs existed. Equally certainly there were many Catholic gangs, and Greene's portrait of Pinkie is infinitely worse than anything said about Colleoni, who comes over as almost an avuncular figure. There are a few references to his being Jewish; when Pinkie is cornered by Colleoni's gang on the race-track he looks around at the Jewish faces surrounding him before he is slashed by a razor. That is about as far as the direct references go.

Shortly after the war Greene became aware that people were uncomfortable about any allusion to characters with a Jewish background in books, for obvious reasons, and he himself decided to remove the few references concerned. When anyone wrote to him to express concern about this aspect of the book he invariably replied. A typical example in a letter in the Greene papers at Boston College makes his view quite unambiguous.

Addressing his female correspondent, he made it clear that he had never espoused anti-semitism and had no memory of holding such opinions at any time. It was obvious that he had not read *Brighton Rock* for some time as he was not sure where the anti-semitic references were. If they were in the dialogue then of course he was not speaking personally ...[11]

This is plain enough. More importantly, on a charge that he spread anti-semitic ideas, the archives at Boston College, which are voluminous and unexpurgated, contain no papers that reflect anti-semitism in any way. There have been anti-semitic groups in the twentieth century and their writings are always immediately obvious.

It would not have been possible to suppress such a theme had either the family or Greene himself wished to do so, for the archives could not then have been left intact without obvious signs of tampering. Greene simply did not move in the world of anti-semitism and the pattern of the letters which survive and the people whom he knew make this abundantly plain. Further, the letter cited here, written in 1961, was to a private person without thought of publication.

The detective story which Greene planned can still be found in *Brighton Rock*. The detective is a woman, a barmaid called Ida Arnold, who had been talking to Pinkie's second victim just before he is killed. She was perhaps intended as a contrast to the type of female detective favoured by Agatha Christie. Before long Pinkie takes over the action entirely; Greene said that the character of Ida never came to life, and the start of the book with its trappings of a detective novel could have been removed without any loss. Pinkie has a girlfriend, Rose, also a born Catholic, who is entirely innocent. He realises that she knows about the murder and arranges a civil marriage so that she cannot testify against him if he is brought to trial, but this is not enough and he decides he has to kill her as well. He takes her up to the cliffs outside Brighton, where he persuades her that they should both commit suicide; he then gives her a revolver. They have been followed, however, and when people approach her Rose throws away the gun. Pinkie always carries around a flask of acid with him and he tries to throw some of it at the member of his gang who has brought the police. The acid instead goes into his own face and, blinded, he struggles off towards the cliff edge, tumbling over before anyone can reach him:

> 'Stop him,' Dallow cried; it wasn't any good: he was at the edge, he was over: they couldn't even hear a splash. It was as if he'd been withdrawn suddenly by a hand out of any existence – past or present, whipped away into zero – nothing.[12]

With the book finished Greene now faced his own leap into the unknown.

The idea of a journey to Mexico came to Greene indirectly, as spin-off from another travel-book project which he and Evelyn Waugh were to write together, describing a trip around the world in emulation of Jules Verne's *Around the World in Eighty Days*, a faint echo of Greene's travels in Europe with Waugh's cousin Claud Cockburn. This proved impossible, and he developed the idea of a journey to Mexico where some of the most intense contradictions in his view of the world were concentrated. Here was the most savage persecution of the Catholic Church in modern times, but here also was Trotsky, writing his biography of Stalin. Although he developed the idea in 1936, he had to make a rapid decision on whether to pursue it or not when the *Night and Day* job was offered to him. He took the job, but this caused trouble with the original publisher for the book, Sheed and Ward.

Sheed and Ward were one of the main Catholic publishers at the time, and Greene mentions his sympathy with such books as Kuhnelt-Leddihn's *The Gates of Hell*, which they published in 1933 with considerable success. They had good contacts with the Catholic hierarchy and were very taken with the idea of a book which would describe what had been happening in Mexico. By the time *Night and Day* had ended its brief run and Greene had come back to them with the project, they had had second thoughts; the trip would be expensive and Greene would require funds to cover every risk; travelling as a Catholic writer for a Catholic publisher, he might even find himself in physical danger – especially as he was going to Tabasco, where the most fanatical persecution in the Church's history had taken place a few years before.

Luckily Greene's links to Tom Burns saved the day. Burns took over the book and backed Greene totally. It was a courageous decision which gave English literature one of the best travel books of the era, *The Lawless Roads*, and one of the greatest novels of the century, *The Power and the Glory*. Having had to leave Vivien behind when he went to Liberia, this time he made sure she could accompany him as far as America, no easy thing to arrange. Paradoxically those who criticised him for going on his Liberia trip without Vivien also criticise him for taking Vivien with him to America to return alone.

Greene's account of Mexico is so brilliant that there is little point in adding to it. However, there were indications of his changed political views that have not been noticed. He was well aware, for example, that Trotsky was living in Mexico City, in Diego Rivera's villa, but instead of going there and describing it he portrays in detail an extraordinary waxwork display which he visited. On the ground floor were typical revolutionary exhibits of monks flogging naked women, which he writes of with amusement. But upstairs he finds something equally astonishing: 'Upstairs there was Trotsky ... He wore plus fours and a little pink tie and a Norfolk jacket – a Shavian figure. Two waxwork hands in a glass case were compared, the worker's and the sleek priest's, but which would Trotsky's have resembled most?'[13] It is safe to say that Greene's attachment to Trotsky, and the ILP, had ended by this time. The last exhibit he mentions was of a peasant woman and a child in a cradle. This was not Mary and her infant; it appeared that this peasant woman had said that her child was foreign to her and that he would grow up to rule Mexico from London in 1997. Greene cites this as an extraordinary example of the superstition that takes the place of religion.

The physical environment in Mexico shocked Greene. It was the beggars and poverty in a civilised environment which most disturbed him – he had not been to India or the Middle East. His biographer Norman Sherry records an almost pathological hatred of the Mexicans to be found in his book. But there is also a moving account of Greene's realisation of how unjust and unChristian he had been in taking this view. It comes when he has gone in search of a priest who can speak English to hear his confession:

So in Orizaba – from a thin, unshaved, impoverished man with a few words of English – one gained a sense of peace and patience and goodness, which includes, like the Roman virtue, courage and endurance. He had lived through so much; what right had an English Catholic to bitterness or horror at human nature when this Mexican priest had none?[14]

Nor was his revulsion at the heat and the dangers as complete as Sherry and others have suggested. If Greene travelled to escape, he found sometimes that he had succeeded in doing so, escaping to the world of Walter de la Mare which he knew even before he had gone to Oxford:

It was like an escapist's paradise – nothing new or dangerous, nothing bitter: little bridges over sharp torrential streams and the mountains pressing in and the clouds falling; hidden squares with fountains and cupids and broken bows, like a de la Mare poem, the grass pushing up; flowers in private patios, and not many people about, a sense of desertion – ' "Is there anybody there?" said the Traveller.'[15]

When Greene returned to England it was to a country not sure whether war would break out immediately – gas masks had been fitted, barrage balloons tested on their moorings and anti-aircraft guns sited in the parks throughout London. Chamberlain succeeded in gaining a further twelve months of peace; it was not the lasting peace all hoped for, but it was nonetheless a vital respite without which the outcome of war when it did come might have been very different. Greene had a ringside European seat through his brother Hugh and knew that war was inevitable and that he would probably have to find some other source of income for his family. At the time of the Munich crisis he had put himself down for the Officers' Emergency Reserve, which meant going to fight immediately, it meant too that his family would have to survive on much less than their normal income, with even worse consequences if he did not return when the war ended.

Greene's first attempt to provide some extra cushion for his family was in the new medium of radio, which he had first attempted as a young student. The early arts programmes had developed rapidly from the hesitant poems read out by Greene and his fellow under-graduates. There were now producers who were as skilled at creating radio drama as any theatre producer. Greene knew one of them, Stephen Potter, later to become world famous for his *Gamesmanship* books, and Potter commissioned from him *The Great Jowett*, a radio play. It was broadcast on 6 May 1939 at eight in the evening and was considered a great success. Jowett was not at first sight an obvious subject, but Potter was an Oxford man steeped in the traditions of undergraduate drama and the Oxford University Dra-matic Society – the OUDS. And, as Greene's narrator says of Jowett:

Perhaps what undergraduates have most to thank him for was the founding of the O.U.D.S. – though the outside world may think it a mixed blessing. For all those adolescent Hamlets with their Oxford accents, and awkward extras sloping spears in tow-coloured wigs Jowett is responsible.[16]

Like many of the great Victorians, Jowett has been forgotten and seems to have been in need of a revival even in 1939. Balliol men had never forgotten him, and Greene was still very much a Balliol man despite all that had happened to him since he left university. Jowett had been a controversial figure, the subject of the first of the satirical poems known as the Balliol Rhymes:

> First come I. My name is Jowett.
> There's no knowledge but I know it.
> I am the master of this College,
> What I don't know isn't knowledge.[17]

It was an unworthy attack, because Jowett, the great Master of Balliol, was a classics scholar who had been blocked from getting the Mastership as a younger man because of his religious opinions, or lack of them. Greene has his narrator give a more balanced view which reflected the origin of his own interests and the line he took in his play:

You wouldn't have called a man like that a leader – and yet, somehow, between the dinner parties to the great and the translations from the Greek, he created an atmosphere in which leaders were born – Arnold Toynbee, the philanthropist, statesmen like Milner, Asquith and Curzon, writers like Mallock who in his *New Republic* gently caricatured his master. Not the greatest men, perhaps, who emerge from stormier worlds than Balliol ... but men with a sense of philosophy and common sense, who didn't, any more than Jowett, expect too much of the world.[18]

The author of the *New Republic* Greene refers to here was W. H. Mallock. Greene had recorded in his diary at Chipping Camden that he had obtained a copy of this book and compared what he thought its perfect style with his own efforts. Mallock's caricature of Jowett set Greene thinking about him and his contribution to Oxford, ultimately creating the play in a medium which had not even been thought of in Jowett's day, less than a lifetime away. The resigned note here, with his philosophical reference to not expecting too much of the world, reflected the atmosphere in Clapham reported by visitors like the writer Julian Maclaren-Ross. Greene was thirty-five, a married man now with two children (a son Francis had joined his daughter), worried about what a future war would bring. His political ideas had vanished and were only to appear much later when his children had grown up and his married life had ended.

There was one aspect of working on a play which appealed to Greene: the possibility of interacting with the producer and the players while the final shape of the play was being hammered out at rehearsals. The author's profession is an isolated one, with countless hours being spent alone, reading, writing or typing. Greene was to find the cut and thrust in rehearsing a script more and more attractive. He had the first experience of this in rehearsals for *The Great Jowett*. Greene's own copy of the Roneoed script has survived. It is marked for him to attend on the penultimate rehearsal the day before the broadcast, lasting three hours. The text had reached almost its final state but still Greene hurriedly wrote in new material to develop points and create effects which sounded well over the microphone.

Towards the end of the play there is an excellent example of this. Greene is describing Jowett's setting up of an Indian Institute at the university. The original text covers the bare facts, in the narrator's voice. Then suddenly a new idea occurred, pure radio, with loud voices shouting out the taunts of undergraduates from other colleges because Balliol had Indian students: 'Balliol, Balliol, bring out your blasted Blacks!'[19] As Greene scribbled in these lines he perhaps had in his mind for a moment Ieuan Thomas' fate for trying to involve the Indian students in his branch of the Communist Party. Greene answers the sneering taunts with words from Jowett: 'I see no reason why an English blackguard should not be sentenced by a respectable native.'[20]

The play may have been a great success but it did not lead anywhere. In terms of a career it was the producer who gained most from success in the medium. Greene knew that his basic problem had not been solved. The only way to secure Vivien's and the children's financial position should war break out was for him to write a thriller as fast as possible and sell the film rights. He succeeded brilliantly with *The Confidential Agent*.

CHAPTER SIX

Benzedrine and the Blitz

The Confidential Agent was a novel Greene was so unhappy about that he wanted it published under a pseudonym. Reading it now it falls squarely into the pattern of Greene's work at the time and his turning against it can only have been a reaction against the way he was forced to produce it. The writing was concentrated into six weeks' intense effort, working in the mornings only, under the influence of benzedrine, which he presumably obtained from his brother Raymond. He was to say later that he blamed the acute stress brought on by the drug, which he had not used before, for the breakdown of his marriage to Vivien. But there was another factor.

Greene was already working on a novel, *The Power and the Glory*, in his study at Clapham, with his family around him. Like many an author before, he felt he had to find some refuge from the daily domestic disturbance to enable him to work. George Gissing rented rooms away from home when his family arrived to enable him to work; later writers such as T. S. Eliot found the answer in working for a publisher with their own office. Greene adopted Gissing's solution and looked for rooms in Bloomsbury. He found exactly what he wanted in a house in Mecklenburgh Square. The landlady and her daughter lived in the basement flat and it was the daughter, Dorothy Glover, who showed Greene the rooms. Greene recalled how they stood in the room watching the barrage balloons rising in the first air-raid practice and realised that war was certainly coming.

It was also the start of their affair.

Dorothy Glover was the daughter of an electrical engineer. She had been born not far from Clapham Common and had at first gone on the stage as an actress. She was three years older than Greene but seems to have concealed this from him as she used to talk of her time as a mite on stage during performances of the popular musical *Chu Chin Chow* at the end of the war when in fact she had been well into her teens. Little is known of her life before she met Greene. He was very protective of her privacy and kept their friendship and even more their affair very secret for over nine years. But this is not the only reason for the paucity of information about Dorothy. When she died in 1971, aged seventy, all her estate went to her mother, who outlived her by six years. When she in turn died, intestate, no relative could be found despite extensive search and her estate went to the Crown. The contrast with Greene's family background could not be greater.

When war broke out Greene found himself in an awkward position over Dorothy and his affair. Quite by chance the editor of the *Spectator*, Wilson Harris, also lived in Mecklenburgh Square, and, as luck would have it, his wife was a local air-raid warden in charge of the shelters for the square. Harris was a Quaker and did not see eye to eye with Greene over a number of things. It would have been very difficult for Greene to appear in the air-raid shelter with Dorothy and her mother, because Harris, who had been Greene's editor for years, knew that he had a house in Clapham Common which he was meant to be looking after, having found somewhere in Oxford for his wife Vivien and his family to live safely as long as the war lasted.

Another move was clearly necessary and by the time the Phoney War showed signs of turning serious Dorothy and Greene were living together in a cottage in Gower Mews, originally the coach-houses for the north side of Bedford Square. It would be difficult to imagine a more convenient location, or one with more evocative memories of Bloomsbury. Immediately opposite the entrance to the Mews, in Gower Street, was the London town house of Lady Ottoline Morrell, which Greene had visited in the 1920s. On the corner, a few yards away, was the London School of Tropical Medicine – foundation stone laid by Neville Chamberlain – whose basement was the air-raid shelter for the neighbourhood and a night-time home for Greene and Dorothy, who were both air-raid wardens. Parallel to the Mews was Store Street, which was as close to a village street in a small town like Berkhamsted as any to be found in London.

There was a chemist, a small garage and other essentials including a restaurant popular as a meeting place among intellectuals swept up into the war effort at the Ministry of Information, housed in London University's Senate House. There was also a staff hostel for Bourne and Hollingsworth, then a well-known Oxford Street store, and some studios used by artists. One of these, Mervyn Peake, got to know Greene and Dorothy during the Blitz and Greene happily recommended his book *Titus Groan* to friends of his at Eyre and Spottiswoode, as we shall see. Any reader of Greene's books can almost plot the geography of this village, for it haunted him for the rest of his life; and with every memory of it there was a memory of Dorothy.

The Confidential Agent is dedicated to Dorothy Craigie, Dorothy's professional name when she was on the stage, and one she also used when she became a graphic designer, specialising in book jackets and illustrations. Her flat in Mecklenburgh Square features in the novel, and the owner of the flat is given her real name, Glover. The hero of the book, the confidential agent, is a middle-aged man who had been a medieval scholar in Spain before war broke out there. He remembers with nostalgia his days spent researching in the British Museum and contrasts war then with war in the twentieth century echoing Greene's own views:

> Fighting was better in the old days. Roland had companions at Roncevalles – Oliver and Turpin: the whole chivalry of Europe was riding up to help him. Men were united by a common belief. Even a heretic would be on the side of Christendom against the Moors: they might differ about the persons of the Trinity, but on the main issue they were like rock. Now there were so many varieties of economic materialism, so many initial letters.[1]

Earlier he had referred to a friend who had died because he belonged 'to an organisation with the wrong initial letters'. The significance of this is of course that Greene, as we have seen, was a member of the ILP and then, by proxy, of the POUM in the Spanish Civil War. Greene is saying that he sees the war in terms which are simply not comparable to the modern ideological world, where an acronym can damn a man. His confidential agent is on the side of the Spanish government; there is another agent, who is with Franco. Greene neatly sums up the contrast in a simple conversation between the two men when Franco's agent, known as L in the book, tells D that he admires his work on Roland and that he had had a medieval manuscript of Augustine's *City of God* but only for D's comrades to burn it along with his pictures and books.

D's contacts in London met in a language school that taught one of the numerous artificial languages flourishing at the time, like Esperanto. But this one, Entrenationo, was of Greene's invention. One of the few words of Entrenationo given in the book is *korda*, meaning heart. Many critics have pointed out that Greene is referring to the film magnate Alexander Korda, using his name as he had Glover's. But there is a double joke here, for Korda's name is an artificial one modified from his signature to his early articles written as a young man, 'sursum corda', a phrase in the Latin Mass where *corda* does indeed mean heart. It was said to have been Korda's wife who suggested that the C be changed to K when he was looking for a new name for himself.

The plot of the book is aimed consciously at the mass market with the film-rights sales the central object – use of Korda's name was more than just a doffing of the hat. The confidential agent is lucky enough to have the daughter of the coal-mine owner Lord Benditch fall in love with him, and the book ends happily with D being joined on the deck of the tramp steamer in which he has made his escape by the girl, who has boarded earlier when the boat sailed because she knew he was to be brought out to it. There is a prescient touch during D's journey to the coast to catch the boat. He gets into the back of a car with two men whom he thinks are policemen: 'A third man sat at the wheel.' We are never told anything more than the third man's christian name, Joe, but the phrase was to linger in Greene's subconscious.

An uncanny feature of the book, which was published in 1940, echoes Zoe Richmond's suggestion made later to Norman Sherry that he could foresee events: there is repeated mention of bombing raids and the effects on people caught in them. The accounts are so realistic that at least one critic has mistakenly suggested that the book drew on Greene's experiences in the Blitz, even though he wrote it before the war began:

She lay there stiff, clean and unnatural. People talked as if death were like sleep: it was like nothing but itself. He was reminded of a bird discovered at the bottom of a cage on its back, with the claws rigid as grape stalks; nothing could look more dead. He had seen people dead in the street after an air raid, but they fell in curious humped positions – a lot of embryos in the womb.[2]

There are other brilliant descriptive touches:

The raid was over and the bodies were being uncovered; people picked over the stones carefully for fear they might miss a body; sometimes a pick wielded too carelessly caused agony ... The world misted over – as in the dust which hung for an hour about a street.[3]

The cumulative effect of eight or more such passages evokes the horror of war to such good effect that it is not surprising that readers have supposed Greene to be describing what he had actually seen. But they can only have come from his imagination, aided by what he had seen in the press and on newsreels, and perhaps by the stories of refugees he had met when trying to get to Spain in 1937. Unless Greene was a bad judge of his own work, these parts of the book alone suggest that he should have been proud of it. Perhaps it was the private references to Dorothy Craigie that worried him. But when his publisher pointed out that using a pseudonym would mean a much lower advance he had to capitulate: it was for money that he had gone through the hell of writing the book in six weeks.

In the autumn of 1939 he was called before the draft board of the Officers' Emergency Reserve. He did not embarrass the officers facing him by asking, as did so many others, for one of the more exotic branches of the armed forces – although that was where he ended up. Instead he simply said he saw himself in the infantry. He added the rider that he was an author and that he thought that he needed another six months or so to finish his current book. This was agreed to and his call-up date postponed to June 1940. Greene's biographer Norman Sherry has pointed out that he had finished the book *The Power and the Glory* by mid-September; but it is possible that Greene had found fault with it, or thought he might, and that he genuinely needed the time. The more likely reason is that he had been advised to take the steps he did, perhaps by his uncle Sir Graham, who was still active despite his age. The result of the postponement sits too pat when contrasted with the normal response made by the board to someone who simply wanted to join the infantry – one of immediate acceptance.

In April 1940 Greene joined the Ministry of Information (MOI) to organise the work of writers who were being used in the war effort to produce propaganda. He joined Tom Burns, and it is probable that the introduction to the MOI came from him, for he knew that Greene was unsure what to do and had been casting about for a new book. Burns had suggested a biography of Father Damien, the missionary who had worked with lepers and died from the disease. Greene had not been able to come to grips with this subject, although he had a number of projects which show that the intense experience of writing *The Confidential Agent* was still having its effect. Augustine's *City of God* was still in his mind and he proposed a book describing the terrible nature of the modern world, and contrasting it with passages from Augustine. This conceptual idea would have won many admirers later in the century, but at the time it went over the heads of the publishers to whom it was proposed. Burn's suggestion of the MOI brought Greene down to earth.

The MOI was brilliantly parodied by George Orwell's *Nineteen Eighty-Four* as the Ministry of Truth. Besides housing the propaganda sections it also co-ordinated all censorship of the media and such unsavoury functions as the collation of reports from mail censors. Mail censorship is essential in wartime, both to prevent the disclosure (innocent or otherwise) of useful information to the enemy and to reveal the state of morale in the country.

Greene was lucky to be working for one of the more respectable propaganda sections of the MOI, and there are many of his letters known asking authors for propaganda contributions to war campaigns of one kind or another. A particularly interesting example was H. V. Morton, who wrote a book called *I James Blunt* about an England after a Nazi victory. The book impressed Churchill, who invited Morton to his Atlantic meeting with Roosevelt in August 1941. It also profoundly impressed Orwell, who reviewed it when it came out; the resemblances with Orwell's vision of a totalitarian Britain are striking. Greene commissioned this book, but also entirely rewrote it, as he later revealed, because he thought Morton's prose too good for the mass public the MOI aimed at. When Greene worked for the publishers Eyre and Spottiswoode after the war he was to make great use of these editorial skills.

The MOI was not without its critics. The propaganda may have been witty and original when it left the office of Greene or Waugh or even Muggeridge, but then it struck bureaucracy, which killed stone dead virtually anything with a spark of originality. A book appeared with the suggestive title *999 and All That*, referring to the widespread belief that there were precisely that number of bureaucrats in the towering white block. Duff Cooper, the original Minister of Information, was ineffectual and soon went in July 1941, a shake-up taking place initially after the fall of France in May 1940. Greene was one of those to go. He said afterwards that he had been sacked, a blunt term for Greene, but that he was glad to go. There was a little more to it than that.

The Second World War differed from the First in one crucial aspect: it was politically based. Britain was fighting against Nazi Germany and Hitler, not Germany the imperial power. The enemy was Nazism, which was engaged in a fight against world communism, despite the temporary respite supplied by the Nazi–Soviet pact. The entire conflict was rooted in the political struggles that had also caught up Greene and his brother Hugh. However, there were many in England who supported fascism and had done so since the days when Britain funded Mussolini and his party at the end of the First World War. The government were fully aware of this and had passed an Emergency Powers (Defence) Act, under which Regulation 18B provided for the detention of people of hostile association. When William Joyce, the broadcaster known as Lord Haw-Haw, fled to Germany just before the outbreak of war he had two brothers and a sister working for the BBC in various capacities. All were arrested on BBC premises, with other suspect persons, in the greatest secrecy on the day war broke out and were detained while they were checked. All proved entirely innocent and were eventually released. The detentions were widespread, but they did not include people such as Sir Oswald

Mosley and his party, the British Union of Fascists, who despite their political allegiance were fierce patriots. They were against the war, with a slogan adapted from their pre-war trade slogan 'Mind Britain's Business', but many members joined the forces immediately, eager to fight and die for their country: 18B clearly could not be stretched to apply to them.

In May 1940 when the Nazi hordes swept over Europe, a panic developed in Britain over the so-called fifth column of collaborators on the continent who had made the rapid advance possible. Churchill's answer to this was his classic phrase 'Collar the lot!' and 18B was extended to include Mosley's party and many other small fringe groups, including some pacifists who were duped into believing that Nazi radio propaganda broadcasts in English were from a pacifist station somewhere in England. One of these was the British People's Party established by the Duke of Bedford just before the war. Amongst its members was Ben Greene, Greene's cousin, and Kim Philby's father H. St John Philby, who had contested a parliamentary seat for the party. Ben Greene was a devoted Quaker and pacifist and there was no question of his joining the armed forces; he was detained, along with H. St John Philby and other party members, their pacifism seen as objectively pro-German. The Duke of Bedford was confined to his house, and the House of Lords; it was said that only the likely effect on American public opinion prevented his actual imprisonment.

Once Ben Greene had been detained it would have been very difficult for Greene to have remained at his post in the MOI. There was no question of an arrest or detention, but he and Tom Burns both left the propaganda ministry. Tom Burns had been appointed to a far more senior position, press attaché at the British Embassy in Madrid, where he stayed for the rest of the war. Graham's position was more difficult, exacerbated by the fact that he was known to have travelled in Liberia with Ben's sister, and she was not merely of hostile association but actually married to a German aristocrat and living in Germany. She stayed there throughout the war.

The position of the Greene family was additionally complicated by an unusual event at the time of the Saar plebiscite in March 1936. Ben Greene had been appointed an invigilator to oversee the plebiscite, nominated by the Labour Party. Shortly after he took up his post, the Prime Minister's office received a telegram from Graham's eldest brother Herbert. Without disclosing that Ben was his cousin he asked tersely whether it was known that Ben Greene's mother was German, adding that it was essential that the plebiscite be seen as impartial, which meant that Ben should therefore be removed. There has never been any indication of the reason for this outburst. Herbert had returned from Brazil some while before where his uncle, Ben's father, had arranged employment for him in the family business. He had failed at this job as he had failed at so many other things – Graham Greene identified him as the model for the anti-hero of *England Made Me* – and perhaps he was bitter about Ben's prominence. After a rapid exchange of telegrams the authorities realised that some domestic feud was at the root of the problem and took no further action. But Ben's card had been marked. MI5, in the person of Maxwell Knight, was convinced there could be no smoke without fire and paid special attention to Ben Greene. When no obvious reason for his detention could be found in May 1940, it set about creating some, with complete success. The morale of the family was not improved by the decision of Greene's cousin Christopher Isherwood to spend the war on the west coast of America pursuing mystical religious cults, still living in the world of Ouspensky and Madame Blavatsky that Greene had shrugged off twenty years before.

Luckily, other arms of the British government were well aware that Greene and his brother Hugh, a fanatical anti-Nazi who had been expelled from Germany before the war, were entirely free of any hint of pro-Nazi activity. Most telling of all, Greene's sister was already working for MI6. There Maxwell Knight's machinations cut no ice; later in life when someone suggested to Graham Greene that he had worked for MI5 he replied, 'You insult me. I would never spy on my fellow countryman.' That bitterness stems from this wartime incident.

Greene's experiences over the next year from May 1940 until his recruitment into MI6 in August 1941 were to leave a lasting impression. He had accepted the post of literary editor of the *Spectator* in February 1940 when Derek Vershoyle had been called up. After being sacked from the MOI Greene continued this work but on a larger scale, doing theatre reviews and anything else he could fit in. But all these activities were overshadowed by the Blitz which dominated his life for many months. The effect on British publishing had been catastrophic when the destruction of Paternoster Row near St Paul's, long a centre for publishing, had destroyed enormous quantities of books. The main wholesalers Simpkin Marshall, where James Hadley Chase had worked before the war, were completely destroyed and Chase wrote a graphic account of the destruction which, with his other unpublished letters, contains some of the best descriptions of the Blitz. Greene was affected by this as much as any author in England, but his own memories of the Blitz were those he shared with Dorothy in the area around Tottenham Court Road. It was an exhausting time and Greene had to deal with death and injury as bad as that on a battlefield. But still he was given no news of what the War Office planned for him. He grew so desperate that he once wrote to his mother that he would soon consider joining the fire service, like Stephen Spender.

Then came a hint that something was being planned for him that involved going to West Africa. Liberia, where he had unique experience, would not accept him, for that very reason, so instead he was to be sent to Sierra Leone. In a letter to Evelyn Waugh he had said that he hoped to be helping the Free French in North Africa, so he may have known something of the long-term planning for the 1942 invasion there, but by August 1941 he had been told that he was definitely going to West Africa, and he had been recruited into MI6. Although H. St John Philby's son Kim had not then been recruited to the Iberian section of MI6, of which Greene's station was a part, he had become Greene's immediate head by the time he went to Freetown in Sierra Leone.

After the war it seemed that Greene had been almost banished, along with another awkward customer, Malcolm Muggeridge, who was sent to Lourenço Marques, nominally under Greene's control. But the significance of West Africa when Greene went there was considerable. Vichy France extended to North Africa, and on the map Sierra Leone was on the front line, far off though that might be. The main concern was enemy smuggling of industrial diamonds and other essential war contraband, including information and currency.

Once these reached Freetown they could easily be carried across the borders to Vichy-held territory. As far as Philby's Soviet masters were concerned, there was a very good reason for them to want the fullest knowledge of what was happening in any theatre where action might bring about the overthrow of the Vichy regime. The majority of the leaders of the French Communist Party in parliament were being held by the Vichy authorities in North Africa. If the Allied plans were to break the weakest link in the Axis chain, Vichy North Africa, the Soviets saw the possibility of a new revolutionary France springing from the same soil.

The idea that Greene had been placed in West Africa as an unconscious source for Philby seems far fetched, but there was an extraordinary development when the invasion of North Africa took place in November 1942. The Soviet interest in the area had not abated, and Moscow found it necessary to send one of its agents there with the advancing Allied troops to make contact with the Communist Party members, who had been cut off completely since 1940. The man whom the CPGB managed to get down to North Africa, by complex subterfuge given that officially there were not supposed to be any civilians in a battle area, was none other than Claud Cockburn. He went under the assumed name of Frank Pitcairn and was arrested by the American forces when they found him at an unauthorised meeting of the French communist delegates. By chance a man who had known him at Oxford occupied a high position in the British forces and was able to identify him, though not to avoid an intense diplomatic row.

Paradoxically it had been MI5, the domestic security service, and not MI6 which had been involved in the moves that got Cockburn down to North Africa, ostensibly as a correspondent for the *Daily Worker*, so Greene may not have known of this astonishing incident at the time. It is tempting to read into this that Greene had been placed in West Africa for the same reasons when that region looked like being a potential invasion point. Anyone attempting to follow Philby's tracks would have found this one of the most difficult problems to deal with. If the despatch of the two friends to Africa was not part of some overall plan, it must rank as one of the most remarkable coincidences in the whole sad story.

Greene spent much of his time at this period writing his next novel, *The Ministry of Fear*. The novel he was to write after the war based on his African experiences, *The Heart of the Matter*, gives us a cross-bearing on how he saw his time there. One cannot imagine Claud Cockburn wrestling with such themes, let alone writing about them. As Greene once said, Cockburn really was a communist; Greene was not. What Greene took away with him was a love of Africa.

After the invasion of North Africa by the Allies there was really no point in having an MI6 station in Freetown, and Greene was recalled. While he had been in Africa there was a remarkable development at home in connection with Ben Greene. Shrewd detective work and prompt action by his solicitors had enabled them to identify an *agent provocateur* who had provided the evidence for Maxwell Knight at MI5 to justify his detention. The man was trapped and forced to admit what he had done, enabling Ben to be released. The effect of this was far-reaching, for at the time Knight's main concern was the rising influence of the communist threat, even in 1944. He wrote a paper entitled 'The Comintern Is Not Dead', but it was ignored: as a result of the blunder over Ben Greene, he had been discredited.

Ben Greene's release may well have prompted Graham to write *The Ministry of Fear*, a savage account of the world in which many of Knight's informants lived.

CHAPTER SEVEN

The Ministry of Fear and Philby's Empire

The Public Record Office at Kew is not on the normal route for people engaged on literary quests, but it seemed worth checking the Foreign Office's excellent indexes of its files – the indexes are sadly now no longer being printed or made available – for references to Greene and his family. The most revealing material found was in the MOI files, which explained fully the world with which Greene, George Orwell and so many others had had to cope. It was a world of censorship, political intrigue and fear that at times seemed almost to betray the men fighting for their country in the field.

The Ministry of Fear evokes better than any other novel the atmosphere of wartime London in the Blitz. The detailed observation is remarkable, and the book is full of broad perceptions, for example that a 'front line' ran across London, with areas that were frequently bombed situated right on the line, and elsewhere no damage inflicted at all. But every word of the novel, another of his 'entertainments', was written in Sierra Leone, West Africa. Throughout it there is an aching nostalgia for London and for the camaraderie of the war and the Blitz. In Sierra Leone, Greene soon became annoyed and isolated. One can sense his growing isolation and an almost desperate longing to return to London.

The two central characters in the novel, after the hapless victim Arthur Rowe, are Anna and Willi Hilfe, two Austrian refugees who are working in England for a farcical do-gooder organisation called the Comforts for the Mothers of the Free Nations Fund, which is a cover for fifth-column activities. The inspiration for Anna is clearly Barbara. Perhaps Greene's memories of her with him in Sierra Leone before the war, and the knowledge that she was now in Germany, suggested this element in the book. Anna's brother in the novel, a more committed, thoroughgoing agent, perhaps then resembles Barbara's husband rather than her own brother Ben, who was still detained under the Emergency Powers regulations, and with whom Greene had great sympathy. The closest Greene gets in the novel to a direct reference to the hidden reality of the Greene family's own suffering under the Ministry of Fear is a comment about a senior figure whose position places him above suspicion. Some top-secret papers have gone missing, a mainspring of the plot, but are later found to have been in his supposedly safe hands all along: 'The papers never left the possession of ... Somebody whose word you had to take or else one of you would go to Brixton, and you could feel sure it wouldn't be he.'[1] Brixton was where the majority of the 18B detainees went first and where Ben had been held.

The world which Ben Greene was accused of belonging to was remarkably like that portrayed by Greene in the first part of his book. Anyone who doubts that such an absurd set-up could possibly create any danger or that such people existed needs only to read the surviving MI5 papers in the Public Record Office dealing with Maxwell Knight and his officers. This was the world of Anna Wolkoff and the Tyler Kent affair when Kent, a cipher clerk at the American Embassy passed telegrams from Churchill to Roosevelt on to Wolkoff who supposedly was in touch with Germany. But Greene at the same time creates a brilliant parody of the genuine pacifist fringe groups, to which Ben Greene belonged, and which had no hostile association at all. There is even reference to vegetarians and eccentric bohemian poets. Harmless, you imagine, until the Ministry of Fear's all-embracing filing system gets to work and you find yourself detained. Greene's portrait in *The Ministry of Fear* of a gentle giant of a man held in a cell, even at one point in a straitjacket, must have derived from his worst fears about the actual conditions in which Ben Greene was being held.

One brilliant piece of dialogue captures the pacifist line as it was pumped out over the German English-language radio night after night and, it was feared, absorbed by deeply committed pacifists such as Ben Greene:

'The stupidity of this war,' he said. 'Why should you and I ... intelligent men ...?' He said, 'They talk about democracy don't they. But you and I don't swallow stuff like that. If you want democracy – I don't say you do, but if you want it you must go to Germany for it. What do you want?' he suddenly enquired.

'Peace,' Rowe said.

'Exactly. So do we.'

'I don't suppose I mean your kind of peace.'

'We can give you peace, we are working for peace.'

'Who are we?'

'My friends and I.'

'Conscientious objectors?'

'One can worry too much about one's conscience.'[2]

Ben Greene really had been entrapped by just such a conversation with an agent of Max Knight's acting as an *agent provocateur*.

One of the vignettes created by Greene in wartime London featured some book-auction rooms in Chancery Lane. Like so much else, this was drawn from life, but Greene's absence in West Africa distorted his memory slightly. He had visited these rooms before the war, and many years later, in 1982, a member of staff, Fred Snelling, identified them in his memoirs, *Rare Books and Rarer People*:

> There is one famous scene in Graham Greene's *The Ministry of Fear*, quite obviously set in Hodgson's Rooms which he knew quite well, although he got his geography and topography all wrong. He put the big clock at the wrong end of the room, and he had a character spying out from the shelves towards a detective agency along Chancery Lane towards the Fleet Street end ... as it happens there *was* a detective agency in the direction he indicated, but he put it on the wrong side of the road.[3]

From where Greene was sitting when he wrote his description he seems to have held the picture remarkably well – and can there have been many others in the club in Freetown preoccupied with such memories? But the extraordinary thing about Greene's portrayal of the book trade is that one of the fifth-column agents who gives Arthur Rowe a bomb in the novel is the antiquarian bookseller first seen at the auction rooms. In 1955 Peter Kroger, the leader of the Portland spy ring, which was uncovered in 1961, made his first appearance in London at Hodgson's, those same auction rooms Greene had described in *The Ministry of Fear*: reality following fiction. To round off the picture, in his later novel *The Human Factor* Greene portrayed a lifelong committed communist who worked as just such a bookseller.

The first part of the book ends, in best thriller style, with Arthur Rowe, who has innocently become involved with the fifth-column pacifist German agents, being knocked unconscious by the bookseller's bomb which had been designed to kill him. He awakes in a private hospital suffering from amnesia and with a false name to which he is taught to respond. The second part is set in the hospital, which has uncanny parallels with an enlarged version of the Richmonds' clinic, with their interest in spiritualism, moved to open countryside. It contains an extremely savage criticism of psychiatry. Later in 1953 some critics were to attack Greene for his treatment of the profession of psychoanalysis in his play *The Living Room* – as we shall see. They cannot have grasped quite how savage was Greene's portrayal in *The Ministry of Fear*. The psychoanalyst was a Dr Forester, with an assistant Johns:

> 'What about Dr. Forester?' Rowe asked...
>
> 'Oh,' Johns said enthusiastically, 'he's sound as a bell. He's written a pamphlet for the Ministry of Information, *The Psychoanalysis of Nazidom*. But there was a time when there was ... talk. You can't avoid witch-hunting in wartime. You see, Dr. Forester – well he's so alive to everything. He likes to know. For instance spiritualism – he's very interested in spiritualism, as an investigator.'[4]

And in a brilliant sketch of Johns' character Greene describes him in terms that would have fitted what he knew of Richmond closely: 'He was not qualified, though the doctor occasionally let him loose on the simpler psyches.' The account Greene gives of the attempts to bully Rowe into believing that he is someone else, and getting him to remain where he is, rather than go to Sick Bay, is called 'Conversations in Arcady', perhaps the most ironic title for a series of psychoanalytic sessions ever created. The Sick Bay means detention in a room, with a straitjacket if needed.

The book ends when Rowe escapes and goes to the police; the story he has to tell is finally believed. He is not guilty of the charges levelled at him and is free to go, precisely mirroring what happened to Ben. But the final tying up of the plot takes him back to Anna Hilfe and her brother, who have escaped capture. Willi has the vital microfilm of the stolen papers and almost escapes to Ireland, but Rowe catches him in Paddington station and, in the appropriate environment of the gentleman's lavatory on the station, Willi shoots himself with a gun which Rowe, sure that Willi is not going to shoot his way out, has given him. The resemblances to the finale of *The Third Man* are striking.

Elsewhere in the book there are other themes seen later in *The Third Man*, for example the misuse of medicines. In *The Ministry of Fear* Rowe's character is given a twist, like the scar on the face of Pinkie in *Brighton Rock*, but his is a secret from his past. He had murdered his wife in a mercy killing and for a brief period had been detained as insane. The drug used to kill her is carefully described – hyoscine. And this is the very poison with which the agents attempt to kill Rowe. Greene describes vividly Rowe's shock as he realises what the strange taste in his tea is:

> Rowe took a sip of the tea; it was too hot to swallow ... an odd flavour haunted him like something remembered, something unhappy ... He took another slow slip and then he remembered. Life struck back at him like a scorpion, over the shoulder. His chief feeling was one of astonishment and anger, that anybody should do this to *him*.[5]

Knowledge of hyoscine and its properties came from Raymond, like the benzedrine which enabled him to write *The Confidential Agent*.

A note struck repeatedly in *The Ministry of Fear* is the absurdity of crime, even murder, during war. Murder is around everyone all the time, glorified by the name of war; there are no inquests in wartime and, as Greene's detective remarks, 'So many bodies waiting for a convenient blitz.' And yet it is the individual crime, the unconsidered murder, that is the key to the larger evil. Greene could see that the great consumption of thrillers in wartime, despite the war on their doorstep, was significant. It was only on the very smallest scale that the ordinary man in the street was able to understand what was happening. In a dream Rowe is talking to his dead mother, describing the insane world of London at war:

> You remember St. Clements – the bells of St. Clements. They've smashed that – St. James's, Piccadilly, the Burlington Arcade, Garland's Hotel where we stayed for the pantomime, Maples and John Lewis. It sounds like a thriller doesn't it but thrillers are like life ... the world has been remade by William Le Queux.[6]

Le Queux is a forgotten novelist now, but Greene retained an affection for his work right through his life, and his remark here is an allusion to one of his most famous books, *The Invasion of 1910 With a Full Account of the Siege of London*. When it was published in 1906, the chapters on the bombardment of London were thought alarmist nonsense. But the world *had* been remade by Le Queux. The Luftwaffe bombing was worse than anything he foresaw.

Greene made the point more acutely when he described in the novel some books as the History of Contemporary Society and then reeled off the names of a string of novels by Edgar Wallace and Conan Doyle, with Le Queux thrown in for good measure. And in writing his book, as he sat in the tropical heat of Freetown, Sierra Leone, Greene was adding to this history. Greene's policeman remarks:

> One must avoid self importance, you see. In five hundred years' time, to the historian writing the decline and fall of the British Empire, this little episode would not exist. There will be plenty of other causes. You, me and poor Jones will not even figure in a footnote. It will be all economics, politics, battles.[7]

And of course, as with all Greene's 'entertainment' novels, politics is one of the themes he explores, here with particular subtlety and originality. Like many other writers Greene had a habit of reading with a pencil so that, as he put it, he made each book his own with marginal comment and markings. It turned reading a book into a dialogue, and an examination of such annotations is an essential basis for scholarly comment.

In *The Ministry of Fear* it is the doctor whose books are marked, and Greene adopts the clever device of identifying as having been marked by Doctor Forester the quotations from Tolstoy that he wants to use to make his point. Tolstoy's words defend internationalism against patriotism, and are typically those that one of the myriad pacifist groups might have taken up, even, perhaps, his cousin Ben Greene himself. The whole of Tolstoy's *What I Believe* is distilled into a few brief extracts culminating in a short: 'I cannot acknowledge any States or nations ... I cannot take part ... I cannot take part.' Then these are curtly dismissed: 'He couldn't be bothered with Tolstoy any longer ... it was all very well for Tolstoy to preach non-resistance: he had had his heroic violent hour at Sebastopol.'[8] And for a moment the mask drops and we realise that it is either Greene who has made the markings and noted the texts or Greene's understanding, perhaps, of comments made by Ben.

In parallel with this investigation into pacifism Greene makes a series of comments about murder and murders. One seems to come straight from his favourite quotation from Browning's 'Bishop Blougram's Apology':

> Our interest's on the dangerous edge of things,
> The honest thief, the tender murderer,
> The superstitious atheist...[9]

Greene has a tender murderer: 'Murder was infinitely more graceful because it was the murderer's object not to shock – a murderer went to infinite pains to make death look quiet, peaceful, happy.'[10] And on the very next page he seems to parody Browning in twentieth-century terms by referring to broken illusions of childhood: 'the V.C. in the police-court dock, the faked income tax returns'. The VC must have killed in war, but perhaps is in the police-court dock for murder; and income tax evaded is honest theft – in Greene's case it had to be, for his salary paid by MI6 was outside the tax system. And in one culminating contradiction Greene has Rowe a murderer 'as other men are poets'.[11] The reader suddenly finds himself forced into looking at a murderer as if he were a pacifist, and Greene's skilful creation of his thriller has engaged his sympathy for a man who is actually a murderer.

The writing of this book shows all the signs of acute creative stress,

as prominent almost as those in George Orwell's *Nineteen Eighty-Four*.
In passing he makes a wry comparison with his travel book *Journey
without Maps*: 'It's as if one had been sent on a journey with the
wrong map.'[12] At the end of the book he finally comes full circle,
reaching an understanding of what would happen to Barbara's
husband, or even to Barbara herself, if they were back in England:
'He thought for the first time, "It's her brother who's going to die".
Spies, like murderers, were hanged, and in this case there was no
distinction. He lay asleep in there and the gallows were being built
outside.'[13] And this was the reality that his family had been plunged
into by the accidents that his cousin had a German mother and had
married a German, and that another cousin had been a dedicated
Quaker and pacifist when his country was at war.

But Willi does the decent thing. And Arthur Rowe walks off with
Anna Hilfe in a happy ending tailor-made for the cinema. Greene
could not have been surprised when his agent told him that the film
rights had once again been sold in Hollywood, this time for over
£3,000, before the book had been published. He already knew that
the film would not represent the book truthfully; but then who but
a handful of people at that time would perceive the overtones in the
book and the personal struggle he must have had in dealing with
these most sensitive issues affecting his closest family?

While Greene was developing his thesis about the thriller as real
life, an extraordinary court case was being pursued in London. In
the inter-war years there had grown up the very tough 'hard-boiled'
school of American fiction, itself a reflection of the gangster world
created by Prohibition. There were respected practitioners of the art,
but the vast majority of the books published in the genre that reached
England were anonymous pulp fiction, much of it brought over as
ballast for ships engaged in general trade with North America. With
the coming of the war this trade had stopped and there was a dearth
of supply. James Hadley Chase, who, like Greene, had been very
worried about how his wife and family were to cope financially if
war came, had written a pastiche of the genre, *No Orchids for Miss
Blandish*. Owing to the shortage of American pulp fiction the book
sold astonishingly well and his publishers had pressed him hard for
more of the same.

Chase was said to have written *No Orchids for Miss Blandish* in six weeks, but his papers show clearly that he had been at work on it for almost a year. He did not have Greene's background as an author; the only way he could keep up the supply was by drawing directly on other books he knew in the genre, sometimes in the most general way. He did so in his thriller *Miss Callaghan Comes to Grief*. Anyone who knew Greene's work and chanced to read Chase's novel would have been struck by the name of the villain, Raven, taken directly from *A Gun for Sale*. Some of the most explicit acts of violence in the book bear a close resemblance to incidents in Greene's book, although Greene's descriptions certainly beat Chase's in their detail and impact.

Miss Callaghan Comes to Grief was an extremely violent account of the white slave traffic, set entirely in America, which James Hadley Chase had in fact never visited. It caught the eye of the authorities, who decided to suppress it. On 19 May 1942 the author and publishers were found guilty of causing the publication of an obscene book. The case aroused considerable scandal and Chase received support from many literary figures, including John Betjeman and H. E. Bates, who both knew Greene and had worked on *Night and Day*. Chase's papers reveal that he was very friendly with the police, even meeting them socially; they were extremely embarrassed about the affair and privately gave him an outline of the prosecution case so that he would not be caught unawares. They behaved in this unusual way not just because James Hadley Chase had by that time become the most sought-after best-selling author in the country, but because they also knew that under his real name René Raymond he was working for the Royal Air Force as editor of its internal magazine. An anthology of some of the best poems and essays he commissioned was published after the war by Greene at Eyre and Spottiswoode.

Chase's addiction to thrillers seems almost inexplicable to us today but reflects the place they occupied in English life at the time. He had watched the sales figures of the hard-boiled school of fiction when he worked at Simpkin Marshall, the book wholesalers, and had been drawn to the genre. The films of the school interested him as they did Greene. His fascination for the American culture of violence in literature was attacked savagely by George Orwell in his critique of *No Orchids for Miss Blandish*, although even he took care to say that the book was brilliantly written. Orwell was close to Christopher Hollis, who was in Air Force Intelligence and knew of Chase's other life; whether he inspired Orwell's article or not there were others in the air force who resented the success that *No Orchids* and Chase's later books had had with the public. Another who objected was Alfred Gordon Bennett, also in intelligence, who had written books before the war with a Christian theme. In his copy of *Miss Callaghan Comes to Grief* Bennett kept information on the case against Chase and the final suppression of the book – though he retained his own copy. It is possible that resentment against the book in these circles helped fan feeling against it and prompted action.

There was one other possible reason for the attack on the book and that was its American content. It was known that Chase had never been to America, so it must have been doubly objectionable, after America had entered the war, for him to write about white slave traffic – technically the transportation of women across state borders for immoral purposes, a wide legal definition – and the involvement in it of black Americans. Greene had suffered prosecution over Shirley Temple for offending American sensibilities and this may explain his making friends with Chase when he returned from West Africa and began a desk job at MI6.

In later life Greene did not hesitate to praise Philby, his chief in MI6, for his abilities and in particular for his leadership during the war, which extended to his covering up the mistakes of his juniors and generating enthusiasm after work in their local in St James's. He especially resented attacks made on Philby by Malcolm Muggeridge, and this resentment grew until he came to loathe him. Muggeridge was a major source for Andrew Boyle's exposé of Philby and the other Cambridge spies, *The Climate of Treason*, and Greene peppered the margins of his copy of the book with comments attacking Muggeridge and his misrepresentation of Greene's view of him at this time when they worked together as a team. Muggeridge claimed that Greene could take Philby only in small doses, which Greene acidly minuted, 'Quite untrue. Untrue.'

When Greene began his correspondence with Philby in Moscow in 1979 Muggeridge was still writing articles about the defector which

Philby found distressing, particularly their personal tone:

> Incidentally, Malcolm [Muggeridge] spread himself on the subject of the
> Blunt affair in Time Magazine, writing again at inordinate length on
> the subject of my stutter. It seems to have become an obsession with
> him; he could surely find more serious ground on which to denigrate
> me.[14]

To Greene this type of vilification of someone who had been a friend
was beneath contempt.

Philby once said that Greene never mentioned Catholicism in his
presence. This suggests they never had any profound discussions and
raises the obvious question of how two people with such differing
views could have got on in the first place. The first point to be made
is that they had one common skeleton in their cupboard as far as
outsiders were concerned, a connection through their family with
the far-right British People's Party, both men having had close
members of their family detained, Philby's father and Greene's cousin.
Philby had the added problem of having worked in Spain during the
Civil War as a member of the press corps attached to Franco. Greene
was anti-Franco. No doubt in the complex situations Greene and
Philby were creating with agents and counter-agents these matters
were regarded as part of a distant past compared to the fight against
the common enemy in which they were currently engaged. Both
men seem to have shared the same sense of humour, and the same
native ability to find agents and create cover for them and their
precarious lives. Another colleague of Philby's commented, 'During
the war I worked pretty closely with him [Philby] from time to time,
and got to know him about as well as most people. He had a
remarkable flair for strategic deception, combining imagination with
audacity.'[15] He could equally well have been talking of Greene. But
despite their good working relationship Greene and Philby appear
not to have mixed socially away from work. On one occasion when
Greene was taken ill, Philby had to help him back to the Mews
cottage, and Greene warned him to make no comment about Dorothy.
Philby was himself living with someone to whom he was not married,
and with their children, in a sociable group which Greene seems not
to have been part of. Greene's own life appears to have settled down

much as it was before. Far from pursuing an espionage life of the kind Philby and his friends Burgess and Maclean could not resist, Greene kept in touch with his Catholic friends. In his diary he records taking the Mathew brothers out to dinner in 1944 and other similar events. David Mathew was now Catholic chaplain to London University, and both he and his brother Gervase had shown great courage in the Blitz. There was another priest, Father Ivor Daniel, who once referred to himself with Greene and the Mathew brothers as a quadrilateral of friends, dating from before the war. Daniel too seems to have been in London, and was closer to Dorothy and Greene than the Mathew brothers. Many years later Dorothy visited him when he was terminally ill, and Greene wrote to him. A common friend of all of them had been the Cecil Court bookseller David Low. Greene left these close friendships unrecorded in his autobiography, although all the letters between them were kept amongst his private papers, now at Boston College. Perhaps they were indeed part of the very private life lived through the Blitz that created the intense bond of loyalty to Dorothy, the breaking of which caused him such intense pain after the war.

Greene left MI6 under mysterious circumstances, in 1944. It was said that Philby offered him promotion as a ploy in some complex game of office politics, the object of which was to ensure that Philby himself ended up running counter-Soviet espionage, as he eventually did. Greene did not wish to take the job and resigned then and there. Tim Milne, who took over Philby's job as head of Section V of MI6, wrote to Greene many years later enclosing a carefully drawn-up chronology of events in 1944, which had led him to believe that the accepted version of Greene's departure was not quite accurate. Milne came to no conclusion. The only immediately obvious alternative explanation is connected with an early anti-communist drive in 1944, about which little is known. If Greene was a pawn in that game, he might have been sacrificed by Philby to protect himself, for Greene's early party membership at Oxford must definitely have been known somewhere in the system, although that proved no barrier to his joining MI6.

Whatever the circumstances, Greene could now return to civilian life. The only problem was that the war would not go away. The air-raids, which had ended for good, they all thought, restarted in a particularly demoralising form: the flying bombs, the V1 and V2. In his diary Greene captured exactly the feeling of surprise and shock that this new weapon created. The bombs left people defenceless, because they came at any time of the day, without warning, so there was no longer the camaraderie of the shelters. In his diary entry for 27 June 1944 Greene recorded graphically the daytime terrors in an incident when he was speaking on the phone one morning to his agent Laurence Pollinger. Pollinger suddenly said 'Stop a moment, there's one coming up Bedford Street.' It was at roof height going past his window. And then, 'It's all right, it's gone off,' only to hear the roar through the phone Greene was holding.[16] The reason of course was that Greene was in Bloomsbury and very close to where the bomb had gone off. He had survived the Blitz in good spirits, but he found the V1s and V2s very depressing, and the concealment of the reality of the damage done by the V2s even more so. In July, writing in his account of the new attacks called 'The Second Siege of London', an unpublished diary in the Texas University archives, he recorded Churchill's message, an uncommon thing for him to do. He was struck by the fact that Churchill's tone was resigned; there was to be no respite.[17] And the situation was worse than in the first blitz for there was no possibility of defence against the larger rockets, nor even a warning of their approach.

The V2s were the background experience to most people's views of the events which finally ended the war, the dropping of the atomic bombs on Hiroshima and Nagasaki in 1945 – a sombre beginning to a dark post-war era. Greene was especially fortunate that he was to live in great luxury over the next few years. It was a strange life for him, one in which he never felt quite at home.

CHAPTER EIGHT

A Publishing Affair

One of the main barriers in my quest for Greene's life in the post-war years was the break-up of Eyre and Spottiswoode after its sale. The conglomerate that now controls the name has a few box files which are effectively inaccessible – a request for a supposed index simply produced photocopies of the spines of the box files, most of which on examination proved to be files relating to Methuen many years later. Personal enquiry was rebuffed. Luckily this setback was overcome by the information that had already emerged. The appointment diaries of J. D. Beresford had recorded an extensive correspondence with Greene while he was at Eyre and Spottiswoode. It was discovered that this concerned a reprint of his book *The Hampdenshire Wonder* for a list Greene was creating that he christened the Century Library. When a full list of the books originally envisaged was found (see p. 115), they could then be researched in Texas, Boston and elsewhere.

By such tangential approaches the quest succeeded. A picture was built up that told a lot about Greene's abilities as a publisher. In one case a book that had been on my shelves for many years proved to have been published by Greene, and it was with astonishment that I realised that the dustwrapper had been designed by Dorothy Glover. Greene often used to say that if he had not been an author he would most have liked to been a secondhand book-seller. On the evidence of this quest he would have been even better at setting up a family publishing business.

When Greene's war ended he moved to the job which had been waiting for him right through the hostilities at Eyre and Spottiswoode, arranged for him by Tom Burns. He had proved his ability to deal with a large number of authors during his time as editor of the ill-fated *Night and Day*. The publisher Douglas Jerrold, also an author, best known for his *The Necessity of Freedom*, was thinking of retiring in a year or two and the idea was to groom Greene as his successor. This did not work out, but Greene retained very close links with the owner of the firm Oliver (later Sir Oliver) Crosthwaite-Eyre, and with his wife. It was an important friendship that Greene was to look back on at the end of his days as one of the happiest of his life.

The description given by Anthony Powell of Greene's time at the firm has some elements of truth in it: 'Greene soon set humming the veteran engine of Eyre and Spottiswoode by no means so broken down an equipage as Duckworth's [where Powell worked earlier in his life], nevertheless a chassis set rattling ominously under the force of the new dynamo.'[1] And a dynamo Greene certainly was. He began a series of innovations to strengthen the fiction list, with an emphasis on crime fiction, and the particular sub-class of this category which especially appealed to him, the Soho thriller. He was to publish Edgar Lustgarten's first book, *A Case to Answer*, the start of a fine career, and Greene's jacket note describes the setting in his best style: 'A woman of the streets is found murdered in her Soho lodging. A young business man with a wife and children is accused of murdering her.'[2] Another supposedly new author was 'Ambrose Grant', whose *More Deadly Than the Male* got stunning reviews from Anthony Powell, John Betjeman, Elizabeth Bowen and others in Greene's circle.

'Ambrose Grant' was the pseudonym of René Raymond, better known as James Hadley Chase. It is not clear how Greene met him, but H. E. Bates was a mutual friend and drinking companion around Tottenham Court Road. Anyone reading the book Greene published for him under his new name will immediately realise that the two men must have worked very closely together on the book. The young thug in the book, Brant, has more than a touch of Pinkie in *Brighton Rock* about him: 'He had a livid scar on his cheek ... then there was a look of starved intensity in his face, and his grey-blue eyes, heartless and bitter, were the most unfriendly eyes George had ever seen.'[3] Pinkie has the same look: 'A boy of about seventeen watched from the door ... a face of starved intensity, a kind of hideous and unnatural pride.'[4] And the eyes: 'his grey eyes had an effect of heartlessness like an old man's in which human feeling had died'.[5]

Perhaps even more suggestively, neither drinks alcohol and both ask for a soft drink in a pub: Pinkie has a grapefruit squash, Brant a lemonade. And both men are adept with a razor, ruthlessly attacking anyone who owes them money or will not play the game.

The phrase 'starved intensity' is Greene's. The Ambrose Grant book *More Deadly Than the Male*, the only book Chase wrote using that name, is so untypical of Chase's normal work that one has to ask just how much input Greene had into Chase's work at this time. It has been suggested that the entire book is largely Greene's work. A close reading shows that this is unlikely. But the extensive auto-biographical element in the book, uncharacteristic of Chase, is a commonplace of Greene's writing. It is as if Greene was doing a very strong line-editing of Chase's work, and there is convincing circumstantial evidence that at this stage of Chase's writing career this was possible, indeed essential.

James Hadley Chase had written little before his first hit book, *No Orchids for Miss Blandish*, and his creative ability and imagination, which he later developed to a high degree, were still largely dormant. Critics had pointed out that *No Orchids* owed a lot to William Faulkner's *Sanctuary*. It was perhaps understandable that Chase borrowed from others' work in his early days, just as he had from Greene. That he did so is not purely speculation: not only was there the *Callaghan* novel, but shortly after his next book *Blonde's Requiem* appeared Chase was obliged to publish a letter in the *Bookseller* admitting certain borrowings from Raymond Chandler. They were not extensive and, partly as a result of Greene's support, which lasted for many years afterwards, he soon rid himself of this doubtful tendency and wrote over eighty excellent thrillers. Greene had rewrit-ten H. V. Morton's book *I James Blunt* largely for stylistic reasons, and no doubt he felt able to take Ambrose Grant's work in hand. If the reviews are any guide, he did so brilliantly.

A successful career as a writer awaited another Greene discovery, Marc Brandel, whose novel *The Ides of Summer* created a stir amongst the critics as a promising début. Beside the usual supporters who responded to Greene's enthusiasm – Anthony Powell, John Betjeman and Peter Quennell, the book got dazzling coverage from Pamela Hansford Johnson and others, now forgotten, who carried great

THE CENTURY LIBRARY

FIRST SIX TITLES

The History of Mr. Polly **H. G. WELLS**
With an introduction by V. S. Pritchett

The Hole in the Wall
ARTHUR MORRISON
With an introduction by V. S. Pritchett

Dialstone Lane **W. W. JACOBS**
With an introduction by Henry Reed

The Green Child **HERBERT READ**
With an introduction by Graham Greene

The Unbearable Bassington **SAKI**
With an introduction by Evelyn Waugh

Widecombe Fair **EDEN PHILLPOTTS**
With an introduction by L. A. G. Strong

OTHER TITLES IN PREPARATION

The Wings of the Dove	**HENRY JAMES**
The Fifth Queen Trilogy	**FORD MADOX FORD**
The Nebuly Coat	**J. MEADE FALKNER**
Antigua Penny Puce	**ROBERT GRAVES**
Israel Rank	**ROY HORNIMAN**
The Hampdenshire Wonder	**J. D. BERESFORD**
The Position of Peggy Harper	
	LEONARD MERRICK
A Waif's Progress	**RHODA BROUGHTON**
The Case of Bevan Yorke	**W. B. MAXWELL**

influence at the time, such as Howard Spring and Ralph Strauss.

Greene must have been particularly pleased with this response for the pseudonym Marc Brandel concealed the son of Greene's old idol J. D. Beresford, Marcus Beresford. His later success in novels and films was to justify Greene's faith in his writing and equalled that of other writers Greene launched. Geoffrey Cotterell seemed to Greene to be one of the best young writers around and he was glad to have the opportunity to be the first to publish him.

Anyone coming across a novel published by Eyre and Spottiswoode while Greene was there can be sure of finding something worthwhile, from the design of the jackets – Dorothy Glover did those for Ambrose Grant and Edgar Lustgarten – right through to the blurb and promotional material. Greene was also a master of a technique, now little used, for establishing an identity for a publisher and his list – putting on the back of a book quotations from favourable reviews of another book by a different author. Edgar Lustgarten's book, for example, featured reviews praising Ambrose Grant's *More Deadly Than the Male*.

J. D. Beresford himself was featured by Greene in his Century Library list, a series reprinting neglected literary masterpieces of the none too distant past; even then literary reputation was evanescent. Beresford, at the very end of his life – he died in 1947 – was all but forgotten. But Greene believed that Beresford's *The Hampdenshire Wonder* was one of the most unjustly neglected works of the era before the First World War, as we have seen, and he set about reprinting it. He also arranged for a foreword by Beresford's lifelong friend Walter de la Mare. The Century Library list (see p. 115) was very much Greene's own idea, and he would approach other authors to see if they had any suggestions. George Orwell's offering – Leonard Merrick's *The Position of Peggy Harper* – shown on the list here sadly never appeared.

Perhaps Greene's most spectacular success was in bringing Mervyn Peake to Eyre and Spottiswoode. Peake was a cult figure at the time and had featured in a series of photographs taken by Bill Brandt of cartoonists and artists who had contributed to the magazine *Lilliput*. Others in the series, published in the March 1943 edition of the magazine, included Osbert Lancaster and David Langdon, a close friend of James Hadley Chase's. Chase and Langdon co-edited *Slipstream*, an anthology of RAF writing, including contributions from H. E. Bates and Chase himself, writing under his own name Raymond.

At this point Mervyn Peake, whom Greene had kept in touch with since their accidental meeting in Store Street during the Blitz, had published only a slim volume of verse. His publishers were Chatto and Windus, but Greene in a considerable coup managed to lure him away for his Gormenghast trilogy. This was another early example of Greene's editorial skills, for Chatto and Windus had turned down the sample of *Gormenghast* which Peake had shown them before Greene joined Eyre and Spottiswoode. Peake handed the manuscript to Greene and asked for his advice. He was shocked when Greene sent him a severe letter drawing attention to the book's shortcomings, focusing on what he called lazy writing. Greene gave positive advice as well on this and other books, and when he went to Eyre and Spottiswoode a Peake book was first on his list.

The social life which surrounds any publisher was always important in the days before giant conglomerate publishing, when an author may never even meet the man who is nominally his publisher, and Eyre and Spottiswoode was no exception. There were two main venues, and also, for close friends, Oliver Crosthwaite-Eyre's own circle. They were the Authors' Club in Whitehall Court near the river and not far from Inigo Jones' Banqueting Hall in Whitehall itself, and a pub, the Lamb and Flag. Lunchtimes were often spent there, over the way from the Garrick Club in London's Covent Garden. Greene's friend Tom Burns has left a memorable description of the gatherings which followed more formal board meetings. The leading trio were Douglas Jerrold, Sir Charles Petrie and Frank Morely, an American who had been a Rhodes scholar. Greene stood out as something of an eccentric in this company. In particular, as Malcolm Muggeridge, still a friend of Greene's in the 1940s, pointed out, Jerrold's opinions were of the far right:

> It would be difficult to imagine two more strangely assorted human beings; both Catholic converts certainly but Jerrold induced thereby to move to the extreme right, as a supporter of General Franco, and Greene to move ever further leftwards as a fervent advocate of Catholic–Marxist dialogue.[6]

In fact, as is clear from Jerrold's book *The Necessity of Freedom*, there would have been much common ground with Greene on serious literary matters. Jerrold was old enough to remember when there had been a reading public in England ready to buy good books in large numbers and he deplored the fact that important and scholarly literary works which before 1914 had sold between 2,000 and 10,000 copies were by 1939 selling in their hundreds:

> There has been a steady decline in the sale of all works of serious scholarship ... it has been calculated that for such books there are in England, out of a population of 40,000,000 not more than 5000

117

potential readers ... it has taken only fifty years of shoddy philosophy and systematic compulsory 'education' to force out literature and scholarship from the markets of at least one third of the world.[7]

Greene was from the new school, a man who could write both serious books and 'entertainments', however misleading that description, and publish James Hadley Chase alongside Bishop David Mathew's scholarly naval histories (another Greene addition to the list).

Anthony Powell also concentrated on Douglas Jerrold in his account of Greene's time at Eyre and Spottiswoode, referring not to the Lamb and Flag, scarcely his stratum of society, but to the Authors' Club, in the same building as the National Liberal Club and with the same late-Victorian atmosphere. There were even some late Victorians still to be found there, notably Morley Roberts, the friend and biographer of George Gissing. But the central figure on the club's committee was Jerrold, who spent much of his time there. He was also said to edit the *New English Review* in the club's lounge, with the magazine's literary editor Hugh Kingsmill in attendance. To Powell this was the world of Eyre and Spottiswoode, and he described the lunches he had with Greene at the club in a vain effort to get Greene to speed up the publication of his books. Greene could only reply with stories of post-war paper shortages.

The inner heart of the publishing house, not surprisingly, was the world of the owner of the firm, in whose family it had been since it was founded centuries before, Oliver Crosthwaite-Eyre. It was a strongly Catholic world and Greene was frequently a guest at their house in the New Forest, attending Mass in the private chapel, while discussing serious long-term projects, such as the publication of the *Summa* of Thomas Aquinas, to be translated by Father Thomas Gilby, whom Greene had met at Oxford in the 1930s as Bede Jarrett's young assistant.

Father Gilby used to say Mass for them all, but when he was not available another priest, Father Denys Lucas, would officiate. A gifted teacher, Father Lucas was the headmaster of a preparatory boarding school, St Hugh's, attached to St Edmund's Ware, a public school and also the seminary for the Westminster diocese. He was a valued addition to the Crosthwaite-Eyre weekends because, besides being a priest, he had an Englishman's devoted love of the countryside and was also an excellent shot. He went on to become a missionary priest in Uganda and later set up the publishing section of the Pastoral Institute in Kampala. It was at his funeral that I first learned of this Catholic world in which Greene spent so many happy days. When Greene came close to a nervous breakdown over his personal life and his struggle between his duty to Vivien, to whom he remained married until his death, and his involvements elsewhere, it was Oliver Crosthwaite-Eyre and his wife who gave him shelter at their Austrian home.

When Douglas Jerrold did finally retire, some years later in the 1950s when Greene had already left, Crosthwaite-Eyre tried one last time to get Greene to rejoin the firm and run it at a very generous salary with time to write his own books. Greene sadly declined; by then he had become wealthy enough to dispense with such employment and had also got into the habit of extensive travel which was to remain with him to the end.

Greene's first continental travels after the war were devoted to matters of business. He records going to Amsterdam to buy paper for Eyre and Spottiswoode as the result of a shortage caused by rationing in Britain. To his amusement he discovered that much of the paper he was buying had been exported from Britain in the first place. This was the world of barter and exchange in war-torn Europe which the young Robert Maxwell, now attached to the book wholesalers Simpkin Marshall in London, was to make his own. Anyone involved in that world seems never quite to have lost the wheeler-dealer attitude to business which those days engendered. Greene's somewhat cavalier attitude to financial matters first developed on these journeys and was reinforced by the fact that his payments from MI6 for off-the-record briefings – he was no longer employed by the service directly – were unknown to the tax authorities. His man-of-the-world view of such matters was to return to haunt him in the 1960s, but for the moment the post-war years were halcyon days for Greene, far removed from the austerity which crippled the lives of ordinary citizens.

Greene later used Amsterdam as a setting in his play *The Complaisant Lover*, but it was Paris which drew him more than any other city in

Europe. It became a home-from-home for him and he acquired a flat there, with his French literary agent conveniently occupying the flat above. Greene succeeded in persuading François Mauriac to allow his works to be published in English translation through Eyre and Spottiswoode. In exchange Paris learned a lot more about the contemporary English thriller writers whom Greene was enthusiastically supporting. He was perhaps closest to James Hadley Chase and introduced him to his own Paris agent, who quickly arranged publication of Chase's books. It was a connection that lasted well into the 1970s; in consequence Chase became as well known in France as Greene and was frequently mentioned with him in critical acclaim of the English version of the American hard-boiled fiction.

The view of Greene which James Hadley Chase gives in letters at the time is revealing. He admired him as one of the finest English writers of fiction and was extremely proud that Greene had taken an interest in him. Greene told him candidly that he had given up the idea of writing any more novels himself. He wanted to carry on publishing and encouraging young writers, but for his own work he wanted to concentrate on the cinema. When Greene said this, in 1946, he was discussing a film project with his friend Alberto Cavalcanti, the Brazilian film director, but this came to nothing. It later re-emerged much altered as a novel, *Our Man in Havana* (1958). There may have been other failed projects, for by the following year, 1947, Greene had changed his mind again and was working on a new novel, *The Heart of the Matter*. When he visited New York on business for Eyre and Spottiswoode that year the novel was far enough advanced for him to be discussing it with Viking Press, which published the American edition in 1948. The obvious conclusion that Chase drew was that Greene must also be having doubts about going on with publishing. As Chase knew, writing at Greene's level was a full-time occupation. He was right, and it only needed the right episode to bring about a parting of the ways with Eyre and Spottiswoode.

In his autobiography *Faces in my Time* Anthony Powell makes the positive statement that he was the cause of Greene's going. The story went that Powell had tired of Greene's excuses and become more and more annoyed by the delay in bringing out *John Aubrey and his Friends*, which Eyre and Spottiswoode had originally scheduled for

1946. Now publication was set for autumn 1948. Powell confronted Greene over lunch at the Authors' Club when Greene casually announced that he had decided to postpone production once more to the spring of 1949. Greene rubbed salt in the wound by saying that the book was anyway very boring. This was too much for Powell: 'I said it was to be presumed that Greene's words implied release from a contract that offered further books of mine to Eyre and Spottiswoode. Greene agreed that consequence was implicit in the view he had expressed.'[8] Powell goes on to say that there followed a row in Greene's office about the way he had treated Powell which led to his leaving the firm. Greene denied this vigorously, saying that in his opinion the book *was* dull, and stuck to his own explanation for leaving – that a row had developed over a thriller bought for the firm by Jerrold when Greene was abroad. Greene was very annoyed, because the book – never identified – was a very bad pastiche of *Brighton Rock* filled with soft pornography. Crosthwaite-Eyre, then on his estates in Africa, was said to have burned the copy that was sent to him.

The acquisition of this book may have been a ploy by Jerrold, who had become not a little cynical about Greene's view of the world. And there is one good clue about the possible background to what happened. It concerned Dorothy Glover. Even today surviving members of families long associated with the firm were unaware that the artwork signed 'Craigie' on many of the books Greene produced was actually done by Dorothy Glover. Though much has been published on the relationship between Dorothy and Greene since, they did not know of it at the time nor did they know that the pair had been living together right through the war. The clue came when Greene went a stage further than just using her jacket-design work and published a children's book which he wrote and Dorothy illustrated. The contracts signed for the remaining books they did together – not published by Eyre and Spottiswoode – identify Dorothy Craigie as Dorothy Glover (it was normal for writers using pseudonyms to have their contract in their own legal names).

Even today for an editor to use the artwork of his live-in girlfriend without letting anyone know of the relationship would be frowned on; had it been known at Eyre and Spottiswoode it would have been a very great scandal indeed. Douglas Jerrold would have been especially outraged. Had he found out that Dorothy Glover was the woman who had featured in one of Greene's more celebrated practical jokes he would have been even more upset. Dorothy had phoned the firm pretending she was an author whose manuscript had been lost – an all too frequent occurrence even today. Endless calls ensued which went on for weeks and caused chaos. A combination of Greene's detailed planning and Dorothy's acting sustained the joke effortlessly until finally it assumed a life of its own. Someone unknown to either Dorothy or Greene phoned from Edinburgh and seemed to know all about the manuscript. They decided that enough was enough.

Greene and Dorothy probably thought they were quite safe because their affair had been going on for nine years without anybody in his formal life learning of it. The split between Greene's 'entertainment' novels and his serious work reflected a similar split in his private life. The Soho and Tottenham Court Road environment that he knew during the Blitz was to him the real world of which his other friends, and even his family, knew little or nothing. There were people whom he and Dorothy knew who might have crossed over from one world to the other – the bookseller David Low, for example, who was later to publish his correspondence with Greene, *Dear David, Dear Graham* in 1989 – but when discovery came it was by complete chance.

Greene had recently met an American woman, Catherine Walston, married to a wealthy landowner, Harry (later Lord) Walston. They came to know each other through an unusual chain of circumstances. Catherine Walston was an admirer of Greene and his novels, and when she decided to become a Catholic, partly under this influence, she wrote to Greene asking if he could become her godfather. She had initially telephoned Vivien, whom she knew through mutual friends, to ask whether she could do this, and in the event it was Vivien who attended the baptismal ceremony as Greene could not appear. Greene finally met her through the introduction, it seems, of another Catholic, Robert Speaight, who had been at Oxford, much involved in the OUDS, for part of Greene's time there as an under-graduate. Speaight had learned of Dorothy Glover's existence through theatrical gossip. Greene said in a letter to Catherine that gossip about him and Dorothy was spreading, though there had been none for nine years, and he was sure that it was through Speaight, whom she knew well.

The chance encounter which revealed the situation had occurred in 1947 during the filming of *Brighton Rock* in Brighton itself. One day Greene brought down Dorothy and introduced her to everyone as Dorothy Craigie. At the end of the day he gave her a copy of the script on which he had been working, inscribing it to Dorothy as Dorothy Craigie, illustrator of *The Little Train* and *The Little Fire Engine*, mentioning that it was a corrected shooting script. The two titles were the children's books which he had written and she had illustrated, but the secret affair, put in inverted commas by Greene, was something only they knew about until then.[9] Unfortunately one of the staff on the set had previously been involved with a small hotel behind Paddington station which Greene and Dorothy had visited before the war in the early days of their affair. She recognised them. The exact progress of gossip is difficult to chart and usually scarcely worthy of attention, but here the results were to be traumatic for Greene. As soon as Catherine Walston heard of it, the news spread and the relationship between her and Greene also changed. In a short while Greene's life became an open book in Catherine's circle, which included Barbara Rothschild, who was to marry Rex Warner, a close friend of Cecil Day Lewis and others from Greene's time at Oxford and later. The situation was complicated even more because Greene and Catherine, who was in her early thirties with four young children, had started an affair in 1946 shortly after they met. Greene was therefore in the scandalous position of being a Catholic author, with a wife and family, living with one mistress and having an affair with another. It was a situation which had to be faced.

Greene did not take his relationships lightly despite comment in numerous biographies which depict him as a classic philanderer. Nothing was further from the truth; from his days with Zoe Richmond he was never fully in control of situations which were liable to engulf him completely when the right stimuli triggered them. Indeed there are distinct resemblances between Zoe and Catherine, physically as well as in their domestic life, both relatively young married – even happily married – women with children, who had for some reason grown away from their husbands.

The conflict between a relationship of this kind and the real-world relationship with Dorothy which had borne the intense experiences of the Blitz is obvious. Greene hurt Dorothy, who knew she was fighting for his loyalty; he knew he was being heartless and once inscribed a book to her as from 'Graham the bastard'. But the real problem was that Catherine moved in the same circles as his wife, so the harm caused to Vivien was of a different order. Even Greene's mother sided unhesitatingly with Vivien and was damning in her comments on Catherine's character. But Greene was still tied to the scenario Zoe had created all those years before. He struggled free only at the time of his play *The Complaisant Lover* in 1959.

Vivien Greene never despaired of the situation and was even able to notice objectively that her husband became harsher and less affectionate towards his family when he was involved with Catherine Walston than he had been when he was living with Dorothy. A lot of this she attributed to the great luxury with which Catherine Walston surrounded Greene. A classic example she described to me was an occasion when Greene was going to miss an appointment on a visit to Vivien and his family at Oxford; Catherine solved the problem in a moment by arranging for a light plane to fly Greene over. On another occasion Greene had arranged for François Mauriac to receive an honorary degree at Oxford. The reception afterwards was prepared by Vivien with food which it had taken her weeks to gather together from her rations. Catherine was present with Greene and the others and it was clear that the effort meant nothing; the Walstons lived in a world on which rationing could never impinge.

In 1948, when Greene left Eyre and Spottiswoode, these personal problems were still gathering force. He left publishing without regret, although he came back to it more than a decade later when his regular publisher Heinemann became the subject of a takeover. He was to move to the Bodley Head, in which he took much the same interest as he had in Eyre and Spottiswoode.

CHAPTER NINE

Doctor Harry Lime and James Hadley Chase

Graham Greene disliked the term Greeneland attached to the world he so often described, but, as we have seen, his dislike stemmed not from annoyance at being identified with that world, but from a dislike of the people who used the term and did not realise that this was the real world, the world which the vast majority of their fellow citizens inhabited. The critics, he thought, lived in a narrow, hothouse, London-based world. That Greene's world still existed was brought home to me one day when my quest was at its height. I was visiting a radio studio in London to take part in a programme on Graham Greene presented by the journalist Cristina Odone. Bizarrely, through the magic of radio, the interview was not conducted face to face. Scripted questions were read to me earlier by a producer and my replies were later spliced with the presenter's observations for the actual programme. The listeners were none the wiser and imagined a studio full of people. This surreal experience was counteracted outside a few moments later on the street, back in the real world, when a second-hand bookshop hove into view. It specialised in sheet music and there were various editions of *The Third Man* theme music, including some variants previously unknown to me. The owner of the shop proved to be an alumnus of Berkhamsted with a fund of know-ledge about Greene and links to other booksellers who knew of him. One of these now living in Los Angeles had visited Greene in Antibes and had filled many gaps in my knowledge of Greene's life as a book collector. Remarkably the radio-station people had not made themselves known to the bookshop, although only a few moments' walk away: Greeneland lives.

Originally *The Third Man* was to be set in London. The idea which

Greene showed to the producer Alexander Korda, written on the back of an envelope just as it came to him, has Harry Lime walking down the Strand and passing Martins without any sign of recognition. Martins is stunned, for he has just seem Lime buried. Greene classed *The Third Man* with his 'entertainments', and its relationship to his previous work in the genre, *The Ministry of Fear*, is obvious once the film is forgotten for a moment and the words carefully examined. One detail in the book, missed in the film and by many critics, is that Harry Lime is a doctor – he had qualified but never practised, he once told Martins. We are back in the world of *The Ministry of Fear* and quack doctors who cause terrible damage – in a word, the world of Kenneth Richmond as ever present in Greene's imagination. But Korda was to change all that.

First the setting of *The Third Man* was moved to Vienna; then the leading character Harry Lime became an American. Instead of being an English criminal, to whom Greene would probably have given a Soho background, Lime becomes a gangster in post-war Vienna who is making a fortune from a particularly nasty racket selling stolen adulterated penicillin to people who cannot get it by any other means. Children with meningitis in the local Austrian community are the most in need of the drug, but are barred by occupation regulations from getting it – Harry Lime supplies it. But, as the drug is diluted and contaminated, the children suffer appalling damage.

Greene's other original character, Rollo Martins – changed in the film to Holly Martins because the actor playing him, Joseph Cotten, objected to Rollo – is a writer of pulp fiction, westerns, all set in America, naturally. However, like James Hadley Chase, whose thrillers were almost all written against an American background, Martins has never set foot in America. Since Harry Lime was at school with Martins, Martins also becomes an American. There are other typical Greene references to James Hadley Chase in the book. The narrator of the book is a colonel in the Security Police called Calloway. Martins refers to him as Callaghan, actually the name of Chase's character in the book that borrowed a name from Greene, and goes on calling him by that name despite being quickly corrected. Amusingly, at one point in the book Greene gives a brief parody of Chase's best Callaghan style. Their mutual friend H. E. Bates also finds his name used as that of the sergeant who is killed in the Vienna sewers chasing Harry Lime. Before he dies he tells Martins his name is Bates, and they remember old times in the pubs they both knew in Tottenham Court Road.

A comparison can be made between Greene and Chase in real life and Harry Lime and Martins. Martins idolised Lime as an honest, gifted man who could have been anything he chose from a doctor to a composer of light music – the theme song of the film is one that Lime pretends to have written, and Martins believes him. In fact Lime is the morally corrupt racketeer, and Martins, the writer of savage western thrillers, is the moral innocent who even falls in love with Harry's girl. Chase wrote lurid thrillers, but in his private life was a highly moral person devoted to his wife and family. He looked up to Greene as a Catholic novelist and a great author. In fact Greene was in the middle of his own personal hell with a wife and two mistresses. The contrast mirrors that between Lime and Martins exactly.

Once the decision to move the action to Vienna had been taken, Greene found himself in a world he could recognise. There were even kidnappings across political borders, just as there had been in the Palatinate over twenty years before. It was the world of European politics at its most bitter. To Greene it was as much home as London in the Blitz. The narrator Calloway is a Scotland Yard man who has been seconded to the British occupying forces and given the rank of colonel. As soon as Martins asks him if he is a policeman he reveals he is a Yard man; he refers to his files frequently with an ease Greene himself had acquired in his time in MI6. But the detective is pure police procedure, and the policeman – Calloway not Callaghan – is a ringer for Greene's policeman in *The Ministry of Fear*, and others before him. In the end Greene, like Orwell, never quite forgot that he once wore a policeman's uniform; even if it was worn only for a matter of days the psychological effect is never forgotten.

Through the policeman's eyes the political dimension is scarcely seen. The Russian zone is simply 'Russian zone' and it is taken for granted that kidnappings are masterminded from there, that the Russians do not comply with regulations and have strange quirks like refusing to allow the street-access points to the sewers to be secured – Calloway says the reason was unknown. Greene knew of course that it was because in the days of the workers' uprising in Vienna before the war, when Philby had helped communists to flee, the sewers had been their escape route. Calloway's political comment, when it comes, is short and sharp: 'A racket works like a totalitarian party.'[1]

Thought about politics, already beaten down in *The Ministry of Fear* into just fear and a few quotations from Tolstoy, has now been reduced to a cynical comment by Lime, spoken from high above the war-ruined Vienna in a cabin on the Great Wheel: 'In these days, old man, nobody thinks in terms of human beings. Governments don't so why should we? They talk of the people and the proletariat, and I talk of the mugs. It's the same thing. They have their five year plans and so have I.'[2] And following straight on from this cynical view Greene has Martins say:

> 'You used to be a Catholic.'
> 'Oh, I still *believe*, old man. In God and mercy and all that. I'm not hurting anybody's soul by what I do. The dead are happier dead. They don't miss much here, poor devils,' he added with that odd touch of genuine pity...[3]

Perhaps after a war in which tens of millions had died this is the only kind of morality that can be expected; religion has become irrelevant and human beings mere specks on the face of the earth. Greene had once flown in a bomber before the war, having spent all those civilian flying hours without grasping the potential danger of the pilots losing all moral contact with the people below them. The problem still worried him later in the 1950s when he went in a bomber, for real, in the Indo-China war. But it was in *The Third Man* from the top of the Great Wheel that he has Harry Lime make the classic statement of it, now impossible to separate from the voice of Orson Wells:

> Martins said, 'Have you ever visited the children's hospital? Have you seen any of your victims?'
> Harry took a look at the toy landscape below and came away from the door ... 'Victims?' he asked. 'Don't be melodramatic, Rollo. Look down there,' he went on, pointing through the window at the people

Zoe Richmond, wife of psychoanalyst Kenneth Richmond, in whose house Graham Greene lived as a patient for six months at the age of sixteen. Greene fell in love with her and their relationship haunted him for thirty years. (Private Collection).

J. D. Beresford, left, and Walter de la Mare. An unjustly neglected novelist, J. D. Beresford was Greene's idol when he stayed with the Richmonds. Greene kept in touch with Beresford until he died and republished his best novel *The Hampdenshire Wonder*. (Private Collection).

The menu for the Mulla Mulgars dinner at Oxford attended by Graham Greene and John Buchan. The Mulla Mulgars – Royal Monkeys – were a creation of Walter de la Mare. (Dominic Winter Book Auctions).

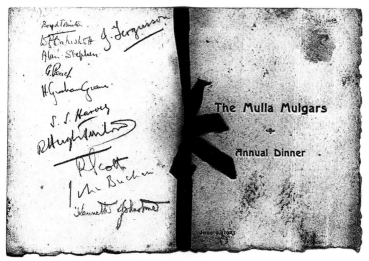

The Mulla Mulgars

Annual Dinner

June 9, 1923

(left) Geoffrey Moss, author of *Defeat* which inspired Graham Greene to visit French-occupied Germany during his university vacation in 1924.
(Private Collection).

Father Bede Jarrett O.P. who received Graham Greene's wife Vivien into the Catholic church and had a great influence on Greene. He died young and his loss was greatly felt.

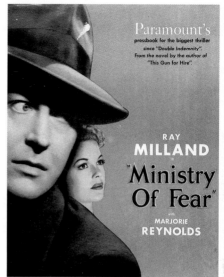

Viscount Cecil of Chelwood. Lord Cecil's evidence at the Royal Commission on armaments in 1935, which Graham Greene attended, echoed Greene's preoccupations in *A Gun for Sale*. His account of the Chaco wars in South America saw Greene on another quest there thirty years later. (Karl Pollak F. R.P.S.).

Paramount's press book for their film of Graham Greene's novel *The Ministry of Fear*. The Hollywood image that culminated in Orson Welles' depiction of Harry Lime in *The Third Man* is already apparent. (Paramount).

Dust jacket for *More Deadly than the Male* by James Hadley Chase using the name Ambrose Grant – the only book he wrote under that name. Graham Greene published the book and he commissioned the jacket from Dorothy Glover, known also as Dorothy Craigie. At the time Greene and Dorothy were living together in London. (Eyre and Spottiswoode).

(left) James Hadley Chase, author of *No Orchids for Miss Blandish* and *More Deadly than the Male*. Later, like Greene, Chase accepted the advice of Tom Roe, a lawyer and financial advisor based in Switzerland whose operations were fraudulent.

(below) Clemence Dane and Noël Coward in 1942 at a reception in London. Clemence Dane was an early and enthusiastic admirer of Graham Greene. She met him at the Richmonds', visited him at Oxford and gave him the title for his neglected second novel *The Name of Action*. (Hulton Getty).

(right) Graham Greene and Catherine Walston backstage at a Noël Coward production in 1953. Greene's involvement with Catherine Walston dominated his life in the forties and fifties, and this photograph gives the 'hint of an explanation'. (Hulton Getty).

(below) *The Third Man* was Graham Greene's most successful film and a major element in the success was the haunting theme music by Anton Karas. The sheet music, seen here, was equally popular. (Chappell & Co.).

Thomas Chambers Windsor Roe – Tom Roe – on the right – with two Swiss police officers after his arrest for fraud and circulating forged $100 bills obtained from the Mafia in Hollywood. He had operated tax avoidance schemes as a front for his other activities and amongst those who fell victim were Graham Greene, Noël Coward, Charlie Chaplin and James Hadley Chase. (Hulton Getty).

George Sanders, partner of Tom Roe in the scam which precipitated Greene's exile from England on 1 January 1966. (Private Collection).

Harry Saltzman, film producer. After Tom Roe's conviction in Switzerland Saltzman visited him in prison and offered him the job of running his Paris operations when he was released. Saltzman's partner, Cubby Broccoli, with whom he created the James Bond films, was not involved in any way in these activities with Roe. (Desmond O'Neill).

Malcolm Muggeridge, second left, at a political meeting in 1956. Muggeridge worked with Greene in MI6 during the war and also when Greene was a publisher at Eyre and Spottiswoode, on a freelance basis. He visited Greene in Paris in 1966 after Greene had gone into exile. In later life Greene became highly critical of him and his betrayal of their wartime friendship with Kim Philby. (Associated Press).

(above) Graham Greene in Moscow in 1987 in the apartment of his friend Genrikh Borovik (far left). Kim Philby is third on the left with his wife Rufina Philby on his left. (V. Krokhin).

(below) Graham Greene, left, with Father Gustavo, centre, the Abbot of the Benedictine monastery of Leyre in Navarra, and Father Leopoldo Durán. In later life Greene spent increasing time in Spain with Father Durán and other priests. These friendships echoed earlier ones in England with Father Bede Jarrett and Father Thomas Gilby. (Father Durán).

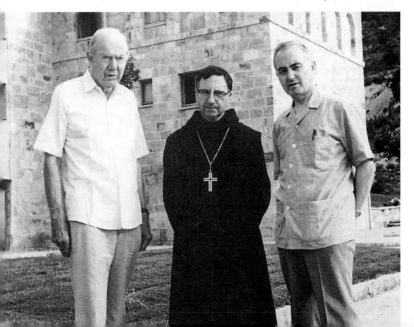

moving like black flies at the base of the Wheel. 'Would you really feel any pity if one of those dots stopped moving – for ever? If I said you could have twenty thousand pounds for every dot that stops, would you really, old man, tell me to keep my money – without hesitation? Or would you calculate how many dots you could afford to spare? Free of income tax, old man. Free of income tax.'[4]

And was there really any difference between the racketeer who speculated on how profitable his murders might be, and the leader who threw away tens of thousands of lives without even that thought, since he had a political justification for what he did? The criminal pays no income tax, so he is even free of the moral stain of the crimes committed by the state of which he is a nominal member.

Like the other Greene novels, and even his travel books, there is the obligatory return to childhood and the hero-worship, or more often the sufferings caused by the acts of his classmates. But in *The Third Man* there are signs that Greene was beginning to shake off this artificially induced preoccupation. It is almost as if he is realising that it is not the childhood pain that worries him, but the false emphasis placed on it by Richmond in his daily sessions of analysis. The incident that destroys the childhood illusion is Calloway's showing Martins his file on Harry Lime.

The facts revealed about Lime ruthlessly destroy Martins' loyalty and every detail of his childhood friendship. Greene uses the chilling image of nuclear contamination. All these moments of intimacy and comradeship were tainted 'like the soil of an atomized town. One could not walk there with safety for a long while.' The comparison is so acid that, knowing Greene, one looks for a possible source in his own life. The only likely comparison is Greene's school friendship with Claud Cockburn. If Greene saw Cockburn's security services file and its record of political activity and even betrayal during the period of the Nazi–Soviet pact, this could have created the level of disillusion on which Martins' revulsion at his old friendship was based. But there is no evidence in the public domain, nor ever likely to be.

Although the changes suggested by Korda were driven by his need to get an American co-producer on board and to attract American audiences, the result was a vast improvement. Greene worked on a day-to-day basis with the director Carol Reed and greatly enjoyed it. As he says in his introduction to the book, if there was a change in the film from the published book it was not a case of his ideas being overturned; he might very well have been the person suggesting the change. Greene and Reed went to Hollywood to meet the American producer David Selznick, crossing the Atlantic on the *Queen Elizabeth* in August 1948. Their discussions with Selznick were conducted at night, according to Greene's biographer Norman Sherry, never finishing before 4 a.m. They came away with masses of notes and the suggestion that the title *The Third Man* be changed to *Nights in Vienna*. Greene trusted Reed implicitly and none of the suggested alterations were taken up.

The publication of *The Third Man* as a book, never intended by Greene, helped scotch rumours that Orson Welles had written many of Lime's lines, if not all of them. The only contribution he made was the celebrated observation that 500 years of peace and brotherly love in Switzerland had produced nothing but the cuckoo clock. A more serious challenge was made by Greene's unauthorised biographer Michael Shelden; he suggested that Greene had obtained the idea of the penicillin racket from a freelance journalist called Peter Smolka, a friend of Philby's and later identified as a Soviet agent. Smolka does appear in Korda's records as having had a contract and having received a payment for some script work, but the nature of this is never specified. Korda was then much involved in espionage as well as film-making, as he had been before the war, and it is possible that this contract was cover for some other less avowable reason for payment. The only witness to the contract was also involved in Korda's other activities. Whatever the background to this murky affair, letters amongst Greene's papers in Boston College confirm that the idea was his, and where he got his facts from.

In 1950 a Catholic priest wrote to Greene asking him for the origin of the story of the penicillin racket. The priest had actually worked in one of the hospitals concerned and could not believe the story. Greene replied that the story was true and that he had got the information from the Chief of Police in Vienna. Greene's statement here is convincing because, like his letter rebutting the charge of anti-semitism, it was written without any thought of publication. He could not possibly have imagined that it would become a matter of dispute forty-four years later. It also provides further indirect evidence of the seriousness of his Catholic beliefs – many an author, many a biographer, would have brushed aside such a letter in his mail and left it unanswered. In his volume of autobiography *Ways of Escape*, written thirty years after the priest's original question, he gave further details of how the idea came to him and of whom he was referring to as 'the Chief of Police'. He had had difficulty finding his story and the time had almost come for him to leave Vienna. Then the solution fell into his hands:

> On the penultimate day I had the good fortune to lunch with a young British Intelligence Officer (the future Duke of St. Albans) – my wartime connection with the S.I.S. [MI6] used to bring me useful dividends in those days ... At lunch the officer had told me of the penicillin racket and now ... the whole story took shape.[5]

There were other rackets going on in Vienna, and one of the unforeseen results of Korda's making Lime and Martins American was that the American character whom Greene had already incorporated into his plot, Colonel Cooler, had to go. Cooler was a friend of Harry Lime's, involved in his rackets, though his own private racket is relatively innocuous, $25,000 salted away from black-market tyre deals. Greene's description of him, seen through the eyes of the Scotland Yard man Colonel Calloway, is revealing:

> The Englishman who objects to Americans in general usually carries in his mind's eye just such an exception as Cooler: a man with tousled grey hair and a worried kindly face and long-sighted eyes, the kind of humanitarian who turns up in a typhus epidemic or a world war, or a Chinese famine long before his countrymen have discovered the place in an atlas.[6]

Whether Greene himself felt like this is another matter, but it is difficult to see a reason for his portraying as a crook the type of American for whom most people the world over might feel admiration. The earliest appearance of an American of this kind in Greene's work is the armaments dealer in *The Name of Action*; its reappearance here was to be the beginning of a very troubled relationship between

Greene and America. The year after *The Third Man* appeared, in 1950, Greene found himself in Brussels for a debate with François Mauriac. He happened to mention to the American Chargé d'Affaires in Brussels that he had once been a communist for a few weeks as a student at Oxford. The American diplomat, Robert McClintock, had raised the subject of the newly passed McCarran Act, which excluded all 'alien communists' from the United States. Greene was outraged and McClintock agreed with him. His report continued: 'I suggested that, if Mr. Greene should wish to become a *cause célèbre*, I should be glad to take his application for a visa.'[7] Greene did not give the matter any further thought, but two years later he discovered that he could not get a visa without formal application for exemption through the American Embassy in London. Russia may have lowered an Iron Curtain, but America had in turn lowered a plastic one, as Greene later put it.

This was an unhappy state of affairs and an inauspicious end to a cinematic undertaking whose successful linking of English and American contributions created one of the greatest films to appear since the war. But there had never been a political dimension – it had been a question of sensationalism or the imposition of a happy ending. Ironically, in *The Third Man* Greene had provided a happy ending, with Martins walking away from Harry's second funeral, the real one, with Harry's girl Anna. It was almost an exact repeat of the ending of *The Ministry of Fear*; even the girl's name was the same. But Carol Reed thought the ending wrong; it should end with Anna walking past Martins without even noticing him.

CHAPTER TEN

Faith-Healing and *The End of the Affair*

If the vast archives of the Public Record Office seem an unlikely place
to pursue a literary quest then Companies House in the City of
London, the equivalent of the SEC in America, might seem a desert.
Here, as a result of the wisdom and experience of the Victorians, and
successive Companies Acts, all limited and public companies trading
are obliged to lodge particulars about themselves and their annual
reports. This applies to all, high and low, from hundred-pound
companies to billionaire conglomerates. For the payment of a small
fee the reader obtains an envelope containing the records of any
company on microfiche. The information is precise and detailed.

The result of typing 'GRAHAM GREENE' at the catalogue com-
puter terminal was a listing for Graham Greene Productions Limited,
a company set up by Greene together with the company number.
After a request for papers and a short wait, a fresh section of my
quest for Graham Greene began. Greene would have been well aware
that the information he supplied would be available to the public, for
he had already been a director of Eyre and Spottiswoode. Had he
wanted to keep this aspect of his business affairs secret he would not
have set up such a company but would have made use of one of the
myriad private arrangements that could be made then. In fact he
wanted complete openness and transparency, for once, in an area
where others might naturally look to concealment. The company's
records have been available for all to see since it was founded in
1950. Yet they are a source which the numerous biographies have
ignored, perhaps because their authors did not know of their existence.

The Centaur Press was also listed, of course, and from Jon Wynne-
Tyson's archives and the leads he provided came even more infor-

mation about the themes underlying Greene's *The End of the Affair*.

The End of the Affair is dedicated to Catherine Walston and is one of the most personal of Greene's books. He would later refer to difficulty he had 'in my private life', but the book is far more complex than even Green realised at the time. He was certainly driven to the point of breakdown trying to resolve personal problems, and Catherine Walston was at the heart of them, but there was far more in the book, and in the play *The Living Room*, than that.

In 1948 J. D. Beresford died. He was largely forgotten, and his autobiography, which he had struggled to finish, could not be published owing to the objections of his wife, from whom he had separated on bitter terms to live with Esme Wynne-Tyson. Whatever the rights and wrongs of this sad affair, Esme Wynne-Tyson had written several books with Beresford and he felt she had helped him greatly. But she had also seen the autobiography evolve and had worked on that too, and this was an insuperable barrier as far as his wife was concerned, and the rights in the book were hers. Greene was aware of these problems as an outsider, he had seen the books published, and he was still very much part of the world which he had first joined as such a young man. He repaid his debt to Beresford by the Eyre and Spottiswoode publication of *The Hampdenshire Wonder* and by help given to his son's first book. But he also examined Beresford's life and his philosophy over his later years in *The End of the Affair*.

Greene referred to his book as his 'I' book, and it is written in the first person by a narrator who is an author. But the author is definitely not Greene himself, as his objective description of the 'I' shows. The physical description of the author is that of J. D. Beresford, and one which Beresford himself used rather than the description Greene gave of him in *A Sort of Life* as crippled by infantile paralysis. In fact Beresford had had an accident which was left unattended and resulted in his having one leg shorter than the other. He used crutches throughout his life.

The characterisation was not carried through in further domestic detail. The book is not a *roman-à-clef* in that sense. However, further aspects of Beresford's work were transferred on to another character in the book, the central figure Richard Smythe, a rationalist who lives with his sister and who is also disfigured with a strawberry mark on his face which plays a vital part in the ending of the book.

The book is set on Clapham Common and its timescale is displaced so that any literal comparison between the affair of the title and that of Graham Greene and Catherine Walston would not be possible. The affair in the novel has gone on through the war years between the narrator Bendrix and Sarah, the wife of a friend of his called Henry Miles and bears a superficial resemblance to his relationship with Dorothy, though here the mistress is conveniently placed on the other side of Clapham Common rather than far away in Mecklenburgh Square. In the 1940s there were speakers on the Common and one of these is Smythe, who explains to any people he can get to listen that there is no God. His sister hands around small visiting cards to people and is frugal enough to pick these up carefully when people discard them. He speaks nominally for the Rationalist Society of South London, although, as he later confesses to Sarah, he has very few followers – she is the first for a very long time to call at his address for instruction. In describing the speakers on the Common, Greene makes an amusing joke of his own earlier enthusiasms: 'There were speakers out on the Common: the I.L.P. and the Communist Party, and the man who just tells jokes, and there was a man attacking Christianity.'[1]

In a complex reworking of the way in which Catholics are instructed, Greene has Sarah going to see Smythe to confirm her belief that there is no God, but as he goes through the arguments over a period of years she slowly comes around to believing that he is wrong. She starts calling at Catholic churches when she wants refuge from the chaos of her personal life – a private detective who has been employed by Bendrix to follow her to establish who the unknown person she is visiting might be discovers this – and finally commences real instruction with a Catholic priest. The priest is given Catherine Walston's maiden name Crompton in a typical Greene joke.

But the reversal of the normal relationship between preacher and disciple goes further, for Smythe finds himself being drawn towards the Church as well. The book ends with an incident which worried Greene when he wrote it, and it attracted much comment: Sarah kisses the birthmark on Smythe's face and he wakes up the next day to find that the mark has gone. A few days later she dies. Despite much discussion on this very unusual happening, quite untypical of the type of Catholic reference Greene normally places in his books, there has been no understanding of anything other than the 'miraculous' view of it. When Smythe rings up to tell Bendrix he himself believes this:

> He said with an awful air of conspiracy, 'You and I know how. There's no getting around it. It wasn't right of me keeping it dark. It was a ...' but I put down the receiver before he could use that foolish newspaper word that was the alternative to 'coincidence' ... I thought, He's so proud that he must always have some kind of revelation. In a week or two he'll be speaking about it on the Common and showing his healed face. It will be in the newspapers: 'Rationalist Speaker Converted by Miraculous Cure.'[2]

But the other explanation was more prosaic, that of faith-healing. J. D. Beresford had written a novel on faith-healing, *The Camberwell Miracle*, which Greene had read when it came out in the 1930s, but more important was Beresford's direct treatment of the subject in *The Case for Faith-Healing*. The argument here was a rationalist one and there is much discussion of psychological factors with reference to the exceedingly complex state of psychiatry at the time. Bendrix is angry with Smythe's weakness on such questions and wishes to stop the spread of the idea of a miracle as swiftly as he was able to slam down the telephone. When he has to explain to Sarah's widower, who has been beside him when he took the call, what Smythe wanted he mentions the cure and swiftly invents a rational explanation:

> 'His face has been cured, that's all. I asked him to let me know the name of the specialist. I have a friend...'
> 'Do you mean they've grafted skin?'
> 'I'm not sure. I've read somewhere these marks are hysterical in origin. A mixture of psychiatry and radium.' It sounded plausible. Perhaps after all it was the truth. Another coincidence, two cars with the same number plate, and I thought with a sense of weariness, how many coincidences are there going to be...[3]

The reference to car numbers and coincidences comes earlier when

Bendrix is trying to explain some striking coincidence to Henry and he gives the example of many occasions when he has seen two cars with the same number in their number plates standing side by side in traffic. Greene himself played games of this kind, a final desperate attempt to make sense of the way things happen in the world of chance which dominates our lives, like the numbers in a lottery.

Despite *The End of the Affair* finishing on this crucial question and the writer desperately trying to reject his dead lover's Catholicism by resort to untrue rational explanations, the entire theme, indeed Smythe himself, has been ignored by critics of the book. Greene pursues it ruthlessly to the end. After a bitter outburst against God which ends with the often quoted line, 'I hate You God, I hate You as though You existed,' Bendrix goes on to rationalise his hatred: 'Hatred is in my brain not in my stomach or in my skin,' and then decides to go and seek a cure for it:

> I thought, in the morning I'll ring up the doctor and ask him whether any treatment exists. And then I thought, better not; so long as one doesn't *know* one can imagine innumerable cures...[4]

Throughout the book Greene places in the mouths of his characters different phases of the same argument, and always doctors, medicine and rational thought are at the heart of the matter. Part of the original structure of the book is a diary which Sarah keeps. It is stolen from her flat by a private detective Bendrix has hired who reads it into the narrative. In real life Graham and Catherine Walston were said to have kept a double diary, each writing a page. There were precedents for this, and even for the publication of such diaries. George Orwell and Inez Holden embarked on a similar venture, although the two diaries proved incompatible and were eventually to be published separately many years apart.

Greene transposes large extracts from Sarah's diary as one section of the novel. Sarah is going through her struggles relating to the existence of God and Catholicism, just as Catherine did – it is often forgotten that Greene met her after she asked him to be her godparent and that her struggles before becoming a Catholic were real and complex. She is obviously the inspiration for Sarah in the incident where her husband had explained some crude statues in a Spanish church with painted blood by referring to the materialistic nature of Catholic belief: 'Materialism isn't only an attitude of the poor. Some of the finest brains have been materialistic, Pascal, Newman. So subtle in some directions: so crudely superstitious in others. One day we may know why: it may be a glandular deficiency.'[5] Again the harsh note of twentieth-century medicine, which Greene counters later in the same diary with compelling force:

> Am I a materialist after all, I wondered? Have I some glandular deficiency that I am so uninterested in the really important superstitious things and causes – like the Charity Commission and the index of living and better calories for the working classes? Am I a materialist because I believe in the independent existence of that man in the bowler, the metal of that cross, these hands that I can't pray with?[6]

It was an inspired creative stroke to amalgamate the struggles of Catherine Walston over her religious conversion with the arguments of Beresford and his circle. Greene's revived interest in him, and his sudden death just at the time he was becoming involved with Catherine, had obviously left a profound mark, and it was not simply a question of religion. Memories of Zoe Richmond and the half-forgotten world around the back of Paddington station and what he called the vicious hotels there also reappear in the book. Without exception they have been attributed to Greene's affair with Catherine.

There are other references to that earlier half-forgotten world. Greene published a collection of short stories in 1947 called *Nineteen Stories*; J. D. Beresford's most successful collection of short stories had been called *Nineteen Impressions* – a coincidence, like two adjacent cars with the same number, or a doffing of the cap to someone to whom a just debt was owed? Greene had originally intended to include eighteen stories but at the last minute changed it to nineteen. Although the story added came from before the war, the only recent story in the collection, the one with which it begins, was 'The Hint of an Explanation'. The narrator is travelling on a train with one other person in his carriage. After a while they begin a conversation. He soon realises that the man with him is Catholic, while he, the narrator, is agnostic, though with a firm desire to believe if proof were available.

The stranger tells him a story of his schooldays when a man in his village, a baker, tries to get him to steal a consecrated host for him to examine under a microscope and experiment with; for reward he offers a clockwork train set which he has let the boy play with. The boy agrees at first but then cannot bring himself to give the host to the baker when he calls late at night. Instead he swallows it, and the baker suddenly bursts into tears. He ends the story with his own explanation, that the baker had been an instrument of some Thing, and that it had relied on him as a weapon: 'Now I had broken in its hands and it wept its hopeless tears through Blacker's eyes.' When his companion gets up, the narrator realises that he is a Catholic priest. There are parallels here with the hopes that Beresford and his circle had for Greene, only for them to find that Greene had become a Catholic. Beresford felt bitter towards the Church because he attributed the break-up of his marriage to the increased Catholic tendencies of his wife, and it must have been a shock to find Greene supporting his neglected masterpiece and reprinting it. The story, in a collection with the flattering title, indeed offered 'The Hint of an Explanation'.

Even more interesting, and something which suggests that Greene had at last begun to ask questions about this crucial part of his past life nearly thirty years before, are details in his letters, and in one of his mother's letters. This was a time of acute stress for Vivien, who was trying to understand what was going on, and writing to Greene's mother. The question of Richmond's influence was raised. Greene's mother wrote, on 29 June 1948:

> I wish I had not torn up Kenneth Richmond's letter about [Graham]. I cannot now remember how we took Graham to him but he was a different person after the treatment ... Kenneth R. felt being able to express himself in writing would help so much.[7]

The reality of Richmond's suggestion that Greene 'express himself in writing' was seen in his linking the idea that he might be a writer as good as Dostoevsky to the suggestion that he too might have epilepsy. That specific ambition, to equal Dostoevsky, was so deeply implanted in Greene's mind that it resurfaced in a letter to Dorothy. He had been reading *The Brothers Karamazov* and had found on second reading that it was not as good as he thought. He added: 'Maybe I can write as good as D[ostoevsky]. Cut larger chunks of the new novel and after all it is good.'

Any doubts that Sarah is a portrait of Catherine seem even less easy to sustain given the correlation between Henry and Harry Walston (he was christened Henry), were it not that Greene's own first name was also Henry. And on close inspection there are differences between the two men. The job which the fictional Henry has been given in *The End of the Affair* is that of a senior civil servant, the head of a Royal Commission. Harry Walston had held government office but it is more likely that Greene was harking back to the sort of dry personality whom he had seen presiding over the Royal Commission he had attended before the war. The most striking difference between the fictional Henry and the real one is that in the novel Henry had had no children. The Walstons at that time had four children and were to all outward appearances happily married. By the moral standards current in the post-war world, particularly amongst the extremely wealthy, which the Walstons undoubtedly were, their marriage might be happy if somewhat unusually open. When Evelyn Waugh was invited to their house, through Greene, he found himself in a world of which he had before known nothing, and his travels in society had been wide. A Dominican priest who visited the household found the wealth so overpowering that he felt it was almost as though they did not know quite how to spend their money. At dinner, wine was drunk out of silver goblets, immensely valuable paintings were everywhere. While most of this was simply a result of the Walstons patronising modern artists and authors, including Greene, such details as the wine in silver goblets suggested something outside normal English experience even at the most aristocratic levels.

The contrast with Henry Miles could not be greater. Miles epitomised the higher English civil servant and drank modestly at home, or in his club. When his wife Sarah dies – from pneumonia, because the doctors were not brought in early enough to give her the penicillin which would have saved her – he even suggests that Bendrix move in to his house, as someone who had meant as much to Sarah as he had. Many wondered why Harry Walston did not take action over the book and the very open affair which was going on between his wife and Greene, but the sharp differences between the fictional Henry and himself would have made that difficult. On Catherine Walston's side it could soon have been established that there were other models possible for the character supposedly based on her. The affair that ended might just as easily have been that with Dorothy, or indeed Zoe herself, still alive and a blameless widow. Harry must have thought that this was the price to be paid for becoming involved with one of the undisputed masters of English fiction of his generation; he was obliged to become a complaisant husband. Indeed there would have been no shortage of people aching to be put into Greene's books, however prominently.

Greene was so obviously the person who was suffering most in the situation that the results of pursuing him would probably have caused more harm than good, particularly to the Church, of which Catherine was an ardent supporter. Greene was well known as a Catholic novelist, even if he preferred to be called a novelist who happened to be a Catholic. Had Harry Walston taken any kind of action, the publicity would have been immense and, since Greene kept his private life scrupulously secret, he (Greene) would not initially have been the focus of it. The assumption would have been that he was blameless, the victim of Catherine's obsessions.

Part of the difficulty in understanding how Greene's mind was working at this stage in his life stems from the view of the world he developed during his time with MI6. Enveloped in secrecy that keeps every detail of his day-to-day life away from even his closest family, playing games with people's lives at every level of his work, can create in an MI6 man a cynicism or plain lack of understanding of ordinary existence which can be experienced to the same extent only by the very wealthy. For example, Greene assuaged the guilt he felt about deserting Dorothy by arranging for her to go on tour to Africa on one of the Elder Dempster steamships which he had travelled on during the war. It was almost as if he was arranging for an agent to go off somewhere in one of his wartime espionage assignments. She went off contentedly, leaving Greene with a simpler life. But even then his wife Vivien, by now in the house in Oxford which remained to the end of Greene's life his matrimonial home, remained completely in the dark about such details.

Greene had coped with Dorothy, distancing her, but he was still obsessively involved with Catherine Walston, and both knew that this was causing great problems in their families, and with their religious advisers. The only answer was for Greene to spend more time away from England. From the late 1940s he substituted himself for the agent in a peacetime version of his wartime games and decided to go on ever more extensive and complex travels to world trouble spots, often with the co-operation of MI6, although he was not working for it formally. Greene did not stop seeing Catherine; instead he took a very unusual step in making her a co-director of the limited company he set up to handle his business affairs, Graham Greene Productions. He and Catherine had equal shareholdings and were listed on the firm's notepaper as the sole directors. Greene's logic seems to have been this: if they could not get married – and it seemed that an annulment of their marriages was impossible – then it would have to be business. Later, when their affair had subsided almost completely, other shareholders were brought in, including both Dorothy and Vivien, but Catherine remained a director until the day she died.

In parallel with these traumatic happenings in his private life, all more or less skilfully interwoven with his writing, Greene was developing the interest in the theatre that had begun with his pre-war radio play *The Great Jowett*. It started with Basil Dean and an attempt to make a play of *The Heart of the Matter*. The original idea for the production came from Rodgers and Hammerstein in New York. They had acquired the rights in Greene's book and were trying without success to get an adaptation that would work for the stage. Basil Dean, having worked with Greene on projects over many years, saw an opportunity: 'I offered to lend a hand, making my usual stipulation that the novelist must approve of me and join in the work.'[8] People have said that Dean was difficult to work with in his later years, and the difficulty can be heard in these few words. It was Greene who had to feel able to work with him, not the other way around; in the event he agreed to do so, but the result was a disaster.

At first Greene thought he would work with Dean in America, but he ran up against an unexpected barrier – the Bank of England would not allow him enough money under the stringent exchange-control regulations for dollars to cover the costs of his journey. The post-war Labour government was obliged to guard Britain's foreign currency holdings rigorously and, as far as the Bank of England was concerned authors were beneath the salt when it came to the allocation of scarce funds, however prestigious the project. Greene wrote a letter in protest to *The Times*: 'Writers are creeping up on industrialists as dollar earners, but one department of the Bank of England still appears to regard us as an inferior race, or at least as distinct outsiders.'[9] He went on to describe in detail the difficulties he had experienced with the control authorities and did so to such great effect that Sir Stafford Cripps, the Chancellor of the Exchequer, himself dealt with the question when it was raised in the House of Commons by Christopher Hollis. Cripps protested that Greene had not made it clear that he had already got a contract for the work he wished to do. Greene responded in a further letter to *The Times*:

> I had not expected when I wrote my first letter to you on the subject of 'dollars for authors' that the matter would go as far as it has done. I had no desire to have my personal case used as political propaganda but only to draw attention to what seemed a general attitude on the part of the Bank of England to people of my profession.[10]

But that was exactly what had happened and the whole row was one of the earliest of Greene's newspaper exchanges which became a hallmark of his in later years, culminating in the publication of *Yours Etc.: Letters to the Press 1945–89*.

Despite the relaxation of the Bank of England's rules to allow Greene funds, the American trip did not take place, for he had meanwhile walked into even worse difficulty over his visa. By contrast, Basil Dean made a point of boasting of his own close relations with the powers that be, in the person of Chuter Ede, the Colonial Secretary in the Cabinet with Stafford Cripps, when it came to arranging a trip to Sierra Leone to research their adaptation. Dean went out of his way to portray Greene in an unfavourable light when he wrote about the trip in his autobiography. Having arranged flying permits and official approval of the visit he remarked that Greene was 'unpopular in official circles there because they claimed that the chief part of

Major Scobie in *The Heart of the Matter* was a reflection upon their police service'.[11] Dean went one stage further, adding that although he stayed with the Governor of Sierra Leone Greene was obliged to stay in what he called a 'rather dubious hotel'. In fact, as Greene says in his letters home to Catherine, this was the hotel from which Wilson, at the beginning of *The Heart of the Matter*, sees Scobie; he was writing his letter from the very balcony which opens the book: 'Wilson sat on the balcony of the Bedford Hotel with his bald pink knees thrust against the ironwork. It was Sunday and the Cathedral bell clanged for matins ...'[12] Wilson is joined by a colleague who points out Scobie walking down the street below:

> it seemed to him that no particular interest attached to the squat grey-haired man walking alone up Bond Street. He couldn't tell that this was one of those occasions a man never forgets: a small cicatrice had been made on the memory, a wound that would ache whenever certain things combined – the taste of gin at mid-day, the smell of flowers under a balcony...[13]

The adaptation was not a success. The play was due to open in Boston before going on to New York and Broadway, but frantic messages to Greene in London from Rodgers and Hammerstein alerted him to more than normal teething troubles at final rehearsals. In his autobiography Dean says that the scenes between Scobie and Father Rank were Greene's work and implies that the ultimate failure was caused by Greene. Everyone else took the opposite view. Greene's letters and comments show that he was still struggling with Dean's work and trying to rescue the production for him until the end. Perhaps if Dean had stayed at Greene's 'doubtful' hotel rather than with the Governor he would himself have got closer to the heart of Greene's book. Instead, ironically given that Dean had insisted he get the author's co-operation, it was Greene who finally wrote and said that Dean's adaptation could not be saved and that he did not wish to do any further work on it.

Greene did not let Basil Dean's failure put him off the theatre. He had discovered its attractions as a living art form. In the cinema he had no control over what use was made of novels; writing a screenplay with a director he trusted was a step forward. Writing for radio in the recording room during rehearsals was better still; but the theatre was the final liberation. He could alter his work with the cast as the production developed. It was what Greene called a new drink and he took to it with fervour. His first attempt after the Boston failure was to go to the Group Theatre. This had triumphed before the war with productions of Auden and Isherwood, and Greene now became involved in its revival. His name appeared in the host of literary and other advisers, which included T. S. Eliot, Herbert Read, Lennox Berkeley and the artist John Piper, who came to the formal launch party on 5 May 1950. Greene obviously hoped that they might put on his own adaptation of *The Heart of the Matter*.

Sadly the only production to appear from the Group Theatre was an adaptation of Sartre's *The Flies* in November 1951. Greene's project was still on the stocks but could not be carried through because of the costs. Greene may have felt that the advantages of the theatre in terms of the author's living involvement with actors was more than counterbalanced by the difficulties in getting a production going; with a novel, once a publisher was found, little remained for the author to do. However, Greene's involvement with the theatre deepened when he decided to write something entirely for the stage, as he had written *The Great Jowett* for the radio. The result of his determination was *The Living Room*, which was accepted for production in 1953 and was received by the critics with the highest praise. Even Kenneth Tynan, the most acerbic of the rising young theatre critics, was won over: '*The Living Room* may easily be the best first play of the last half-century.'[14] Greene's wireless play had been forgotten, probably because it was not published until 1981, but Tynan's praise was an important boost for Greene.

The producer of the play was Peter Glenville. Greene had not worked with him before, but their relationship was successful, and was carried through to later work on Greene's film adaptation of his novel *The Comedians*. It is surprising therefore that there seems to have been nothing written on Glenville and how he came to work with Greene.

Peter Glenville was a product of the Oxford University Dramatic Society. He had shared digs in Oxford with Terence Rattigan and after a start in acting had gone on to work as a director and producer closely associated with Rattigan, and was the force behind many of Rattigan's best plays. Greene had not agreed with many of Rattigan's script ideas for *Brighton Rock* and had ended up doing the adaptation himself, a disagreement which would normally have put Glenville out of consideration. However, fortunately for Greene, Glenville and Rattigan had fallen out and were not on speaking terms when Greene was finishing *The Living Room*, and Glenville was therefore available. Not only did he fill the gap left by Basil Dean, he brought over Eric Portman to play the key role of Father James Browne, which ensured that the play would be well reviewed as a potential hit from the start. Portman had met Rattigan through another producer, Anthony Asquith, early in the war and had starred in many of his plays – he was to make a great success of Rattigan's *Separate Tables* a few years later. He did equally well for Greene, and Glenville was obviously the catalyst. Glenville got on equally well with Catherine Walston, to whom the play was dedicated, and she and Greene became part of his circle. It was a world far removed from that of the other women in his life, Dorothy with their shared memories of the Blitz, or Vivien in Oxford with the children.

The Living Room was eventually premièred in Stockholm in October 1952. This was to have unfortunate consequences for Greene which neither he nor Glenville nor anyone else could have foreseen. The play is set in the living room of the title, and the three leading characters are a psychologist, Michael Dennis, a priest, Father Browne, and a young girl, Rose, a niece of Father Browne, played by Dorothy Tutin. The girl's mother has just died. On the day of the funeral the psychologist, who is also Rose's trustee and guardian, has made love to the girl and said that he is going to leave his wife and go away with her; she is twenty, he is in his mid-forties.

The play is a harrowing exploration of what happens in the few weeks after the funeral to the lives of these people. The climax is reached with the appearance of the psychologist's wife, who confronts Rose and even stages a suicide attempt in front of her by swallowing pills – obviously without seriously intending to kill herself. The girl is so torn by emotions with which she cannot cope that as soon as she is alone she herself takes a fatal dose of the sleeping pills. She is successful.

The play had a shocking effect on the audience, but at least one of the critics who saw it, Artur Lundkvist, savagely attacked the play for its ruthless exposure of the psychologist: 'The play consists of Catholic propaganda of the most vulgar type, to which is added artistic and intellectual cheating ... The most dangerous and unpleasant thing about Greene's play is the way in which it attacks modern psychology.'[15] Lundkvist chaired the Nobel committee for the literature prize and it was said that Greene's continual exclusion from the prize was a result of his hostility. But the situation was far more complex than that. The play was written from entirely within Greene's experience and the trauma he had suffered as a result of his own experience with psychoanalysis. He had not sat down with Catholic theologians and concocted the play as active propaganda. Even the priest who appears is clearly a development of his own ideas – one can see the start of this character, perhaps, in the priest in his railway carriage in the short story 'The Hint of an Explanation'. If the picture torn bleeding from Greene's own life was upsetting to Lundkvist, that was only a measure of the accuracy of Greene's exposure, far ahead of its time. It is only within the last decade that anyone has taken stock of the damage wrought by the excessive dependence on so precarious a science. Despite its rather humorous title, Stephen Farber and Marc Green's *Hollywood on the Couch*, forty years later, makes closely similar observations on the effect of what they call 'the overheated love affair between psychiatrists and moviemakers' in Hollywood. Greene was no stranger to Hollywood, but perhaps even he did not realise that film stars like Marilyn Monroe were going daily to their analysts – not even Father Browne would consider hearing daily confession from the most grievous sinner. The concept of a parasitic profession had not yet emerged, but Greene knew of it first hand. He never disowned the experience as long as Zoe Richmond lived, but in *The Living Room* he showed that he was at last beginning to understand what had happened to him. Dr Ralph Greenson, Marilyn Monroe's psychiatrist, tried to adopt her into his family; Greene had lived through that as well.

In fairness to Lundkvist it is clear to us now that Greene still regarded Richmond and his circle as genuine psychiatrists. His character Michael Dennis states his belief just as Richmond must have done: 'I believe in the analysis of dreams, but sometimes I have had a dream so simple and brief that there seems to be nothing there to analyse – a shape, a few colours, an experience of beauty, that's all. Then I refuse to look further.'[16] The analysis of dreams is a very early stage in the development of the edifice now known as psychoanalytic theory. Greene's understanding of the subject can perhaps be seen in Father Browne's outburst against Dennis: 'You're the psychologist. Let's hear the wisdom of Freud, Jung, Adler. Haven't they all the answers you need? You can only get a priest's answers from me.'[17] At the end of the play, after Rose's suicide, and not knowing where his wife is, Dennis has a moment of self-reproach: 'It's a funny thing. I'm supposed to be a psychologist and I've ruined two people's minds.'[18] To which Father Browne replies, 'Psychology may teach you to know a mind. It doesn't teach you to love.'[19]

When the play came to Britain it was greeted everywhere as a brilliant success. Starting in Edinburgh Greene saw many performances and was able to monitor the play time and again as he explored the nuances the actors created. The play stayed with Greene so much that he decided to arrange for a film to be made, but intended to produce it himself so that he could maintain his involvement. As we shall see, the financial arrangements proved more complex than he expected, and the film was never made.

Greene continued his interest in the theatre and the way it could explore intimate personal relationships. The best of his plays, *The Complaisant Lover*, was produced in 1959, but it is worth looking at here, despite a slight break in the chronology of his works, because of the related themes.

The complaisant lover is an antiquarian bookseller called Clive Root, thirty-eight years of age and at the moment in love with Mary, the wife of a dentist, Victor Rhodes, who is some years older than her. The play opens at a dinner party at the Rhodeses' house. Amongst the guests is a local bank manager, his wife and their nineteen-year-old daughter Ann. Ann is a little in love with Clive and when they are left alone together in the first act she suggests that they go away for a while and start an affair. She does not know that Clive is already involved with Mary Rhodes. The discussion between them is remarkably frank, and Ann is provocative. Nevertheless the replies Clive gives are revealing. The audience must have found their conversation riveting. And as so often in Greene's work this is a sign that there are echoes in his own life.

> *Ann*: You'll be able to boast now, won't you, that you've had an immoral proposal from a girl of nineteen.
>
> *Clive*: I'm not the boasting kind. I've been trained in a different school, Ann. You see the first woman I loved was happily married.
>
> *Ann*: Have you loved a lot of people?
>
> *Clive*: Only four. It's not a high score at thirty-eight.
>
> *Ann*: What happened to them, Clive?
>
> *Clive*: In the end the husbands won.
>
> *Ann*: Were they all married?
>
> *Clive*: Yes.
>
> *Ann*: Why do you choose married women?
>
> *Clive*: I don't know. Perhaps I fall in love with experience.
>
> *Ann*: One has to begin.
>
> *Clive*: Perhaps I don't care for innocence. Perhaps I'm trying to repeat that first time. Perhaps it's envy of other men, and I want to prove myself better than they are. I don't know, Ann. But it's the school I have been brought up in.[20]

Knowing of Zoe, the temptation to see this as a piece of self-analysis is well nigh irresistible. Greene is exploring his own problems through his characters. The parallel between his situation and Clive's is not exact, of course, but he points it up directly later in another conversation with Ann. At the end of the dinner party Clive has said he has to go early because he has to work on a catalogue the next day. Mary does not want him to leave so soon and says surely he can choose his own time to do that:

> *Clive*: You wouldn't understand how important a bookseller's catalogue is.
>
> *Ann*: It must be like writing a novel.
>
> *Clive*: Yes, I think it is. One has to know what to put in and what to leave out.[21]

This is inexplicable unless read as a hint from Greene that he is once again examining his own position. He often said that the profession he would most like to have followed if he had not become a writer would have been that of a second-hand bookseller.

The rest of the play follows Clive and Mary as they try to arrange some time together in Amsterdam. It is of course trite to say that this is a portrait of Greene's involvement with Catherine Walston, since arrangements of this kind, with their petty deceptions and surprise confrontations, are the commonplace of all affairs of people at that age. But Greene was fifty-five when the play was put on, and had been Clive's age, thirty-eight, when his affair with Catherine was at its height; and he visited Amsterdam frequently.

There is one other reference to Greene's own life at the time which he puts in Clive's mouth. It concerns finance and exchange control. Clive has given Mary a pair of diamond earrings. She knows that he could not have paid for them out of his sterling allowance of £100. Clive explains what has happened:

> *Clive*: There are always ways. I went to a little man in Knightsbridge. There are quacks for every known disease – even for a collapsed currency. The currency quacks are especially smart. They have deep carpets and the receptionists are sexy and frankly impertinent because they think you may be a film magnate.
>
> *Mary*: Why a film magnate?
>
> *Clive*: All film magnates suffer from collapsed currencies. It's rather like visiting a fashionable abortionist.
>
> *Mary*: You could go to prison for this.
>
> *Clive*: So could he. Everything is on trust between two crooks. No letters. No cheques. Just cash and guarded telephone calls naming no names...[22]

As we shall see in Chapter Thirteen, this is taken directly out of Greene's own life and he was engaged in just such transactions, though ironically he thought them legitimate and his advisers far too respectable actually to risk prison through any shady dealings. All Greene's transactions were open, with cheques and eminent names at the bottom of them. But the warning Mary gives Clive could equally well have been given to Greene.

CHAPTER ELEVEN

Poland, Indo-China and *The Quiet American*

As a result of an approach to the Cabinet Office made under the 'Waldegrave initiative' (Mr William Waldegrave, then Chancellor of the Duchy of Lancaster, had, in 1992, invited historians and researchers to indentify particular closed government records to which they would value greater access), the government agreed to provide me with a briefing based on the records of Greene's service with the Secret Intelligence Service (SIS), generally known as MI6, for the purposes of this book.

The briefing took place in the Cabinet Office library, its walls lined with official histories of the two world wars and voluminous back-numbers of *Who's Who* and *Who was Who*. Strangely, like something out of a Greene novel, the name I was given as a contact was that of a poet and playwright whom I thought had been dead for many years. The name was extremely unusual and it transpired that, coincidentally, it had been randomly generated to create an identity that it was thought no living person could have. It was a surprise for those running the office I dealt with to see the handwriting of this supposedly non-existent person in a book of his I possessed. For a moment I wondered if he had really been an MI6 officer himself. Not for the first time there was an uncanny feeling that the quest for Graham Greene had somehow become part of the plot.

Greene's earliest independent links with the Soviet bloc came very early on in the Cold War. In 1948 the Polish government announced that it was convening the Polish World Congress of Intellectuals in Defence of Peace, known as the Wroclaw Cultural Congress. Greene was approached by the Polish authorities organising the event and must immediately have realised that his early career as a member of the Communist Party of Great Britain was still remembered in Moscow. His name was on the list of distinguished guests alongside that of A. J. P. Taylor and other people who had been members of the failed Oxford movement. By chance the very next name on the list was Mulk Raj Anand, and as I read his name on the list in the Foreign Office file on the conference another piece of the puzzle fell into place. Ten years before I had visited Anand in Bombay, hoping to learn something of his old colleague George Orwell and their mutual friend the author Inez Holden, the most likely original for Julia in *Nineteen Eighty-Four*.

Mulk Raj Anand was in England in 1996 for a reception at the Indian High Commission on the occasion of his ninetieth birthday. We met soon after at the house of a friend not far from Queens Park in London. He had met Greene himself on only a few occasions; he remembered being at Eric Gill's home with Herbert Read when Greene came along. But far more interesting was his account of the Cultural Congress and his own visits behind the Iron Curtain, as it then was, and even more surprising was his information about Charlie Chaplin, which tied in with other information already discovered in the original cache of James Hadley Chase papers.

Anand had been invited to the Congress because of his close association with the movement for Indian independence, and his standing with the far left in England, where he had spent the war. Although he was never a member of the Communist Party in those days, he vividly remembered Harry Pollitt, leader of the party in Britain, telling him and a group of friends that they would not be allowed to join the party for tactical reasons. Anand was also a supporter of the international society PEN – Poets, Essayists and Novelists – and that was the organisation which handled British representation at the Congress. Anand's interest in PEN may have misled the Polish authorities into thinking that the society's British section was sympathetic, if not composed entirely of fellow travellers; they were soon to be disillusioned.

The Foreign Office heard from PEN that they intended to send a very strong team to Poland, including Hermon Ould, then a well-known author and arts-establishment figure, Osbert Sitwell, Bertrand Russell, Desmond MacCarthy, again a well-known figure at the time, an essayist and critic, and perhaps also E. M. Forster. The line they put to the Foreign Office was that this strong team offered an unusual chance to publicise the West's ideas. They said pointedly that 'one of their intentions is to counter the influence of any fellow-travelling Britons who might be there'.[1] If the Foreign Office objected strongly they would withdraw their acceptance – and presumably the Foreign Office could itself have blocked the visit in those days of currency control. In the end after giving the project careful thought the Foreign Office agreed. However, in all its negotiations with PEN's British office there was never any mention of Greene, although his name was on their list. Whether they knew it or not, Greene had already made direct contact.

Greene decided to treat the invitation from Poland as if it was an ordinary matter of business. He asked his secretary to ring up the Foreign Office, giving her his contact's name. As a retired MI6 officer he had special access, but his secretary seems from the files to have dealt directly with the Foreign Office, asking its officials if it would be all right for Greene to go to Poland. If Greene was thought a suitable addition to the delegation organised by PEN then he would work through his MI6 contact. Had he gone, presumably PEN would have been informed; but there is no further mention of a role for him in the files. Anand attended the conference, and was on the platform on one occasion but did not remember Greene being there. The congress became famous for A. J. P. Taylor's outspoken attack on the political views of his hosts. Anand recalled that the speech was broadcast by loudspeaker to audiences in outside halls and the results of Taylor's outburst were spectacular and embarrassing.

The Polish government authorities did not forget Greene; if he did not respond to their approaches then, that simply left his position unclear. A few years later, in the early 1950s, they tried again, the backdrop being the need for Greene to secure publication of his works in perhaps the most Catholic country in Europe. He found himself corresponding with Tadeusz Murek, a Polish publisher, who in turn suggested that he meet the writer Jan Dobraczynski, giving a Polish priest in Paris, Father Florien Kaszubowski, as a contact. Greene's Catholicism here undoubtedly opened doors, but as was clear from the Cabinet Office briefing every letter he received or sent was deposited with MI6 and formed part of an overall plan. Greene often took his own line in his exchanges with his contacts at MI6. They warned him against Dobraczynski, pointing out that he had been involved in the World Peace Congress in 1950, an event with which Mulk Raj Anand had also become closely involved. They gave a very damaging personal reference for him, saying that, though nominally a party man, he was out for his own ends. This probably made him sound very useful to Greene, with his wartime skills in handling agents and double agents; at all events, Greene went ahead and met him, and was soon on good terms with him.

As Greene's relationships with Polish friends developed, MI6 decided that it would be a good idea for Greene to visit Poland. It is important to emphasise this, as Greene's visits and subsequent trips to Moscow during the 1950s were later seen as confirming his status as of the left to the point where he was almost a fellow traveller. One MI6 official remarked, 'Greene went to Poland at our instigation.'[2] The ostensible purpose of the trips was to deal with publication of Greene's books through the government-backed Catholic organisation called PAX. MI6 was particularly keen to know about this organisation, which seemed to bridge the gulf between Church and state. Greene's own position was unambiguous and he did not deceive his Polish hosts. Writing to Wojciech Ketrzynski at PAX he commented that while he criticised the organisation for bringing politics into religion, as he had with the Spanish authorities when they had brought politics into the catechism, he was still sympathetic. He moved onto more dangerous ground when he suggested that he visit again with the opportunity to see more people. His difficulty, he implied, was that he had been under supervision during his visit without any chance of seeing a wider group of people. He had been in PAX's hands.[3]

As he was in the hands of MI6, Greene might have added. He visited Cracow, Stalinograd, Oswiecim, Czestochowa, Warsaw and Lublin, all in full co-operation with his Polish hosts. But there was definitely another side to Poland which Greene pursued on his own. He talked at length to journalists from Poland who had been reporting the Indo-China War, but from the communist side. He became close to a journalist called Zukrowski and mentioned him in a letter to a member of his family as having been very much in the front line facing the French forces.

It now becomes clear why Greene's trips to Poland and links with Polish and political contacts in Paris have to be considered as background to his time spent in Indo-China, and to the struggles he had with the French military authorities there. It also proved to be vital in the development of his next novel *The Quiet American*, set in Indo-China. The missing link in any discussion of what was going on was the Catholic Church. Talking to Polish journalists must have given Greene invaluable insights, which would have been conveyed to MI6, and they would not have been possible without the Catholic Polish connection; but even more important were Catholic Vietminh priests who were in Poland at the time. The information he reported having obtained in discussion with them was invaluable both to MI6 and as background to his understanding of the situation in Indo-China and of the importance of Catholic warlords and priests on the ground.

It was ironic, in view of the attack on America's role in Indo-China, and later Vietnam, contained in *The Quiet American*, that Greene first went to the country as a writer through an American introduction. He had been visiting an old friend from MI6 days in Hanoi, Trevor Wilson, now consul there and still working for the old firm. Greene mentioned this to his editor at *Life* magazine in New York, with which he had a close connection. They had featured him, with a cover photograph, when *The End of the Affair* was published in 1951 and he had written several articles for them since, some with exclusively Catholic themes such as the nature of Catholic devotion to the Virgin Mary. He had actually visited Wilson on his way back from Malaya, where he had done a report for *Life* on the communist insurgency known by the low-key name of the Malaya Emergency. His brother Hugh Greene was in charge of propaganda in Malaya, so Greene had the best introductions.

On his return to London Greene found a telegram from his *Life* editor Emmet Hughes asking for more information about Indo-China. Until then Greene had had no particular interest in the country, or the war going on there, which, unlike the Korean War, involved the

French exclusively. He quickly accepted their assignment and was to spend four years going back and forth to Indo-China, passing his winters there. He explained his presence, first by the *Life* commission, then by saying that he was writing a detective story set in Indo-China. It is true that *The Quiet American* is about a murder, but to describe it as a detective story was grossly misleading.

General De Lattre, the Commander-in-Chief of the French forces in Indo-China, suspected Greene from the beginning of being a spy. He was no doubt relying on reports from the French intelligence services, who knew Greene was fishing in some very murky waters in Paris, which was the centre of his espionage operations throughout the 1950s. He kept his flat there from 1946 after the war ended until just before he died. The Sûreté – the French police – followed Greene in Indo-China, so it is more than likely that they followed him in Paris. There they would have seen him meeting with James Hadley Chase, whose books were very popular in France, often being turned into equally popular films. One of these was directed by Joe Losey, who, like Charlie Chaplin, had fallen foul of the McCarthy witch-hunts in Hollywood. Greene got to know him well. More interesting still, as a pointer to possible communist connections in Paris, were his meetings with Vietminh groups, which he recorded in detail in his reports. One of these resulted in his visit to see Ho Chi Minh a few years later in the run-up to the Vietnam War itself.

De Lattre knew that both Greene and Trevor Wilson were Catholics and that they had been to visit the Prince Bishopric of Phat Diem a short while before his own son had been killed there. De Lattre felt that Greene and Wilson may have been in some way responsible, if unwittingly, and insisted that Wilson was *persona non grata*. Wilson was withdrawn from his post in Hanoi, though Greene remained. The police kept him under constant surveillance, only to find that General De Lattre refused to believe what he was being told. Greene had assured him that he was not involved in espionage and he believed him. In his autobiography Greene recorded an interview with De Lattre. He gives his own account of what the General said to him, and what must have happened afterwards:

'I have told the Sûreté, Graham Greene is my friend. I do not believe what you say about him. Then they come again and tell me you have been here or there and I say, I do not believe. Graham Greene is my friend. And then they come ...' He shook hands [with Greene] warmly, saying how glad he was to know it was all a mistake, but next day, before he left for Paris, his misgivings returned. I had received yet another dubious telegram, again unsigned – this time from my literary agent in Paris. 'Your friend will arrive on Thursday. Dorothy under instruction from Philip' ... I knew he was a spy ... Why should anyone come to this war for $400?[4]

Greene fixes on this detail to make fun of De Lattre, for he had actually told him he was getting $4,000 from *Life*.

But everything Greene had said was untrue, not least when he had assured De Lattre, after the Frenchman had stated that he knew for a fact that Greene had been with the security services during the war, that he had had no connection *after* the war. Greene was acting as an agent, as the Sûreté knew full well. It is difficult to see why, writing in 1980, Greene went to such lengths to conceal this; he could quite simply have passed the matter by. It is possible he was writing for the benefit of his old colleagues in MI6 who had cut him off after the Philby affair, showing them both that he had lied for them and that he had kept his mouth shut about it and was continuing to do so. In the event the questions about Greene's espionage activities turned out to have more significance for the Americans than the French.

The idea for *The Quiet American* came to him, Greene maintained, when he was the guest of another Frenchman, Colonel Leroy, who was effectively the king of a small area in the marshes of Bentre in Indo-China. An entertainment had been arranged and Greene was meant to be flattered by *The Third Man* theme music which echoed around them as they ate. On his way back he found himself listening to an American who talked in idealistic terms of a third force which would take the place of the old colonial powers on the one hand and the communists on the other. Apart from this single incident, and the personality of an American journalist, Greene claimed that the entire book – the story of an idealistic American who is murdered after getting involved in Vietnamese politics – came from his imagination. American critics and journalists frequently said that he modelled Pyle, the quiet American in the book, on Colonel Edward Lansdale. The charge was repeated many times, for example by William Colby, a director of the CIA, who remarked in his memoirs, when talking of South Vietnamese President Ngo Dinh Diem:

> The dramatic exodus of Catholic refugees from North Vietnam during this period, demonstrating in this way their preference for a society in which their religion could flourish, also added to his [Diem's] support in the United States, especially from Cardinal Spellman. And then, too, there was CIA's backing: Ed Lansdale proffered political advice (for which he was pilloried by Graham Greene in *The Quiet American* ...) ...[5]

Colby had arrived in Vietnam in 1956 after Greene's time and was clearly reflecting the common wisdom about the book. In fact Greene denied that he had ever meant Lansdale when he drafted the book, and careful research seems to confirm this. The best source of all, of course, is the undeniable evidence of the text itself. Close scrutiny of this shows that it has its roots in *The Third Man*, exactly as Greene suggested.

Pyle works with the Economic Mission sent by the United States, but there is one aspect of his work that Greene concentrates on: the medical teams. In the course of an argument he makes the offhand remark, 'Medicine's a kind of weapon isn't it?'[6] There are repeated references to the work of Pyle's teams. Finally in a discussion between Pyle and Fowler, the English journalist narrator, Pyle gets close to saying what he is really doing when he is being pressed about why he is supplying plastic to a small local political group whom he takes as the basis for a third force: 'We don't like details of our aid to get around. You know what Congress is like – and then one has visiting senators. We had a lot of trouble about our trachoma teams because they were using one drug instead of another.'[7] And earlier, when Pyle mysteriously appears in the front line where Fowler is chasing a story, he does so with full military kit and steel helmet. Fowler comments on this and receives the reply that this was standard kit for the travelling medical teams. The charge that Greene is making is clear: that in the guise of sending medical teams to help the local people the CIA was arming one small part of the complex political groupings. We are once again in the world of phoney doctors, drugs being adulterated or put to wrong use and criminal activity under the guise of aid which was the backdrop to *The Third Man*.

The numerous critics of *The Quiet American* have not noticed the savage nature of this attack, and Greene himself makes no mention of it. He, and others, have concentrated on Pyle as an American who represents a misguided American attempt to help the Vietnamese, threatened by communist infiltration. Greene seems already to have built up a stereotype of a bad American, beginning with the arms dealer in *The Name of Action* and ending with the grey-haired, far-seeing American colonel in *The Third Man*, who also happens to be in on a number of rackets, from tyres to fake penicillin. In *The Quiet American* he takes this a stage further by having Pyle on his medical mission smuggle bomb-making equipment which he knows will be used for a terrorist bombing campaign, even though he does not realise quite how devastating the results will be. There was no mistake in Greene's message.

The attack on America's presence in Indo-China which Greene places in the mouth of his narrator descends to an insulting level. Using the parallel first developed in *The Confidential Agent* he talks of the medieval world, long past in Europe but still to be found everywhere in Indo-China. The very idea of a prince–bishop had been forgotten by people in America except historians. Early in the book, when Fowler and his girlfriend Phuong are going along in a trishaw, they pass a column of French armoured cars:

> ... each with its jutting gun and silent officer motionless like a figurehead under the stars and the black, smooth, concave sky – trouble again probably with a private army, the Binh Xuyen, who ran the Grande Monde and the gambling halls of Cholon. This was a land of rebellious barons. It was like Europe in the Middle Ages. But what were the Americans doing here? Columbus had not yet discovered their country.[8]

This was the kind of deeply offensive old-colonial attitude which the Americans were trying to dispel as much as communism; perhaps that was why Greene put the comment in, to develop Fowler's character.

159

But beyond the sideswipe at America for not being a medieval power, and using its medical aid teams to smuggle bombs to doubtful political groups, Greene goes a stage further and suggests that they co-operated in bomb atrocities to the extent of arranging for their own citizens to be away from the place where a bomb was hidden before it was timed to go off. Greene based this event in the novel on a real incident and was convinced of the truth of the charge he was making. He advanced the circumstantial evidence that a photographer from *Life* had been positioned with his camera aimed at the bomb in the main square of Saigon and had taken a photograph the second it went off. Greene remembered the detail of a rickshaw driver with his legs blown away who had not yet fallen to the ground. He added the final detail in his autobiography *Ways of Escape*:

> This photograph was reproduced in an American propaganda magazine published in Manila over the caption 'The work of Ho Chi Minh', although General Thé [one of the rebellious barons] had promptly and proudly claimed the bomb as his own. Who had supplied the material to a bandit who was fighting French, Caodaists [followers of a religion invented in the 1920s with considerable power] and communists?[9]

But although Greene believed in American complicity in the bombing in 1980, when the second volume of his autobiography was published, and the same belief had informed *The Quiet American* written at the time, he was mistaken. The photograph had been taken quite by chance by a local photographer who sold it to the magazine. Americans near the explosion were saved through good fortune and had certainly not been warned. Greene had simply got it wrong. But why was there this quite extraordinary animus on Greene's part against the American presence in Indo-China in the 1950s? In reality there were fewer than a hundred men on the ground with the various American missions. Greene was said by some to have clairvoyant powers – did he foresee the carnage that was to come? Or did he have a sudden and profound understanding of what was likely to happen if a modern industrial power became intimately involved in a war in what was essentially a medieval situation which was so complex that even an old colonial power, France, was having difficulty in solving it?

It is possible that Greene himself was not fully conscious of some aspects of his anti-American theme. The characterisation of Pyle had its origin at least partly in themes taken from *The Third Man*, but nothing there can really explain the hatred for America's fight against communism which seems inextricable from the fabric of *The Quiet American*. From a religious standpoint William Colby's reference to Cardinal Spellman of New York is significant. Greene strongly disliked Spellman's views; he stood for an America typified by the House Un-American Activities Committee. Greene's visits to Catholic Poland, which was living under a Marxist regime, and his comments on PAX, show the way his mind was working. The way forward was a reform of that kind of system and a union of Catholic and Marxist philosophies. It was an ideal he was to proclaim to the end of his life, finally having the honour of expressing it to an audience in Moscow when well into his eighties.

There is a vignette of the medieval Catholic world which still operated in Indo-China in *The Quiet American*. Visiting one of the Prince-Bishopric's headquarters Fowler asks about the treatment of the wounded in the war. The priest he is talking to says simply that he does what he can; only then does Fowler notice that his soutane is sprinkled with blood from the operating table. This was a world that Greene could identify with; he remembered another priest who said Mass for people in the war zone and lived in acute poverty. It was an image that first entered his mind in Stevenson's portrait of Father Damien and was never fully to leave it. And it was with the image of a leper that Greene makes the most profound comment on the relationship between Pyle and Fowler:

'... I had better look after Pyle.' That was my first instinct – to protect him. It never occurred to me that there was greater need to protect myself. Innocence always calls mutely for protection when we would be so much wiser to guard ourselves against it; innocence is like a dumb leper who has lost his bell, wandering the world, meaning no harm.[10]

In this warning there is a stern truth which would indeed have saved many lives.

When *The Quiet American* appeared in 1955 Greene's former colleagues in MI6, to whom he had been reporting, were worried that the CIA might think that they had had some input into the book. They were well aware that Greene's connections with MI6 were an open book to the CIA, as a result both of his wartime activity and of mutual co-operation since. In the end they decided to say nothing, on the basis *Qui s'excuse, s'accuse.* The Cabinet Office briefing made no mention of an incident involving Greene and the FBI that occurred a year before the novel was published. If MI6 were aware of FBI interest, it might have wanted to give some explanation of how Greene came to be flying its colours while at the same time giving a very good impersonation of a genuine fellow traveller.

In August 1954 Greene decided to visit Haiti, possibly at the suggestion of Peter Glenville, although he also met Truman Capote there, who was in close touch with the Chaplins, particularly Oona, and it may have been she who mentioned the country to Greene. When he came to return to England he chose to do so by travelling to Puerto Rico, then on to New York and back across the Atlantic. Greene knew that he would have difficulty getting a US visa, but he spoke directly to the American Ambassador in Haiti and seems to have got from him an assurance that, if he stayed within the transit perimeter and did not pass customs and immigration, he could go by this route without a visa.

On arrival at San Juan in Puerto Rico, Greene was asked if he had ever been a member of the Communist Party and replied immediately that he had. He was taken out of the line and detained. After a brief interlude he was informed that he would be sent back to Haiti by the next plane. In his autobiography Greene discloses that he knew he would not be able to do this because, although Americans did not need visas for Haiti, British subjects did, and he had no such visa. Chaos ensued, with lengthy telegrams being sent from the local FBI linkman to the FBI headquarters in Washington. Amusingly, the FBI at first did not realise that Greene could not return to Haiti and had him down as going on the next Delta flight back. In fact Greene persuaded the pilot of the plane on the tarmac, who conveniently happened to be an ex-Hollywood man who had been drummed out of the film industry in the McCarthyite purge, that he should fly him on to Havana, the plane's next stop after Haiti. When the plane reached Haiti the Delta Airlines manager had been informed of the Greene problem and thought he was going to have to make personal representations with the authorities to allow the visa-less author to stay. Greene informed him that, courtesy of the captain, he was going on to Cuba, not Jamaica as the American authorities had requested.

Greene was to tell the story many times over, but the press headlines worldwide were reward enough. In *Ways of Escape* he suggests that he took that route home by chance, it simply seemed the shortest way. In fact the entire saga was planned in meticulous detail, child's play to a man who had been regarded by Philby as one of the great experts at creating cover stories and direct political-action proposals in MI6 after he returned from West Africa. The detail he could not resist disclosing in 1980, that he knew in advance that he would not be allowed to return to Haiti without a visa, shows that the entire episode was a provocation.

The remarkable thing about Greene's acting-out of this stunt was that he stuck to his guns on his political innocence, just as he had when confronted by De Lattre. He was quoted in the press as saying that the whole incident was absurd and that nobody could be less communist than he, and he repeatedly brought out his Catholicism as a final line of defence. He painted a most convincing picture of himself as a man who had once on a whim when a student joined the Communist Party for a few days, with the idea of getting free travel to Russia. Now he was being persecuted for it decades later when he had become a well-known novelist and a Catholic.

It is difficult to find a convincing explanation for this disinformation exercise. Evelyn Waugh believed that Greene was deliberately creating a favourable image of himself for the benefit of the Soviets for some deep Cold War game. But a more likely clue can be found in an event which occurred in Switzerland in June 1954, two months before Greene set out for Haiti. The occasion, now completely forgotten, was the awarding of the Lenin Peace Prize to Charlie Chaplin by a delegation from Russia which included the novelist Ilya Ehrenburg and Mulk Raj Anand. Chaplin had been given the award in acknowledgement of the role he had played during the war in raising funds for Russian War Relief campaigns, and also because he had been banned from returning to America on account of his pro-Soviet sympathies. The cancelling of his visa while he was at sea on his way to Europe caused an international outcry, and Ehrenburg and his colleagues seriously hoped to persuade him to defect.

Greene had followed Chaplin's plight closely since he published an open letter to him welcoming him to England and attacking America's conduct over the visa. From the timing alone it seems possible that Greene's provocation over his own lack of a visa was planned as a sequel to the honour granted to Chaplin. When Greene had last visited New York in 1953 he had made a point of saying that McCarthy was a Catholic and that it was the duty of every Catholic in America to object to his activities. This was of a piece with his objections to Cardinal Spellman and does indeed make some overall sense of Greene's position. Presumably if Pyle in *The Quiet American* had been an American Catholic who objected to McCarthy, he would not have acted as he did and Greene would not have pilloried him. Ultimately he would no doubt have sympathised with Catholics in Poland who co-operated with the state.

Before Greene finished the writing of *The Quiet American* he had a pleasant break working on a short novel, in which Korda's yacht the *Elsewhere* had a walk-on part. There is a mystery here, for Greene wrote in *Ways of Escape* that he had written the book in a mood of escape *after* he had finished *The Quiet American*. The evidence which establishes what happened was found in the Cabinet Office files, of all places. On 21 April 1955 Greene wrote a letter to his Polish friend Tadeusz Murek, who had written asking about a novel that he had heard Greene was writing from their mutual friend Dobraczynski. Greene specifically identified this book as *Loser Takes All* which was to be filmed that summer. He warned Murek that he might find it a surprise as it was light-hearted with a happy outcome. Greene then mentioned that a more serious work on Indo-China – his novel *The Quiet American* – would be finished later. It is clear that *Loser Takes All* had already been written as a film treatment to exactly the same plan as *The Third Man*, well before his Indo-China book was finished. Greene's books had had happy endings before but the light comedy element in the book was new – and very successful it was too.

Korda features in the book under the alias 'Dreuther', as Greene later confirmed, a powerful business tycoon who suddenly transforms the life of a junior accountant in his firm by suggesting that he get married to his fiancée in Monte Carlo, and have the honeymoon on his yacht. The couple agree and book in to the most expensive hotel with very limited funds, only to wait for days running up enormous expenses as Dreuther and his yacht fail to appear. The story was extremely funny and rang true to anyone who had unwittingly got caught up in one of Korda's schemes. All turns out well in the end, although Greene's mention of a happy ending is partly ironic, for the accountant has initially won an immense fortune at the casino, only to lose it – but regain his wife, whom for a moment he lost. Happiness is the person you love, without the boredom of unlimited wealth.

Greene's long involvement with Korda ended with his death in January of the following year from a heart attack. A good insight into the way Greene viewed the world at that time can be found in the exchange of letters he had about Korda with Father Caraman, a priest to whom he was then close. Greene had written to ask if Korda could be remembered in some way, and received an astonishing reply: 'Actually I said Mass for Korda at Brighton as soon as I read of his death in the *Times*. I have often heard you and Catherine speak of him. From all you both said I seemed to know him ...'[12] Any idea that Greene's involvement with Korda and the world of espionage was in some way at odds with his Catholic beliefs, or that he was a different man with Korda, is immediately dispelled by this charming expression of the real nature of Greene's friendship.

After publication of *The Quiet American* Greene continued his visits behind the Iron Curtain. He went to Moscow on at least four occasions, on the last of them, in 1961, catching a rather severe attack of pneumonia. The journeys Greene made were by no means unusual. At the highest level Harold Wilson, soon to become Prime Minister, travelled extensively all over the Soviet Union. Wilson was allowed a far freer hand than mere diplomats, but, unlike Greene, he was not given to sharing his secrets with officialdom. He even visited a well-known defector in his home, to the exasperation of the British representatives in Moscow who had to run interference for him when such visits became known through the press. It is often forgotten that defection was much more common at this time than later. It was not simply Burgess and Maclean, though they were stars. A myriad of smaller fish were caught in the propaganda net as well; the man Wilson visited, Archie Johnston, was well known for having torn his passport up and thrown the pieces through the doorway of the British Embassy.

To his Russian hosts, and to old friends like Ehrenberg, Greene must have epitomised the literary fellow traveller. When *The Quiet American* was adapted for stage presentation in Moscow Greene was no doubt flattered. He became close to the translator and guide who accompanied him everywhere at the time, Oxana Krugerskaya. His hosts would have been astonished, therefore, to learn that Greene was not only reporting back to MI6 but at one point took part in direct political action for his controllers that required most careful and detailed planning on his part. Had anyone faced him with detailed information about his contacts with the Soviets at the time of his visa campaign he could easily have trumped them with this exercise, which involved a journey through China with a group of fellow travellers, one of whom, a senior figure in the Labour Party, the authorities wished particularly to discredit.

The journey took place in 1957. Greene had finally ended his earlier journeys to Indo-China with a visit to Ho Chi Minh, furnished with introductions from a variety of contacts. One of the topics Greene discussed with him was a film which had been made of the battle for Dien Bien Phu, but with the story told from the Vietminh side. A copy of the film had been prepared for him in Hanoi but it had then been sent to Peking for him to collect. Two years passed, but he was eventually able to collect it on this journey to China, and bring it back to England. The question naturally arises – were the Vietminh aware in advance that Greene was going to China? There is nothing anywhere in the records to suggest how they might have learned of the visit as it was still at an early planning stage when Greene received information from the General Secretary of the Association of Vietnamese Journalists in Hanoi that the film had been sent off to Peking.

Greene's target on the journey was Lord Chorley. A lawyer elevated to the peerage in 1945 he had somehow attracted the severe displeasure of the authorities dealing with internal security affairs in England. It was Greene's task to neutralise the effects of Chorley's propaganda efforts while at the same time finding out as much as he could on a wide range of topics, ranging from military objectives to political ones – the *cause célèbre* at the time was the plight of a dissident named Hu Feng. Greene's later account of his trip, written in 1980, brings in the powers of a local drink as an excuse for the lack of hard military information, but he gives no hint of the commission from MI6 that sent him there.

Greene had been formally invited on the China trip by one of those already in the group, Lady Huntingdon, the novelist Margaret Lane, who was travelling with her husband. Apart from Lord Chorley there was a communist from Hampstead, and a sociology professor. Greene wrote an amusing article about the journey for *The Times* in 1985. He describes in graphic detail how he confronted Lord Chorley at an important dinner when the question of Hu Feng came up, thus causing the peer acute embarrassment. He even reveals how he was to behave abominably to 'the innocent Lord Chorley', going on to say that Lord Chorley was dead and would not be harmed by anything he might now reveal. Any MI6 officer acquainted with Greene's file might have trembled a little in anticipation – but no revelation was forthcoming. On the contrary Greene specifically said he went to China innocent of any espionage intentions. This use of the word 'innocent' so soon after ascribing to Lord Chorley that ever noble attribute would no doubt have caused a wry smile when the article was absorbed and added to Greene's file.

In fact, on 26 June 1957 Greene wrote a full account of the attempts he had made to discover the fate of Hu Feng, amongst other things; interestingly he wrote on Graham Greene Productions notepaper, with himself and Catherine Walston shown as the only directors which threw the question of copyright in the letter into confusion if nothing else. Greene had raised the Hu Feng question whenever he had met a group of authors and also at his birth place Chungking. On all sides he was told that Hu Feng had not been arrested for his writings but because of his political actions. Greene said in his report, and elsewhere, that the totalitarian mindset was such that people believed implicitly that Hu Feng would not have been arrested if there was not conclusive evidence. Accusation and arrest were enough to prove guilt. The new liberal doctrine of 'the blossoms in the garden' allowed freer speech in theory. Greene suggested to the Minister of Culture that experience in Russia where liberalisation had been succeeded by a clamp-down might influence Chinese writers. He was told that nobody had heard of affairs in Russia, presumably because of censorship.[13]

The only way in which Greene could conceivably have been acting within his conscience in denying espionage intentions was if he had in fact deliberately not taken any military information for example and used the joke of the strong local drink as an excuse. But even this suggestion is belied by the fierce correspondence he engaged in with Lord Chorley through the columns of the *Daily Telegraph* after the trip. One paragraph alone conveys the bitter venom he has summoned up about Chorley:

> I should have realised that Lord Chorley in the degree of his incon-
> sistencies and possibly the extent of his credulity belonged with the
> great comic figures of fiction – Don Quixote, perhaps with more than a
> touch of Mrs. Malaprop. But Don Quixote, of course, did not fight in
> defence of windmills.[14]

It was the word 'possibly' that added bite here.

It is not surprising that Greene should have embarked on an espionage novel after years of living on the dangerous edge of things, but the novel he produced, *Our Man in Havana* (published in 1958), has been misinterpreted as a send-up by Greene of MI6, ridiculing its shortcomings. Those in the secret service would have seen it as a brilliant satire of how the public imagined the way MI6 worked. There was no bumbling incompetence in the intricate double game Greene had been playing, or in the information he was able to provide. It was a profoundly complex game, as far removed from *Our Man in Havana* as Ian Fleming's James Bond books were. The world Greene describes in his novel is simply the espionage practised before the Cold War.

Originally, as we have seen, Greene had been asked to write a film treatment for his friend the Brazilian director Alberto Cavalcanti in 1946. The subject was to be espionage and Greene set it in pre-war Europe, in Tallinn, Estonia. It does not take much to see Greene's own amateur experience through this disguise. However, the project came to nothing. Then Greene saw further film opportunities after the enjoyable experience of creating *Loser Takes All* as both a book and a film. He brought the same light-hearted touch to *Our Man in Havana*. Initially he had intended to set it in Spain, but the book would then have been too obviously a parody of his wartime experiences. Cuba was far more amenable to creative treatment, so much so that Greene foresaw in his plot the Soviet missile bases which were to precipitate the most dangerous confrontation of the Cold War a few years later in 1963.

The book still retained a great deal of Greene's own life. The number that Wormald is given, 59200/5, is based on that of his recruiter 59200, and that was Greene's own official MI6 number in Sierra Leone during the war. When Greene took on agents, the fifth man he recruited would have been known as 59200/5. The code actually depended on the country, and it would have been impossible for any agent in Cuba to have such a number; the men at MI6 must have been greatly amused, as they would have been by the spy-craft techniques Greene described. All had been long superseded when Greene was writing his book, as he well knew.

The plot of the book drew once again on the stock of characters inhabiting his subconscious. Like the narrator of *The End of the Affair* Wormald has one leg shorter than the other and walks with a limp. There is a doctor, this time a German called Hasselbacher who, like Lime at the end of *The Third Man*, is shot. But everything soon assumes a new identity as always and the result is a brilliantly comic book which very convincingly captures the atmosphere of Cuba just before the arrival of Castro in the late 1950s. Greene's own current concerns intrude pointedly, for those who knew his difficulties over his membership of the Communist Party and how it had come back to haunt him in the Cold War. In the book it is Dr Hasselbacher who has the problem which exposes him to the blackmail that finally leads to his death. His room has been broken into and papers taken. Wormald asks if they are important:

I should never have kept them. They were more than thirty years old. When one is young one gets involved. No one's life is quite clean, Mr. Wormald. But I thought the past was the past. I was too optimistic. You and I are not like the people here – we have no confessional box where we can bury the bad past.[15]

There is more than a hint here that Greene may have revealed his past because he was being approached by Soviet agents. In reality the invitation to the writers' congress in Poland must have shown him and the other old party members from Oxford that the past had not been forgotten. And Greene did keep his party card all that time and longer, producing it in 1979.

The overtly political statements in the novel are few and almost naive in tone, but they clearly reflect what Greene thought then:

We hear a lot nowadays about the cold war, but any trader will tell you that the war between two manufacturers of the same goods can be quite a hot war. Take Phastkleaners and Nucleaners [Wormald is making a speech as the head of his vacuum-cleaning operation]. There is not much difference between the two machines any more than there is between two human beings, one Russian – or German – and one British. There would be no competition and no war if it wasn't for the ambition of a few men in both firms; just a few men dictate competition and invent needs and set Mr. Carter and myself at each other's throats.[16]

Wormald's problems begin when he is recruited into British intelligence as an agent on the ground, and it is not difficult to see the message Greene is trying to put across. It cannot have been reassuring to those who had employed him in the past, except for the fact that everything else he describes is so much a parody that it must have seemed he was simply commenting on the likely views of the kind of people they were recruiting, the exact opposite of James Bond with his licence to kill. Ironically Wormald does actually shoot Carter using a policeman's gun, but only after he has tried to poison him first.

The novel contains some purely personal allusions, for example to Greene's interest in car numbers, which puzzled many people in

England. He seemed fascinated by them and collected sequences sometimes over long periods. An explanation is provided in *Our Man in Havana*. In Cuba the lottery was a major factor in people's lives – it did not then exist in Britain, which had outgrown the practice a century and more before, with the advent of general education. People became fascinated with numbers, and lottery-ticket sellers used to find the most complex ways to get people to buy tickets. One of the most popular was to search for cars with the same number as that on part of the lottery ticket. Dr Hasselbacher is addicted to the lotteries: 'Like Milly [Wormald's daughter] Dr. Hasselbacher had faith. He was controlled by numbers as she was by saints.'[17] Milly is seventeen and has been brought up as a good Catholic at an American convent school in Havana. Greene paints an endearing portrait of her, and she plays a significant part in the action. With her love of horses she is perhaps a portrait of Greene's own daughter.

The world of numbers dominates the book from the beginning, when a beggar is seen walking along counting his steps. He has reached one thousand, three hundred and seventy as he passes them. Wormald has to encode endless messages with five-number groups; then loses the number of his safe, for which Greene amusingly uses the telephone number of his flat in Oxford before the war. Now the arrival of computers has multiplied the numbers in our daily life; Greene has preserved a time when this process was just beginning.

The book ends on a serious note. Wormald is discovered to have been faking his agents' reports and is called to London fearing the worst. He has earlier wondered if he might be refused permission to return to Britain if some such catastrophe occurred. In Greene's own life that did indeed happen, as we shall see, but Wormald is simply promoted, given an OBE and a job training recruits to the service. He is astonished but is given a simple explanation:

> The chief felt you had valuable experience which should be kept for the use of the department rather than for the popular press. Too many people had written reminiscences lately of the Secret Service. Somebody mentioned the Official Secrets Act, but the chief thought it might not cover your case...[18]

While the powers that be at MI6 might have been amused by the send-up of public perceptions of how they operated, there was a hint here of a sting in the tail. And, as with even the funniest of Greene's books, there was underlying political opinion. Greene's interest in Cuba was serious, but his direct political action took another form. In later interviews he several times referred to a Member of Parliament whom he had briefed to ask questions in the House of Commons about Cuba. The MP was Hugh Delargy, and the questions he asked were pointed, revealing a great deal of inside information which undoubtedly came from Greene.

It is not known how Greene and Delargy met, but both had been interested in action taken against book-auction rings in 1956. A campaign had been got up by Basil Blackwell after some very bad and public examples of rings that had resulted in libraries being sold for far less than their true worth. The matter had been raised in Parliament by the MP for Londonderry, Chichester-Clark. Delargy had spoken in support of him, and in favour of Basil Blackwell's attempts to get all members of the antiquarian book-trade to sign an agreement stating they had not been involved in such activity – only 66 members out of 300 approached had felt able to do so. Greene had supported Blackwell and the line Delargy took.

The most contentious issue at the time Greene published *Our Man in Havana* was the supplies of arms to the Cuban dictator Batista by British firms, an echo of the pre-war arms trade that had prompted *A Gun for Sale*. Even America had stopped supplying armaments. But there was one particular category of arms which caused real anger and that was rockets. Astonishingly the British export-control authorities had licensed the shipment of rockets for use against Castro and his forces. In an attempt to get an emergency debate under Standing Order no. 9 Delargy on 15 December 1958 informed the House exactly what had been going on:

This matter is as urgent as this, Sir. As recently as last Friday 180 Cuban rebels – so-called – were either killed or wounded chiefly by arms supplied by this country. The others have now taken refuge in the mountains and the dictator is badly in need of these rockets to destroy them as soon as he can. An all-out offensive is to be launched next week chiefly with the aid of British arms. This is something which, so far, has been unknown to the British people or to the British Parliament. I am convinced that if the British people knew about it they would strongly disapprove. That is why I said that this deal is being done behind their backs. It is very serious, exceedingly urgent, and is certainly of public importance.[19]

He did not succeed in getting his debate, but the astonishing fact, still astonishing now nearly forty years later, that rockets were being supplied to Batista to attack Castro in the hills explains a great deal. Greene's amusing fiction of Wormald saying that he had found that rockets were being assembled in the mountains assumes an entirely new meaning. Even more interesting is the background this gives to the Cuban Missile Crisis, which broke on the world a few years later. Many have commented on Greene's supposed prescience in making rockets an element of his plot in *Our Man in Havana*. In fact Greene was attacking what he knew to be the case, that British firms had been supplying the government with rockets. He was in effect saying in his book, They might have rockets too! And the Soviet Union soon obliged by sending rockets of its own of an entirely different kind down to Cuba.

For those who believe that Greene's political allegiances had taken him too far and that he was no more than an agent of influence for the Soviet Union, these actions of his seem almost conclusive. Greene knew what was going on in Cuba through direct contact with the 'so-called' rebels and had then arranged for this information to be rehearsed in the House of Commons, a pattern which almost defines the role of an agent of influence. It cannot have been a surprise to those in MI6 when he was retired from the service's active list – even at arm's length – in 1959. However, as we shall see, there was more to it than that.

Greene may have been very well aware that his views chimed in with those expressed in Moscow, but was he actually in contact with them? More significantly in the light of his contacts with Philby after his defection, was he sharing his knowledge and information with him in the late 1950s and after? If so, the Soviet decision to go one better than Britain and send some real rockets – not just air-to-ground missiles launched from planes – a decision which led to the most dangerous moments in the Cold War, may have stemmed from Greene's actions.

CHAPTER TWELVE

The Business of *A Burnt-Out Case*

It was inevitable that in pursuing a quest for Graham Greene there would come a time when the quest began to cover ground that he was also interested in – his preoccupation with Father Damien and lepers was a good example. It was this that surely lay behind Greene's decision to go to a leper colony in West Africa, a journey from which *The Burnt-Out Case* ensued. I had known of Greene's interest in Damien, and had read that Tom Burns had asked him to consider writing his life, but there was some further connection that needed explaining, although there was no obvious clue to what it might be.

Walking through Oxford one day on the way to the Dominican House, Blackfriars, in search of Bede Jarrett's letters, I stopped at a bookshop and found a life of Damien. Knowing Greene's interest I bought it and, reading it some time later, found in the appendix a reprint of Robert Louis Stevenson's letter on Damien. Here was the explanation I had been seeking. The letter was a commonplace when Greene was young. He must have read it many times; he once records going through Stevenson's letters and essays. The passage of over half a century has plunged the commonplace into obscurity. No writer on Greene appears to have made the connection or thought that his interest in Damien and lepers required an explanation. Once again a very simple basic perception in the quest for Graham Greene came from browsing in a bookshop.

If anything could remove the miasma of suspicion and doubt about Greene's political views it was the subject and location of *A Burnt-Out Case*, set in a leper colony in the Congo run by Catholic priests and nuns. There is also a doctor who is an atheist, but he is the absolute reverse of the Catholic doctor Harry Lime with his adulterated penicillin.

The signs that Greene's mind was turning back to his view of the world in the 1930s at Oxford have been noticed in *The Quiet American*. There was the priest in his blood-spattered soutane, acting as priest, doctor and surgeon, and the sudden use of the image of a leper. References to Father Damien, both in *A Burnt-Out Case* and in Greene's diary of his time in the Congo, which he published shortly afterwards, show that he was harking back to his earliest knowledge of Catholicism. Before Greene left for the Congo in January 1959 he contacted his Dominican friends to obtain introductions to Catholic priests there, and through his brother Raymond he met one of the best leprosy experts in Britain, Dr R. G. Cochrane. When he arrived in the Congo he had already gained a detailed theoretical knowledge of what he might find. The contrast between this briefing and the briefing he received from MI6 before he went on his China tour could not have been greater. Whether he went on his trip to atone for his political involvements or not, the result was a profound analysis of his life and what he was doing. When Greene finished *A Burnt-Out Case* – it was published in 1961 – he said he was sure he would never write another book. It was to be a long five years before one appeared.

There was one other source for Greene's desire to return to Africa and that was his brief visit at the time of the Mau Mau insurgency in Kenya in 1953. While there he met his old Oxford friend Robert Scott, now Sir Robert, the High Commissioner for East Africa. Greene never mentions the Mulla Mulgars, Walter de la Mare or even John Buchan in his account of the visit in *Ways of Escape*. But in a strange way Scott's life had become a fulfilment of both men's ambitions under Buchan's influence.

Besides climbing the social heights in the colony, Greene found the real world on the other side of the insurgency. He saw the Mau Mau prisoners who had been condemned to death and the strange hold the Catholic priests had over them:

There was one odd thing about the condemned Mau Mau. Nine out of ten became Catholics in the condemned cell when hope was over.

176

Perhaps it was the personality of one Irish priest who began instructing them as soon as they had been sentenced and spent the last night in the cell with them. The Attorney General walking around the prison one night in Nyeri saw a white man squatting on the floor of the condemned cell with three Africans sitting around him. It was the Father.[1]

Greene added the poignant words of the priest, that the men died like angels and that he did not see many Europeans die so well. The priest had the holy duty of going into the pit where the bodies were left and administering the last rites to the men when they had been executed. The contrast between this and, for example, Greene's account of the bodies of countless slaughtered Vietnamese left rotting in a canal in *The Quiet American* seems to have affected Greene and moved his mind to a more profound view of his life and what he was doing.

Early in *A Burnt-Out Case*, there is a discussion between the doctor, Colin, and the Father Superior of the Order. They have to meet regularly to sort out their accounts. The state pays for the doctor and so they try and shift as much of the expenses from the Order to the doctor's account, much as Dreuther's accountant transferred fuel-oil costs to the entertainment account in *Loser Takes All*, but in a more worthy cause. They later discuss the possible motives of a middle-aged architect called Querry who has arrived among them without notice or purpose. The doctor suggests he might be a leprophil and goes on: 'Sometimes I wonder whether Damien was a leprophil. There was no need for him to become a leper in order to serve them well. A few elementary precautions – I wouldn't be a better doctor without my fingers would I?'[2] The priest comes to Damien's defence, just as Stevenson did, but in twentieth-century terms: 'I'm not as suspicious of leprophils as you are, doctor. There are people who love and embrace poverty. Is that so bad? Do we have to invent a word ending in phil for them?'[3]

Querry becomes aware of the difference in the two vocations as well almost as soon as he arrives: 'He blamed himself for not realising that the area of leprosy was also the area of this other sickness. He had expected doctors and nurses: he had forgotten that he would

177

find priests and nuns.'[4] The other sickness was the sickness of the spirit which afflicted Querry, and which is surely the sickness that Greene had found in himself. Part of this sickness is fame. In a direct borrowing from his own life Greene has Querry appearing on the cover of *Time* magazine ten years before, there because he is a famous architect known for his modern church architecture. The factory owner, who has by chance kept a copy of the magazine and recognises Querry from it, releases the virus of his fame into the one community where Querry had hoped to escape from it. Eventually it destroys him, for Rycker becomes fixated on him as a famous man, 'the' Querry, and when he mistakenly believes that Querry has slept with his wife and made her pregnant, goes mad in his anger and kills him. Marie Rycker is much younger than her husband and her lies told from innocence – a desire to get away from her husband and Africa – are the cause of her husband's anger and Querry's death.

The references to architecture are few, the plans seem as far removed from reality as Wormald's plans of the secret weapon – or vacuum cleaner – in *Our Man in Havana*. Near the end of the book he refers to an architectural student whose name he could not remember 'building in some suburb his bourgeois villas – machines for living in'.[5] This last phrase is the architect Le Corbusier's and there are a few other references to a magazine, the *Architectural Review*, but no real clue to where Greene got the idea of having an architect at the centre of his book. One possible explanation is that during the war Greene had had the Architectural Association in Bedford Square in his warden area; it had a club which stayed open right through the Blitz and there were many connections with friends of his such as Osbert Lancaster and Betjeman; they may even have used his shelter.

Whatever the origins of Greene's choice of architecture as the parallel for the art of an author, the result works brilliantly. Querry talks about his delight at the first successful drawings he produced in exactly the way any author feels about the success of his first book. And when he expresses his anger at what people have made of his later churches he gets very close indeed to Greene's feelings about his own work and the Catholic significance people wished to attach to them:

'The popular priest and the popular architect – their talents can be killed easily by disgust.'

'Disgust?'

'Disgust of praise. How it nauseates, doctor, by its stupidity ... the books they have written about my work, the pious motives they've attributed to me – they were enough to sicken me of the drawing board.'[6]

At the heart of the book Querry tells Marie Rycker a story, a story within a story, about a jeweller who believes in a king. The jeweller has satisfied himself through his own logic when a very young man that the King exists while his parents simply believe in him. He makes ever more magnificent jewelled eggs. But then one day he realises that he is wrong, that he is not being an artist when he makes his eggs, just a skilled craftsman. And he is also sure that the King does not exist.

The King in the story is of course Christ the King, Christus Rex, and the jeweller is Querry, or Greene's devil's advocate. Repeatedly Querry tries to explain why he does not believe, why he is no longer a Catholic, in Greene's terms, and the reader is drawn into believing him, if he is conscious of the parallels in Greene's life, and believing it of Greene as well. But then Querry is killed and the doubts die with him. What is left is the reality of the vocations of the priests and nuns, and even of the atheist doctor, who have given their lives to the sick, as Father Damien had done before them.

There are references in the book to the priest who was most in Greene's thoughts while he was writing the book, Father Thomas Gilby, through allusion to the collected works of Thomas Aquinas, which Gilby was in the process of translating into English for Eyre and Spottiswoode. There is also a passable Latin joke. In celebration of the raising of the roof-tree for the new church, a bottle of Sandeman's port is found. One priest asks if it is permitted to drink it, or whether there is anything against it in moral theology. He receives the reply: 'Only in canon law, Lex Contra Sandemanium, but even that, of course, was interpreted by that eminent Benedictine, Dom ...'[7]

The book is a masterly achievement, but it is easy to see why

Greene thought it might be his last novel. It is an exhausting analysis of what it meant to be a writer, and of his own shortcomings. Like the jeweller in Querry's story he feels that he had nothing new to say and is simply a craftsman repeating the same actions, not an artist. It echoes at a more profound level what he had said to James Hadley Chase after the war: he would write no more but would devote himself to publishing other authors' work. And, as then, that is what he did for the next five years after his return to England and the publication of *A Burnt-Out Case*.

Towards the end of the 1950s Greene had an annoying diversion from the usual smooth running of his business affairs. Graham Greene Productions proceeded normally, but one matter cropped up which was to lead to extraordinary complications.

When *The Quiet American* had been published in 1955 Greene had arranged for translation rights to be assigned to a close relative. There was no difficulty over this until the relative died, when Greene found that he was having to deal with the estate duty that should be paid, through his agents. The tax authorities proved exceedingly difficult to handle, not understanding elementary principles of copyright and demanding onerous payments on the basis of possible future earnings from this one small copyright assignment, which in fact had ended with the beneficiary's death.

The affair seems to have concentrated his mind on the position that would arise on his own death. In 1960 he found what seemed the perfect solution. Exactly who introduced Greene to Tom Roe, a solicitor who acted as an off-shore tax consultant, is not known. They had several mutual friends whose affairs were already in Roe's hands, including Noël Coward and James Hadley Chase. Greene decided that all his foreign earnings would be assigned to a new company based in Switzerland, of which he would not be a director. He would then draw an annual salary in return for his services to the company nominally directed by Roe, what he called a slave contract. As we have noted, Greene thought the book would be his last, and many critics saw it as a classic *vale* – how *could* he go on after such soul-searching at the end of his own quest? It seemed logical to begin to tie up his affairs, which were as complex as it was possible to be, not least on the tax front, where his earnings and expenses from MI6, to look nowhere else, required circumspect treatment. *A Burnt-Out Case* was the first book dealt with under the new regime.

Tom Roe had been born in Brighton in 1917, where he qualified as a solicitor before the war. He made his name in India at the time of independence and gained a CBE for his services to charities in Calcutta, after undertaking the complex task of amalgamating the numerous Christian charities into a single organisation. His administrative abilities had first become apparent in the Middle East during the Second World War, when he obtained an OBE (Military). He returned to England and, after a short period in business, decided to set up a consultancy, Roturman SA, to take advantage of the chaos which would be caused by the European Economic Community and the differing tax regimes. He specialised in setting up tax-efficient companies in Switzerland and investing funds for private clients.

Roturman SA seemed the perfect answer to Greene's problems, present and anticipated. It even had offices in Burlington Street, just around the corner from the flat Greene had recently acquired in Albany. Unfortunately this image is misleading. Roe's company had been set up after discussion with a partner who remained hidden, but far from sleeping – the actor George Sanders, star of films such as *All About Eve*, for which he won an Oscar, and *Death of a Scoundrel*. The tax-efficient companies Roe created focused heavily on the needs of the Hollywood film-makers Sanders knew. The holding company which Roe set up to handle the funds deposited by the eminently respectable figures who effectively acted as a front for the other parts of the business was called Cadco. This unusual name was taken from the title of Sanders' autobiography, *The Memoirs of a Professional Cad*. It is unlikely that Greene or any of the others remarked on the name, or knew of the schemes that Roe and Sanders were evolving to spend the money that was pouring in. Sanders' friend and biographer Brian Aherne was in at the very beginning, although he knew nothing of Greene or his involvement:

Exciting plans were made for this company, including investment in Swiss real estate, the purchase and storage of Scotch whisky in bulk,

Canadian oil wells and other projects about which, it seemed to me, they knew nothing. [Roe] began to invest money that had been entrusted to him by clients in various parts of the world, whilst George bought a new Rolls-Royce and once more talked of abandoning the profession in which he was phenomenally successful in order to become a business tycoon.[8]

The money to pay for Sanders' Rolls-Royce came from Greene and his fellow investors, all eager to 'get out from under' the undeniably onerous attentions of the UK tax authorities. Had he realised any part of this, Greene would have run a mile, but he remained in complete innocence until the end. Roe was an extremely smooth operator who even succeeded in shrugging off the failure of one of his investments for Greene, in the Royal Victoria Sausage Company, in a series of lengthy interviews in 1964 at Greene's flat in Albany.

In the short term things seemed to go well with this project. Established in Brighton, of all places, it absorbed pleasingly large amounts of money, culminating in the setting up of an additional factory in Scotland that was launched with full television coverage in 1963. Roe, Sanders and other businessmen with unusual backgrounds appeared before the cameras to celebrate a grant for their latest coup from the government itself.

Greene's new interest in business led to him becoming involved in a publishing wrangle. An advertisement appeared in the *Times Literary Supplement* (opposite) for a new book of his, *In Search of a Character*. Greene's publishers Heinemann were profoundly shocked, for the publisher of the book was Bodley Head. They quickly found out that Greene was responsible for the advertisement, and the appearance of Eric Ambler, another of their authors. Ambler recalled Greene's fierce determination to protect their mutual publisher A. S. Frere, whose position was being threatened as a result of a takeover of Heinemann by an outside firm, Thomas Tilling. He called a group of Heinemann authors to his rooms in Albany and they talked over what they could do. Ambler recalled: 'Greene said that the only asset a publisher had was its authors and we should all write books for another publishing company – the Bodley Head where he had a connection. I said at once that I had a contract with Heinemann which I could not break.

He replied immediately he did too, but it was for fiction, and he was going to do a small book of two travel diaries. My book, *The Ability to Kill*, went into the list and did eventually appear.'[9]

Greene had also got Walter de la Mare on the list and was soon working away at other projects for his new firm, as a director. The new regime at Heinemann had learned something about publishing. Frere was moved to a nominally more senior post but then felt obliged to resign, in time-honoured fashion. Greene was not to forget him and his next book had a dedicatory letter which praised him unreservedly for his help in the past. By contrast J. B. Priestley decided that he would stay with Heinemann, declaring that the firm had made him and he would not desert them now. It may be coincidence, but his later career faded and he is now considered a minor figure awaiting revival, whereas Greene's fortunes moved from strength to strength.

Greene's friendship with Chaplin developed and strengthened when he worked on the actor's long-delayed autobiography with him. The contract for Chaplin's book had been signed in 1957. In Greene's advertisement it had been promised for 1962; it finally appeared in 1964 and was an instant success, reprinting before publication thanks to the flood of orders.

Chaplin's *My Autobiography* was a classic of its kind and revealed to the general public in poignant terms exactly what hardships had been known by the comic figure who had entertained them since before the First World War. It was a harrowing tale of poverty of a kind which Greene had seen only in Mexico and had dimly perceived as the lot of the villagers in Chipping Camden before the war. But Chaplin was now a very rich man living the life of a tax exile. Greene would be one of the editors who could have lived with the contradiction and seen nothing strange in Chaplin staying loyal to his roots. Nor did Chaplin shirk a full account of his sympathy for Russia during the war.

There are several places in the book where Greene's presence can almost be felt. Chaplin had visited Hong Kong and had been introduced to a young priest from Connecticut who had been working in a leper colony there for five years. When they came to part Chaplin shook his hand and, noticing it felt rough, turned it over and looked at it: 'There were cracks and crevices and in the centre a white spot. "That's not leprosy, I hope," I said jokingly. He grinned and shook his head. A year later we heard he had died of it.'[10] Had Chaplin not had for a publisher the author of *A Burnt-Out Case* this brief sketch might never have appeared.

Chaplin's book ended with a few references to the people he saw regularly as friends in Switzerland, and he lighted on George Sanders and his wife Benita as amongst those closest to him. Ironically Chaplin thought he was naming the elite of the expatriate community, with Tom Roe acting to smooth their path in everything from tax arrangements to schooling for their children. Roe was a pillar of the English-speaking community and by this time his circle included Noël Coward, who would not have settled there without his advice, William Holden, James Hadley Chase and, of course, Greene himself, though only on matters of finance – he had not yet decided to leave England. It was a decision that was soon to be taken out of his hands.

With his Bodley Head directorship it must have seemed to Greene's friends as though he had at last decided to stop his 40,000-miles-a-year travelling. A leisurely life in a gentleman's occupation, as publishing was still said to be in those days, with lunches at the Garrick – what could be more sensible? It was not to be. Boredom was something Greene could never cope with; he always used it as a stand-by reason for everything outlandish he did. And the London publishing scene, even amongst his friends, epitomised boredom to him. Greene had become so involved with his imaginative recreations of his political and religious ideas that he simply had to be up and doing.

In the early 1960s he had been drawn to Haiti by what he had read of the infamous regime being established by 'Papa Doc' Duvalier. There can have been few authors with political interests, anxious to attack Duvalier, who were able to recall the old Haiti and could also write about it. Greene accepted the responsibility gladly; he said once that he had hoped that *The Comedians*, his novel set in Haiti, would strike a severe blow against the Doctor. He succeeded far more than he could have hoped. Perhaps it was his ability to see evil in a medical man, from the days of Harry Lime onwards, that helped him describe the regime in such precise detail that Papa Doc later had a book written to expose Greene. Other critics, despite the tales of the Tonton Macoute, Duvalier's ruthless secret police, still wondered whether there was another side to the story. Certainly there were many in America to whom a doctor was a doctor, someone to be supported in his struggles against communism, for all the world as if there were no doctors in communist regimes. Even Greene does not damn Duvalier completely. He describes how he started out as a country doctor who fought a successful battle against typhoid and was a founder member of the local Ethnological Society.

Seeing things from this side of the fence, however briefly, seems even to have led Greene to make some amends for his unrestricted attack on all things American. *The Comedians* has a portrait of a charming old American couple who are only militant in their pro-selytising for the vegetarian cause. In a penetrating thrust against himself, Greene describes the old vegetarian as having been born with peace in his heart 'instead of the splinter of ice'.[11] He had first used this phrase about himself as a novelist when as a young man in hospital he had forced himself to listen to the anguished cries of a mother grieving over her dead son rather than put on the radio earphones as the others patients had to drown out the sounds. A novelist had to have a splinter of ice in his heart, his said. Forty years later he could see a place for people in the world who did not see things that way, and even more conceded that some of them might be American.

The vegetarian Smiths were also opposed to voodoo and anything in any way dishonourable. Greene's leading character Brown, the narrator, goes to a voodoo ceremony that lasts through the night, and we can see in his fascination Greene's own interest, not least in the carefully transcribed Latin words taken from the Mass which formed part of the ceremony. In passing he says that the voodoo ceremonies have decreased since Papa Doc came to power because he vigorously suppressed them; this gives the reader a fleeting moment of anxiety – perhaps after all there may have been something good about Papa Doc, and if the Smiths were also against voodoo, blameless people, and, undoubtedly, Papa Doc was against communism in all its forms, why then ...

The comedians of the title are those Europeans who arrive in Haiti by boat at the beginning of the book and provide the story. They are more than usually detached from the setting of the novel and one, Major Jones, is an amiable confidence trickster who pretends to have had military experience – in fact he was involved in entertainment for troops and his proudest boast was to have been near Noël Coward once. He believes his own fantasies and persuades the local rebels to believe them too, only to find himself obliged to lead them against the Tonton Macoute. He is killed, and it is the narrator's words about the memorial stone to Jones that begin the book. It is obvious that Greene finds in himself a little of the comedian.

There are some especially direct personal allusions in the book which can easily be recognised. There is the passenger on the boat, Baxter, who entertains the other passengers with a dramatic monologue on his time as an air-raid warden when a bomb hit Store Street in the Blitz. There is the lady novelist who was Brown's secretary in the Political Intelligence Department of the Foreign Office – in reality Antonia White, who worked for Greene. And Greene's involvement with Zoe Richmond and of her letter written to Greene out of the blue a few months before reveals the sharp sting of a throwaway line of Brown's: 'The woman in Monte Carlo had betrayed her husband with a schoolboy, but her motive had been generous.'[12] One may also recognise the more detailed account of how Brown as a schoolboy was first seduced by this woman: 'My instructress was at least fifteen years older than myself, but in my mind she has remained always the same age, and it is I who have grown older.'[13]

This same quality which Greene has recognised in himself through Brown applies to yet another portrait of J. D. Beresford, seen in the character Henri Philipot. Philipot is also still young in his mind, with his limp, 'a slight limp caused by polio' (which Greene had thought the cause of Beresford's disability), and of whom he says, 'I had met him once before in happier days, one of a little group of writers and artists … how far away those times seemed now.' Indeed most of those still alive who could remember those days were twenty and more years older than Greene. In literary terms that brief spell at the Richmonds' house had taken him out of his generation. People later said Greene always seemed a strangely isolated figure; in truth he was simply older than his years.

The Comedians was published in 1966. Greene's dedication took the unusual form of a letter to A. S. Frere which was effectively an apology to him for the failures of the various schemes by which Greene and the others had tried to keep him in his post as head of Heinemann. *The Comedians* was the first novel he had written since they had both left Heinemann, and after thirty years of friendship and association with him as a publisher Greene felt the book had to be dedicated to him. He went on to make a joke about the central figure in the book not being Greene, despite being called Brown.

Although the book appeared in 1966, it is not yet clear when the final writing of it took place. The point is important because in July of the previous year the second act of the Roe saga, which was to affect the rest of Greene's life, had already begun. The last pages of the book suddenly take on a fresh seriousness not found elsewhere, which suggests that he already knew there was something wrong when he wrote them. Brown has been forced to flee from Haiti, having lost the hotel he owned there, which was the only reason he had come back to the country in the first place. He finds that it is assumed he must be a communist. When asked why, Brown replies: 'Because the Tontons were after me. Papa Doc, you remember, is a bulwark against communism. And insurgent, of course, is a dirty word. I wonder how President Johnson would deal now with something like the French resistance. That too was infiltrated (another dirty word) by the communists.'[14] The French resistance and French communism sit oddly with the rest of the book's themes, although Brown was supposedly born in Monte Carlo. Greene is surely stating his position in global terms, for the Vietnam War was now building towards its climax and his views had changed little since writing *The Quiet American*. If anything he seemed to have moved even further towards the communist line, while still sheltering under a Catholic umbrella.

In the final pages he enunciates clearly a line which he stuck to for the rest of his life, repeating it as late as 1987 in the address given in Moscow. His statement appears in the guise of a letter written by Magiot, the honest doctor, read by Brown after Magiot is already dead. The argument relates Catholicism to communism:

> Communism, my friend, is more than Marxism, just as Catholicism – remember I was born a Catholic too – is more than the Roman curia. There is a *mystique* as well as a politique. We are humanists, you and I ... Catholics and communists have committed great crimes, but at least they have not stood aside, like an established society, and been indifferent. I would rather have blood on my hands than water like Pilate.[15]

And here is the central line that runs through Greene's life, from the fight against the Black and Tans, through the underground groups in the Palatinate, the Indo-China struggles, and now here in Haiti, all causes on the dangerous edge of religion and politics that he devoted his life to describing. Both Catholics and communists believed in something and were prepared to stand by their beliefs.

There is no obvious explanation for why Greene should give this masterly summing up of his views on things that were so important to him, unless it was because he knew he would have less and less time to think about such things. As we shall see in the following chapter, Greene was by now almost completely absorbed in the endgame of his involvement with Roe and his colleagues.

CHAPTER THIRTEEN

Blues for Uncle Charlie

There were very few people in Greene's life who completely deceived him, despite his knowing them well. The most important by far was Tom Roe, or Thomas Chambers Windsor Roe, the solicitor who arranged the tax shelters that ruined Greene's retirement. It was somehow appropriate that the leads which helped my quest on at a crucial time came from the Law Society in London's Chancery Lane. For a fee, the Society is obliged to provide details of any of its members who have been struck off the list of those qualified to practise, together with the Society's findings. When these reached me, they were accompanied by a batch of faded copies of press cuttings, mostly recycled reports from newsagencies, but with one from New Zealand that gave important information. It relied on a Los Angeles report, from an unidentified newspaper, but of great interest. The material came in at a fortunate time.

In the case of Tom Roe, the Law Society information had provided some leads which I was following up in Boston, Massachusetts at Boston College. Walking along West Street I stopped at the $1 bookshelves ranged outside the Brattle Book Shop – never a wasted exercise however trivial an exercise it might seem – and happened to glance at a copy of Brian Aherne's biography of George Sanders, *A Dreadful Man*. A few moments' intense browsing – the book had no index – made it obvious that Aherne knew a lot about Roe, whom he called Theodore Lowe, later Ted Lowe, a fitting pseudonym. In among the humour of a very witty book were facts about 'Ted Lowe' which, after verification in the archives, gave fresh insights into material found at the beginning of my quest in the Hadley Chase papers. I was to learn more from the Board of Trade inspectors' report on Roe's companies in Britain a few weeks later in the calm environment of the reading room of the Leicester Square branch of the Westminster Library. Had Aherne's book been found at another time, the Law Society material been less complete, or the Board of Trade inspectors' report been discarded in the periodic purges of vital material to which Britain's libraries unaccountably succumb from time to time, my search for the missing links in the story would have gone on far longer, with uncertain results.

On 28 July 1965 a car travelling on the Geneva–Lausanne highway was pulled over by the Swiss police. The driver was Tom Roe. He had not been stopped for a traffic violation. The police had received information that he had earlier in the day changed fifty-nine forged $100 bills in Geneva and they wanted to know where he had got them and if he knew they were forged. But in the boot of his car they found a further $100,000 in forged notes, so they insisted that he return with them to his home near Lausanne before he could warn anyone there. His house was searched in front of his shocked wife, a well-known society hostess from one of the leading banking families in England.

Tom Roe was charged by the Swiss police on 4 August. The following day his partner, known as Dennis Lorraine, a forty-four-year-old businessman and film producer, was charged in Los Angeles. He had been arrested on his honeymoon, and his best man Mickey Hargitay, recently divorced from the actress Jayne Mansfield, was one of the many shocked Hollywood figures who talked to the press in the days that followed. He had been working with Lorraine on films in Rome, including *The Phantom Execution*, and could not believe that Roe or Lorraine could possibly be involved with forged money.

Lorraine was equally convincing when arrested. He said that the money, which he did not then admit was forged, was funding for a film to be called *Blues for Uncle Charlie* – seemingly a coded warning to Charlie Chaplin – starring Sammy Davis Junior. Roe was an immensely wealthy man, he said, with people like Noël Coward as his clients. Besides he had been chairman of the British Residents Association in Geneva. However, the Los Angeles Police Department announced on his arrest that the American Secret Service, Interpol and the Swiss police had been carrying on a joint investigation and they were sure they had smashed a major currency-smuggling ring based in the movie business. It soon became known that Lorraine's real name was Denis Edwards, born in Bristol in 1921, with previous convictions for fraud.

On 3 August, before Roe had been charged, Graham Greene wrote to his London literary agent Laurence Pollinger from Paris, mentioning the emerging scandal. This was not an example of Greene's prescience – the explanation for his early knowledge of what had happened was more mundane, but revealing. James Hadley Chase was in Paris at the time. His Paris agent, shared with Greene, still lived in the flat above Greene's, and Chase was able to get in touch with his friend quickly and easily at any time. He and his wife were close friends of the Roes and saw them often. Roe's wife contacted the Chases immediately to tell them what had happened and ask for their advice and help. It would be inevitable that Chase would tell Greene face to face as soon as he knew. The chance that Greene was in Paris when the news broke explained the speed of Greene's warning to his agent, who replied that he was sure that the entire affair would prove to be a mistake and things would settle back to normal in a day or two. But there was no mistake.

Laurence Pollinger's optimism was born of desperation. The previous year the collapse of the Royal Victorian Sausage Company should have suggested that there was something wrong with Roe's activities. Certainly Greene realised as soon as he heard of Roe's arrest from Chase that they were faced with a catastrophe. Had Greene, or Pollinger, acted as James Hadley Chase had done and withdrawn all the money lodged with Roe at the first signs of trouble, they might have escaped unscathed. The collapse of Roe's empire began then, and is worth examining in detail.

In 1959 Lorraine had acquired a small butcher's in Brighton. In a fraud worthy of a Pinkie of mature years, he had succeeded in rapidly expanding the company, mainly by pretending that he had found a letter from King Edward VII praising the sausages made by the butcher. The change of the name of the shop to the Royal Victorian Sausage Company followed soon after, and the royal crest appeared on the large fleet of vans that Lorraine acquired to carry the sausages around the country. Roe made his first investment in the company in 1961, using Greene's money mixed in with funds from other investors including Charlie Chaplin. It is not clear how Roe and Lorraine met; both were Brighton men and seem also to have known the same accountant. More and more money came into the company and Lorraine built up the figures through false accounting to create the illusion that it was the kind of business which could make use of such sums. Finally it became obvious that some large project would have to be undertaken to give cover for the cash flow provided by Roe, and it would have to be away from Brighton, because the local people were already puzzled by the supposed scale of what had been a very small concern.

The money Roe was investing all came from the tax-shelter companies that he had set up for Greene and the others. Roe was an expert at tax laws and government grants; he had the idea of making use of British development grants available through the Scottish office for projects set up on greenfield sites north of the border. He finally settled on Glenrothes in Scotland. The project was inaugurated in May 1963 with full media coverage of the likely benefits for local employment. It was only last-minute checking by Roe of the advertisements prepared by Lorraine that stopped Greene and Noël Coward being listed on posters announcing the launch of the new venture.

The entire project collapsed in September 1964, and Board of Trade inspectors were appointed. However, so persuasive was Roe that he convinced Greene and all his friends that he had been the victim of a swindler. In December 1964 Pollinger had advised A. S. Frere that the investors were unlikely to get anything from their stake in Roe's operations in Britain. On 23 December Pollinger even wrote to Roe sympathising with the terrible situation in which Lorraine had placed him, and thanking him for his personal guarantee covering the loss of £10,000 of Greene's money. This welcome offer had been made by Roe to Pollinger in a letter, but Roe was quite capable of carrying off a bluff face to face. On 18 February the following year, Greene entertained Roe in his rooms in Albany and was so convinced by him that he wrote a sharp letter to Pollinger the following day asking whether he had had any figures from one of his publishers which seemed, according to Roe, to be overdue.

Early in April 1965 Greene received a letter from the Board of

Trade inspectors asking him to appear before them a few days later on 15 April as they believed he might have information that could be of assistance to them. Even this did not undermine Greene's faith in Roe, and the shock of Roe's arrest must have been as serious as any he received in his life. Over the weeks that followed, Greene's world collapsed as he realised that the man who had set up his off-shore company and to whom he had entrusted his most confidential affairs had been involved in a major criminal conspiracy. He was not to realise for some years exactly what had happened, because Roe's trial in Switzerland did not come on until 1967. The exact chronology of what Greene discovered and when cannot be determined; it is unlikely that he made any record. However, it is possible to piece together events known to others which tie in with information unearthed by the Board of Trade investigation into Roe's British ventures.

When he first became involved with Roe, amongst Greene's strongest admirers and closest friends were Ian Fleming and his wife. In 1960 Fleming had just left the *Sunday Times*, where he had advanced from being just a foreign manager to their most valued contributor, and was acting as a freelance scout for major projects for the paper. The Bodley Head were known to be publishing Chaplin's autobiography and Fleming decided to try and obtain serialisation rights. Through Noël Coward he obtained an interview with Chaplin and flew out to Vevey to see the world's greatest living comic filmstar. Greene seems not to have been present, but the Chaplins were joined by George Sanders and his wife. The discussion did not lead to immediate success but the connections established were useful.

After the meeting Fleming went to Italy, where he was intent on persuading a retired silver-haired Italian-American called Salvatore 'Lucky' Luciano, perhaps the best-known Mafia boss from the pre-war days, to grant an exclusive interview with the *Sunday Times*. Fleming's biographer Andrew Lycett records that this attempt also came to nothing, and he describes exactly what kind of world Fleming had walked into. Luciano had been in prison on the outbreak of the war but had been involved with the FBI in the controversial use of crime bosses to get the Teamsters and other dock and shipping unions to stop sabotage of ships going to Europe with much-needed supplies. Lycett commented:

> Later, Luciano was spirited back to Sicily where he helped the advancing allied forces make their peace with the local Mafia clans. The role, underwritten by the Americans, helped establish the alliance between the mafia and the postwar Christian Democrat political establishment which bedevilled Italian politics for nearly half a century. Luciano was subsequently paroled and deported to Italy where, during the 1950s he built up a lucrative and deadly Mafia heroin business.[1]

Fleming had merely been flirting with a high-profile figure in this world; Lorraine and Roe soon became actively involved. The allegations about Christian Democrat corruption were not mere gossip. When Lorraine was investigated it was found that he had paid 20 million lire in cash to a party official, Signor Scotti, deputy of a top man, Signor Giulio Pastore. The money was an initial sweetener to allow his various films to get going and to find a place in the queue of companies hoping to get development funds from the Italian government set up to attract foreign investment. Here Roe and Lorraine worked admirably together; Roe knew about obtaining investment grants, while Lorraine had contacts in the Mafia hierarchy that led to the politicians such as Scotti and Pastore whom he needed to know.

This was the background to the relationship between the Hollywood Mafia and Roe's operations, which had been incomprehensible to Greene's agent and Greene himself: granted that there had been something wrong – Roe had after all been arrested – how could forged money provided by the Hollywood Mafia possibly be involved? Roe's defence at his trial in Switzerland was that the shipping of the forged $100 bills had been a one-off exercise made as a last attempt to extricate him and his partners from problems caused by the collapse of Cadco and the Royal Victorian Sausage Company. It had been hoped to make a film that would rescue the situation, although how the forged money became involved was unclear if the film was legitimate. This explanation did not ring true. For Lorraine and Roe to have known how to set up the deal to import forged money they must have been closely connected with the Hollywood Mafia in the first place. It was obvious that such large sums of forged money – nearly half a million dollars in this one transaction – would not have been supplied to strangers. Lorraine seems never to have revealed exactly who gave him the money, which was taken over from Los Angeles by a courier, who was also caught. At Lorraine's trial, which took place in Los Angeles, he was represented by Melvin Belli, who a short while before had defended Jack Ruby, the man who killed Oswald, John F. Kennedy's supposed assassin. Ruby was well known to have Mafia connections; the atmosphere of organised crime was everywhere.

It must have been acutely embarrassing for Chaplin and Greene, with their political sympathies, to have been caught up in the seediest backwaters of international capitalism. They had allowed themselves to be used as frontmen for organised crime and had lost a great deal of money as well. Roe's conviction and sentence did not take place until February 1967. In September of that year, fresh evidence emerged about who was behind the entire operation set up by Roe and Sanders in Switzerland, which, besides establishing tax-avoidance schemes, was also laundering Hollywood Mafia deals of every kind, as the Swiss judge at Roe's trial confirmed. It came in a letter Roe sent from his prison cell to James Hadley Chase, who had been convinced throughout that the solicitor was a victim of blackmail and essentially an honest man. They had corresponded for many months, because Chase was worried about what was to become of Roe when he was released. Roe did not share these worries, as he was sure that his old friends in the film world would not let him down. He had said little or nothing at his trial. What he told Chase was that he had been visited in prison by Harry Saltzman, joint producer with Cubby Broccoli of the James Bond films, who had taken him out for the day, accompanied by a guard, and explained to him over a sumptuous lunch what had been planned for his future. Saltzman and his friends were to pay off all his debts and provide his family with capital to begin a new life which would start with a six-week holiday in the Mediterranean. Saltzman explained that a film company was being set up in Paris which he wanted Roe to run, presumably under a new name, with money no object. Roe accepted these generous proposals, an offer he could hardly refuse. Cubby

Broccoli had no part at all in the arrangements and seems eventually to have parted from Saltzman as a result of just such proposals as those made to Roe.

The visit to Roe in prison by Saltzman at this crucial time suggests, at the very least, that he was working as an intermediary for the men Roe and Lorraine had known in Hollywood. There are few businessmen, particularly not men of wealth and a high public profile, who would think of going to a prison to interview a potential chief executive of a major film company.

These developments were in the future, but the basic facts were all apparent as soon as Roe was arrested in July 1965. As far as Greene was concerned Roe's conviction was a possibility from then on, and he was in prison without bail pending his trial. It was inevitable that all Greene's papers in Roe's possession would become known to the police in Switzerland, and to Interpol. The Inland Revenue in England would certainly get to know that Greene was one of those with funds in Roe's hands. There is evidence in the Pollinger files in Texas that at least some of the earnings which Greene had channelled through Roe had had a proportion retained by Greene's agent for any possible tax liability; but even if that were so the future earnings for the rest would still attract the full rate of tax that even Roe's seemingly legitimate schemes were purporting to avoid. And there was also the actual loss which Roe and Lorraine's criminal activity had caused. The only answer was for Greene to become a tax exile, on account of his actual losses, other possible liabilities we cannot know of and not least the risk of scandal breaking when Roe came to trial.

Greene's diary records his rapid movements as he realised that he would have to leave the country. But his problems were not confined to financial and tax difficulties. In September 1965 Greene's file at MI6 was placed in a category which indicated that he was known to the Soviets as an agent – his cover had been blown. This had always been a possibility since Philby's defection. Greene had not been close to Philby since he left MI6 in 1944, but it surely had to be concluded that the Russians would know that Greene contacted MI6 before deciding whether to go to Poland, for example, or make yet another visit to Moscow as an author with 'left' sympathies.

Greene's usefulness had rapidly diminished. Furthermore, it did not help that Greene's views on America were becoming very well known. The CIA must have been informed of the Roe case by the American Secret Service and would know that Greene was close to Chaplin, who had always been sympathetic to the Soviet cause. Information about the involvement of Greene and Chaplin in the Roe débâcle of a detailed kind would without doubt be in the American intelligence service's hands. They had after all co-ordinated the arrest of Lorraine and uncovered the American end of the scam.

The affect of all this on Greene when he realised it must have been profound. He had developed his anti-Americanism in the context of a professed closeness to Russia when in reality he had been living on the dangerous edge of things, and reporting back all he knew that might be of interest to his old friends in MI6. He had now reached the edge and fallen. On every front there really was no alternative but to begin again in exile.

Having decided to leave, Greene set about providing for his family. He visited Vivien in Oxford; they were of course still married and she was a shareholder in his UK company, which had not been involved in the Roe fiasco in any way. As far as she was concerned Greene's move abroad had few consequences. He no doubt explained what had happened and that he had set up another Swiss company to replace the one Roe had established, this time using a very respectable Swiss solicitor. This would ensure his own and his families' income when he was abroad for Greene referred in his letters to his money earned in England being blocked.

Dorothy Glover presented more of a problem. She was sixty-five and may have been in need of assistance now that Greene was not going to be on hand. There could be no question of her joining him abroad, or living near him, even if either of them had wanted this, because she had to be near her mother who would otherwise be entirely alone. The year before, Greene had arranged for the sale through Sotheby's of the manuscripts which he had given her over the years. Now he decided on a quite remarkable gesture which, besides giving her some additional capital, also served as a memorial to their mutual passion – collecting detective fiction. Greene decided to produce a catalogue of their collection, published by the Bodley Head in an edition of 500 copies, each one signed by Greene and

Dorothy Glover, and also by the bibliophile and authority on detective fiction John Carter, who contributed an introduction.

The collection, which Greene and Dorothy had formed over twenty devoted years, represented the passage of time and the slow accumulation of knowledge in a field which Greene called the modern equivalent of the fairy story. Both developed a sixth sense about where they might find seemingly trivial cheap novels which turned out to be of interest for their collection. One sentence in Greene's own introduction makes the point well:

> Yet even today, on two shelves outside a second-hand furniture shop, Victorian detective novels can still be found (one of our latest acquisitions, a parody of Sherlock Holmes by a fairly well known writer of the time, cost 1/6), and I still hope that in ten years our collection will have doubled in size with the addition of unrecognised titles.[2]

The catalogue appeared after Greene had left the country and, as he must have known, the collection was essentially complete; there would be no more forays around second-hand furniture shops. Perhaps their last time spent together was at the publishers during the hours it took for them both to sign all 500 copies of the edition.

By what we can only infer were the terms of the agreement that Greene had made with the Inland Revenue, he had to leave England by midnight on the last day of 1965. On 1 January 1966 he had to be on foreign soil. Greene was invited to spend Christmas with very old friends of his, Lord and Lady Camoys at Stonor in Oxfordshire. In 1963 Archbishop David Mathew had retired and moved as resident priest to Stonor, one of the great Catholic houses with a history going back to before the Reformation. Greene had visited the house more frequently as a result, though his diaries show many previous visits. His last evening in England, as an Englishman living in his own country, he spent at a party given in his honour at the Connaught Hotel by the Sutros, old friends with whom he had set up the Anglo-Texan Society and many other schemes. He was on the boat in the early hours of the new year.

It took Greene a few days into 1966 to adjust to being in exile, living in his flat in Paris temporarily, until he could find somewhere to settle down. The blank pages in his diary soon began to fill again as he started out on fresh projects and picked up the threads of work started while he had still been in England. He saw a great deal of Peter Glenville, who lived in Paris, discussing their film of *The Comedians*. On 15 January he had dinner with John Barry, who had composed the music for the Bond films, and Joseph Losey. There was a series of visits from Malcolm Muggeridge, although these were never explained. His old friend from MI6, Trevor Wilson, also looked him up when passing through Paris – one friend who never deserted Greene. There were even moments of humour in those early days. When the honours list was announced Greene had been made a Companion of Honour. Unfortunately the Inland Revenue had made it clear that he was not to return to England for some time. In a letter to the poet George Barker in November 1967 he said he was still not allowed back. Fortunately standard practice permitted return under such circumstances. Greene's diary records his attendance at Buckingham Palace at 12.30 on 11 March 1966. Before the day was out he was back on French soil. Many of his friends were puzzled by this rapid visit. The Crosthwaite-Eyres had hoped to join in the celebrations with other old friends, but had to be disappointed.

In his autobiography *Ways of Escape* Greene makes no mention of what had happened. He acknowledges that he was depressed after the publication in 1961 of *A Burnt-Out Case* but suggests that this was because of the pneumonia he had developed on his last visit to Moscow – he was thought for a while to have lung cancer. He then moves in the sweep of a single paragraph to the ending of his depression six years later:

> What swung me out of the depression and into the manic condition in which I wrote most of the stories in *May We Borrow your Husband?* and then started work on *Travels with my Aunt?* I can only suppose it came from making a difficult decision in my private life and leaving England permanently to settle in France in 1966. I burned a number of boats and in the light of the flames I began to write a novel.[3]

It is uncommon for Greene to step outside the façade he creates for his readers, and how tantalising the comment he makes about his private life in an autobiography. And what boats? He never says, but a few lines further on he makes a slip, if not a conscious allusion for those who knew about his affairs. Talking of the paper on which he was writing his new book *May We Borrow your Husband?*, an unusual thing for him to comment on anyway, he says: 'As a symbol of my new freedom I had abandoned the lined variety [of paper] where the lines seemed to me now like the bars on a prison window.'[4] Had he remembered the lines in *The Complaisant Lover* when Clive Root, the antiquarian bookseller, tells his lover Mary Rhodes that he has got involved with a crook in a currency deal and she replies, 'You could go to prison for this'? Or was the fate of Tom Roe, safely locked up in a Swiss prison, preying on his mind? In 1966 Greene was still unaware of the background to what had happened, and of the Mafia involvement. Even after the trials in Switzerland and Los Angeles, when much of the secret history of the fraud became known, he still had nightmares in which the Inland Revenue had decided to reopen his case – as we shall see.

Fortunately for Greene Hollywood came to the rescue of his finances in a *de facto* payback for the embarrassment of the Roe affair and the part the dark side of Hollywood had played in it. (Ironically the company which made the film of his novel *The Comedians*, MGM, came under the control of a Mafia boss in the mid-1990s. He too was caught, but jumped bail in 1997 to avoid serving a prison sentence, escaping to his native Italy.) Quentin Falk, in his unrivalled study of Greene's films *Travels in Greeneland*, remarked: 'The film [*The Comedians*] had everything an MGM big budget could offer – star cast (including Richard Burton at $750,000 and Elizabeth Taylor at $500,000), exotic settings and lavish production values.'[5] The result was the weakest film that had had Greene's full co-operation, despite Peter Glenville's best efforts as producer and director. Perhaps if Carol Reed had directed, some of the old magic might have returned, but Greene's previous film, *Our Man in Havana*, had been directed by Reed and had failed to equal their earlier achievements. Greene never wrote another screenplay for one of his own novels.

The money from the film rights for *The Comedians* enabled Greene to buy the small two-roomed flat in Antibes, overlooking the harbour where Alexander Korda used to keep his boat, a happy introduction to the place which was to be his home for the rest of his life, until the frailty of old age, and a fall, brought him at last to Switzerland. He moved from Paris to the new flat a few months later.

Discussing his writing *May We Borrow your Husband?*, Greene made one of his most revelatory and poignant comments: 'Writing is a form of therapy; sometimes I wonder how all those who do not write, compose or paint can manage to escape the madness, the melancholia, the panic fear which is inherent in the human situation.'[6] He added that all the stories in the collection were written as 'an escape in humour from the thought of death – this time of certain death'.[7] The individual stories came from fragments of conversations he had overheard at nearby tables as he dined each night alone. With his talk of certain death the book seems like the work of a completely alienated and shell-shocked man. Greene talked about suicide often enough in his own life and his work, but had there been any real potential for self-destruction in him then those evenings eating alone as he grasped at echoes of the world around him would have tested him to the limit.

There were two serious elements in Greene's thought at this time which removed any possibility of despair, however much he might have been alienated by the thought of the catastrophe he had brought upon himself and the prospect of spending the rest of his life in exile. First, his Catholic life had acquired a fresh impetus through friendship with a Spanish priest, Father Leopoldo Durán, which began with an exchange of letters in 1964 over Greene's work, on which the priest was writing a thesis at King's College London. This friendship was to develop over the years until it replaced completely the Catholic circle and the priests that he had been obliged to leave behind in England. Secondly, in complete contrast, Greene had started another affair with a French woman called Yvonne Cloetta, who lived near Antibes. It was, once again, a repetition of the scenario created all those years before by Zoe, for Yvonne was married with a family. Happily for Greene, the pattern of these doomed relationships was broken on this occasion and the relationship was to last until his death in 1991.

The one aspect which his involuntary exile to Antibes had raised was the political one. The fact that Greene was now known to the Soviets to have been an agent for MI6 affected his public stance. Greene had objected strongly to the imprisonment of the Russian dissident writers Andrei Sinyavski and Yuli Daniel. Their crime was that they had published work in the West under pseudonyms and this had been discovered by the KGB. They were tried in February 1966 and sentenced to seven years' and five years' imprisonment respectively. Greene felt strongly the deep injustice of these sentences, and this was not just a projection of the anger he felt at what he saw as the sentence which had been meted out to him by the British authorities. He pursued the matter over the next few years, writing to the press and going to the lengths of refusing to accept royalties for translations of his books published in Russia. When he asked for these royalties to be sent to the families of the dissidents he received a very frosty refusal from Moscow, to which he responded by declining to allow his books to be published in Russia at all.

The Daniel and Sinyavski affair had more far-reaching consequences for Greene, for it led to a reopening of correspondence with Philby. Greene had written a letter to *The Times* on 4 September 1967 which began: 'This letter should more properly be addressed to *Pravda* and *Izvestia*, but their failure to publish protests by Soviet citizens at the time of the Daniel–Sinyavski trial makes it doubtful that mine would ever appear.'[8] It was in this letter that he raised the question of his royalties and the failure of the Russian authorities to respond to his request that they be assigned to the dissidents' families. However, the letter also contained some of the most notorious words Greene was ever to write:

> If I had to choose between life in the Soviet Union and life in the United States of America, I would certainly choose the Soviet Union, just as I would choose life in Cuba to life in those southern American republics, like Bolivia, dominated by their northern neighbour, or life in North Vietnam to life in South Vietnam.[9]

This letter caught the eye of Kim Philby, who decided to test the waters by writing to Greene what was in political terms an equally ambivalent letter:

> I saw in some recent correspondence in the *Times* that you have decided not to revisit the Soviet Union until certain conditions have been met. That is your very good right. May I join you in hoping that these

conditions will soon be met, not only because it was a just, proper and decorous thing to do but also because it might yield an unexpected bonus in the shape of those long very long lunches.[10]

This letter bore fruit the following year when Greene agreed to write an introduction to Philby's account of his days as a Soviet agent, *My Silent War*. But there was never any question of Greene defecting himself. When an academic, Professor D. W. Brogan, wrote in the *Spectator* of 15 September criticising Greene, Greene responded immediately:

I never asserted that if I had to leave Britain I would rather live in the Soviet Union than in the United States. I *have* left Britain and I am living in France.

Certainly Professor Brogan knows the United States far better than I do, but I would like to make a single one-upmanship claim [a reference to Stephen Potter]. *I* have been put under surveillance and deported from American territory ... Has Professor Brogan had that experience? To make the occasion even more memorable, they tried to deport me to Haiti, but I slipped into Havana instead.[11]

All Greene's difficulties are here, but it is obvious that he has carefully thought out his position and has decided that the South of France was the place for him.

Greene's preface for Philby's book must have deeply angered his old colleagues at MI6 although with one exception as we shall see. The *Times Literary Supplement* dismissed Greene's comments on Philby's book in slighting terms. The reviewer found Philby's savage personal attacks on old colleagues now safely dead offensive and then attacked Greene for defending them:

Mr. Graham Greene, who, as a wartime colleague, contributes an introduction, calls them [the personal attacks] 'admirable if unkind'; no doubt he finds them forgivable since he learnt that Philby is 'serving a cause and not himself', with which excuse he now says he forgives what he once found disagreeable in his old friend.[12]

The day after this review appeared, Greene met Trevor Wilson, his old MI6 friend, in Buenos Aires. Had Philby and his fellow KGB officers known this they might have drawn a different conclusion from Greene's apparent willingness to condone the stabbing of his old colleagues in the back by Philby.

A close reading of the introduction today shows that Greene had not been disingenuous, but was simply following the dangerous edge once again, along the borders between politics and religion. He compared Philby to Catholics working for the victory of King Philip of Spain in the days of Elizabeth. Like many Catholics who, he said, endured 'the long bad days of the inquisition'[13] for the sake of the future, so Philby had not been diverted from *his* faith by the cruelties of Stalin's reign of terror. It was flattery, but flattery on Catholic ground that left Greene's faith intact.

The introduction to Philby's book is brief, and includes some touching memories of Philby and his wartime team, including Greene, drinking in an old-fashioned pub behind London's St James's Street. But the article represented only a part of Greene's thought about Philby's situation. He had begun a novel about just such a character as Philby, but when Philby's book came out he felt he had to set his own aside, fearing that it would be thought of as simply a *roman-à-clef* based on his story. Writing his introduction to Philby's book was a decision he took knowing that it meant suspending work on his novel. Years later, in 1978, he took it up again and created *The Human Factor*, one of his most successful books.

Through all the chaotic events that filled Greene's life between 1965 and 1968, it is truly remarkable that while such matters as Philby's defection and the plight of Daniel and Sinyavski have been commented on exhaustively, Greene's own struggles and even the reason for his exile have remained completely unknown.

CHAPTER FOURTEEN

A New Life in Exile

The Daniel and Sinyavski affair had a remarkable sequel for Greene. His public stand and letters to *The Times* had caught the eye of a television director, Christopher Burstall. Burstall had directed a factual reconstruction of the dissidents' trial for television under the title *The First Freedom*, broadcast in 1967. He had been an admirer of Greene's for many years and wanted him to appear on television. Greene refused, giving complex reasons for not wanting to appear on screen:

> I'd be afraid of playing a part on screen. Playing the part of whom? I'm not quite sure, playing the part of a writer, the part of a Catholic. I don't know, but I think it would be a little bit of a part. I would cease to be a writer and I'd become a comedian. I feel myself infinitely corruptible. It's just possible that it might be successful and then I'd be tempted to do it again. Like a successful first night with a woman. I'd want to repeat it.[1]

The possibility of success and then repeating the experience was real – Malcolm Muggeridge fell into it and epitomised Greene's fears. But Burstall was persistent and got on well with Greene. Could Greene perhaps appear on the soundtrack alone, rather like a radio broadcast with pictures? Greene was interested, and then Burstall had the ingenious idea of inviting Greene to go with him to Istanbul as the setting for their conversation. He knew that Greene had done part of the journey before writing *Stamboul Train*. Greene accepted the proposal and the result was a remarkable piece of television broadcast in the Omnibus series in November 1968. The title of the programme, *The Hunted Man*, was taken from the opening shots which showed Greene flicking through his passport with his voice in the background:

'East Germany, Sierra Leone, Cuba, Jamaica, India – a liquor permit Dahomey – a whole mass of smudgy entry permits. Vietnam. The hunted man, the dangerous edge of things, psychologically and sometimes politically, these are the main obsessions of my books.'[2]

Burstall's interview with Greene during the slow journey to Istanbul was one of the most interesting he ever recorded; quotations have been used here already. But despite the depth of the questions in a confined environment over several days, Greene said almost nothing about why he was in exile, or of his own personal problems. The only exception was made in passing, and only he knew what it meant. Burstall had cited a remark of Greene's, that the Balkans had always been for him the area of infinite possibility. Instead of commenting on that, and they were after all on a train that was to go through the heart of this area, Greene replied: 'Well, Brighton has taken the place of the Balkans, I think. I've always had very strange incidents happening to me in Brighton . . .'[3] Perhaps realising that he had made a slip, he went on to talk of a man who had sat next to him in a shelter in Brighton and revealed that he was 'Old Moore', the writer of the almanack. But Burstall did not pursue the mysterious reference to Brighton. How far would Greene have gone? Had it not been for Brighton Roe would never have met Lorraine, his investment would not have gone up in smoke, and probably Roe's boat in Switzerland would have stayed afloat. Greene would still have been living in Albany, not on a train to Istanbul making a television programme.

Greene found the Orient Express a sad relic of its former glory. By 1968 it was a working train carrying, besides Burstall and his camera crew, myriads of ordinary people, with more than a sprinkling of the new breed of Western traveller, the hippy. This journey of Greene's and the way he incorporated it in his novel *Travels with my Aunt* was a defining moment in my own quest for Greene, for I realised that I had travelled on the same train a year before him, but in the other direction. I had had my own reasons for leaving Istanbul with relief at that time, and I was amused to notice in his diaries that Greene had also left the city within a day or two of his arrival and returned to Antibes.

To his reading public, unaware of what turmoil Greene was living through, his book of short stories *May We Borrow your Husband?*, with its provocative subtitle *Comedies of the Sexual Life*, came as a surprise. The short story which gave the collection its title was set in Antibes, one of those based directly on the chatter he had heard going on around him as he ate alone. There was some detachment from this depressing reality, apparently, for the narrator of the story was not Greene but a scholar, William Harris, who was engaged in writing a biography of the seventeenth-century rake and poet the Earl of Rochester. At one point in the story Harris is talking to the young woman on her honeymoon, staying at the same hotel, whose husband has been 'borrowed' for the day by two homosexual interior decorators. He describes some of the tragedy of Rochester's life and a bishop lurking by his death-bed to 'snatch his soul':

> 'How long ago did all this happen?' she asked.
>
> 'Nearly three hundred years.'
>
> 'It sounded quite contemporary. Only now it would be the man from the *Mirror* and not a bishop.'
>
> 'That's why I wanted to write it. I am not really interested in the past. I don't like costume pieces.'[4]

But Greene was playing a game with his readers, for this is once again him speaking, bravely declaring that he is not interested in the past – it may all have happened 300 years ago as far as he was concerned. His readers could not know that Greene had written a life of Rochester. Heinemann had rejected it thirty years before, but another publisher had recently come forward with an offer to publish it as an illustrated coffee-table book. Nor would they be any the wiser for a few years to come as *Lord Rochester's Monkey*, Wilson's – that is Greene's – book on Rochester did not appear until 1974.

Greene's description of his stories as having been written as 'an escape in humour from the thought of death – certain death'[5] can now be seen to have come at least in part from his plunging back into the world of Rochester and the seventeenth-century rakes. He saw that world being acted out around him by English visitors who crowded the coast in the summer months, living the life that seemed to characterise what became known as the Swinging Sixties.

As Greene's position stabilised with the income from film rights, ensuring first that he could buy his flat and then that he could live there without interruption and travel when and where he needed, he was able to look back over his entire life to assess what had happened. Critics have remarked that Greene's next novel, *Travels with my Aunt*, is filled with personal allusions, and have suggested that there was some self-indulgence in seeming to make so many jokes that only someone very close to his life would be able to understand. As Greene's biographer Norman Sherry has said, Greene thought his experiences could appear as fiction as long as the reality remained secret. The trouble which now developed was that the secrecy started to break down as the critics and even his supporters began to get closer to him. This was inevitable as he grew older; even Burstall had asked him during the train journey whether he was not speaking with his own voice in some of his novels.

Travels with my Aunt was far more complex than that. There were allusions, but there was also astringent satire directed at those who had caused his exile. If relatively few could see the satire he had the satisfaction of knowing that they were the people he was trying to reach and that in time others would come to understand what had happened. The central characters in the novel are the narrator Henry Pulling, a retired bank manager, whose character stems directly from the accountant in *Loser Takes All*; his aunt Augusta, who turns out to be really his elderly mother; and her lover, a black man from Sierra Leone. The hilarious character of the aunt, played in the film of the book by Maggie Smith, perhaps owes something to a doctor Greene knew in Capri whose memoirs he was to edit in 1975, giving them the appropriate title *An Impossible Woman*. But Aunt Augusta also embodies a perfect antithesis of all the staid attributes to be found in establishment Britain – the BBC, of which Greene's brother Hugh was Director-General, was known universally as 'Auntie'.

'Red means left,'[6] shouts Pulling's aunt as she tries to direct a taxi to her home above a pub before going on to the airport. Later when he asks her what she had in her cases – in fact a vast quantity of smuggled currency – she replies that only one of them is 'dangerous' as far as customs are concerned and she always uses a red one for that purpose. 'Red is for danger,'[7] she adds with a smile. Smuggling money was something that could worry a retired bank manager, but when Pulling finds out he comforts himself with the thought that 'smuggling on such a large scale seemed more like a business coup than a crime' – no doubt the very thoughts of Tom Roe as he ferried hundreds of thousands of smuggled dollars around Europe.

As the book develops it is apparent that the entire plot turns on the work of a master currency forger:

> The man who did that forgery was a genius. He was quite illiterate. A peasant on the prince's estate, but with a wonderful hand and eye. The prince never knew what a treasure he had living there until the police descended ... The prince could never understand how it was his people had become so prosperous ... in socialist circles he gained a high reputation as an enlightened employer ... [8]

It is remarkable how Greene's creative imagination had in a few years recycled the events of 1965 that drove him into exile and created a story which was highly amusing in itself, even when only a handful of people would have realised the part which forged and smuggled currency had recently played in his life. Even the Bank of England, which controlled currency export, was lampooned in the book. On their first travels abroad, to Istanbul, Pulling and his aunt are being interrogated by a very forceful police chief, Colonel Hakim, about illegal investments – this time a gold bar his aunt has smuggled into Turkey. She responds to his interrogation sharply:

'Surely you are not working for the Bank of England, Colonel?'

'I am not so fortunate ...' the Colonel replies, before returning to the chase. [9]

Some of the most bitter satirical attacks in the book are directed against the CIA, which is neatly introduced through a girl Pulling meets on the train going to Istanbul, an American hippy called Tooley. She announced blandly that her father works for the CIA and, in a coincidence which is worthy of some of the coincidences in Greene's second novel *The Name of Action*, he also happens to be the CIA's man in Paraguay, which is the destination of Aunt Augusta's final journey. Greene's lampoon of CIA agent Tooley's actions in the field is every bit as pointed as his send-up of the old MI6 in *Our Man in Havana*. Where Wormald sends reports from fictitious agents and invents drawings based on the vacuum cleaners he sells for a living,

Tooley senior philosophises at length to Pulling on the amount of time spent in a year at the urinal. He presents him with a column of figures giving the time spent each day in this way and adds it up to give a figure for the year. Agent Tooley intends forwarding his figures to the CIA medical specialists in case it is of some assistance to them.

The point of the satire is heightened when it becomes obvious that Tooley had been in Vietnam before coming to South America. And, whatever he was doing in Vietnam, in Paraguay he is liaising with the director General Stroessner and his extreme right-wing authoritarian regime.

There are many other personal references in *Travels with my Aunt*, some of which Greene was later to identify. He named the English detective who pursues Wordsworth, Aunt Augusta's black lover, after John Sparrow, Warden of All Souls, Oxford, although when he revealed this in 1980 in *Ways of Escape* he simply said that this was a private joke which no reader would understand. Here I found once again that I had crossed Greene's path, for a publisher of mine had once considered publishing in England a book of Sparrow's in which he was described as a 'literary detective'. The book, published in 1967 in America, was his study of the findings of the official examination of Senator Warren's report *After the Assassination: A Positive Appraisal of the Warren Report*, when the jacket notes on Sparrow carried the 'literary detective' accolade. It was thought an amusing description and Greene's use of it probably reflects his feelings about Sparrow writing favourably on American themes. It was indeed a private joke, of the kind appreciated in Oxford common rooms.

The structure of *Travels with my Aunt* is an unusually simple one for Greene, with only two parts. The second, much smaller than the first, seems to be an afterthought. It is set in Paraguay and is important, not simply for the book, but because it is the first indication of a continuing preoccupation with the continent that Greene carried on into his eighties. To the growing amazement of his friends and those who followed his adventures he continued travelling on an ever wider scale, covering tens of thousands of miles a year. He would respond to the prompting of a story or sometimes to others' suggestions, for example when out of the blue the ruler of Panama,

General Omar Torrijos, sent him a first-class return ticket to Panama with the request that he join him as his guest.

Like so many other things Greene leaves the origins of his interest in Paraguay unexplained, but there is a clue in his novel. Greene describes the veterans on parade for the National Day in Paraguay, saying that they had fought in the Chaco Wars in the 1930s and still had pride in those days. The Chaco Wars had been completely forgotten when *Travels with my Aunt* appeared in 1969, but Greene remembered them from his days sitting in the Middlesex Guildhall listening to the evidence being given at the Royal Commission on Armaments that inspired *A Gun for Sale*. In his autobiography Greene makes a further allusion to this forgotten war, saying that he had somehow become unwelcome on his visit to Paraguay before writing *Travels with my Aunt*, and adding that the transport he had arranged to take him to Chaco did not materialise. The Chaco Wars had been fomented by British armaments manufacturers. Now, thirty years later, he found the country with an extreme right-wing government protected by the United States and the CIA and notorious for sheltering fugitive Nazi war criminals.

Greene, as an author, was extremely clever at concentrating a wide range of themes and observations into his novels, but the appearance of Nazi war criminals might seem almost a random association of ideas about Paraguay rather than something he might have come across in reality. Nothing could be further from the truth. In 1967 he had visited Israel for the first time and had been caught up in some of the fighting in the aftermath of the Six Day War. He found himself trapped in some sand-dunes for over four hours as shells burst around him. The force of the experience can be gauged by his imaginative response – he recalled times of panic fear in his life. The first was when the police charged the crowd at one of Mosley's British Union of Fascists demonstrations in the East End of London before the war. Then he remembered the same feeling when he was lost in ground between Vietminh troops and French patrols outside Phat Diem during the Indo-China War. He shrugged off the Israeli incident which prompted these memories, but his description shows he was deeply affected:

After every explosion we looked back – they were still overshooting, and at every sound in the air we flattened into the sand. I took silly precautions like taking off my sun glasses in case they broke into my eyes. I remember the blitz, but the blitz had one great advantage – the pubs remained open.[10]

It is plain from Greene's account of his visit to Israel that he was very sympathetic to the Israeli cause. He knew that the Israelis had agents looking for war criminals, describing them in an article he wrote for the *Daily Telegraph*, 'The Worm Inside the Lotus Blossom', which appeared in January 1969. They got no help from anyone because no one wanted to stir up trouble. But did Greene himself get involved in the search for Martin Bormann, for example, whose son he had heard of in the Congo, where he was a missionary priest? Greene had been great friends with Korda and unquestionably knew of his espionage work. It is certainly possible, and the very idea that he might have been acting for any Israeli intelligence organisation, taken with his friendship with Korda, and the sympathy expressed on his visit, shows the final absurdity of Shelden's charge of anti-semitism.

If this was the background to even part of Greene's activity in Paraguay it is not surprising he became unwelcome. It was time to leave the country. His stay had been so memorable for the authorities there that ten years later in 1977 Greene was shunned by Stroessner and his staff when he met them in Washington at a reception for the signing of the Panama Canal Treaty.

There is one final area where, as might be expected, Greene took an unusual line, that of the role of the Church. He described in his *Telegraph* article how the Jesuits had protected the native population from the Spaniards in the seventeenth century, and attributed the survival of the native language Guarini to them. He spoke of what they did in anachronistically political terms: 'In Paraguay there have always been dictators, civilian, military, ecclesiastical, the cruel and the kind. In the seventeenth century there was the benevolent communist rule of the Jesuit missions who protected the Indians from the Spaniards ...[11] And he later ties this in with communism in its correct chronological context by referring to Father Camillo Torres, who was with the guerrillas in Colombia and was later killed, calling him 'the Catholic equivalent of Che Guevara'.

We are back here in uniquely Greene territory the world of underground struggle against the state by Catholics who might be priests or who might not even believe in God but fight on the right side. It was a world he first saw in those early days in Ireland and the Palatinate and looked for ever after: the humane face of communism. He sought the ideal of religious care and charity found in the middle ages and rediscovered in the life of Damien and, perhaps, in the Fathers struggling in the jungle with the peasants whose souls were in their care.

Travels with my Aunt does not have this overtly Catholic element, found in his reportage for the *Telegraph*. Instead Greene reverts to the Victorian world of Palgrave's *Golden Treasury*, ending with the triumphant quotation from Browning:

> God's in his heaven –
> All's right with the world![12]

To Greene's family this might have suggested that he had at last decided to settle down. If you had to find a quotation from Browning that was an antidote to 'the dangerous edge of things', this was it. Greene said that he thought he was writing in the last decade of his life, as he put it, and that he had written *Travels with my Aunt* purely for the fun of it. He had never done this before, he said, and perhaps too he hoped that the cycle of depression and elation which had started forty years before was over. He began the kind of work which an author with a lifetime's writing behind him is usually encouraged to do, collections of his essays, of his film criticism, and even a first volume of autobiography, *A Sort of Life*.

Greene said that he was encouraged to write *A Sort of Life* by a new Catholic psychiatrist he used briefly after one last recurrent bout of depression. But in his archive in Boston there is a letter from one of his old literary contacts, Cecil Roberts, telling him that he should not delay in writing an autobiography if he was ever going to do it, or he would find, as Roberts had done, that his memory was not up to the task. Wherever the idea came from, it was to have quite the reverse effect from that intended. From the happiness of Browning's

'All's right with the world' Greene swung around to his old driving enthusiasms and was off on his travels again. When he published an account of his travels to Chile in the *Observer* on 2 January 1972 it actually appeared under his other favourite quotation from the poet: 'Chile: The Dangerous Edge'.

An insight into the real problem he was having after the finishing of *Travels with my Aunt* as opposed to the psychiatric metaphysical description of it can be found in the extraordinary speech he gave when receiving the Shakespeare Prize at the University of Hamburg in June 1969. Entitled 'The Virtue of Disloyalty' his speech approached Shakespeare through the same theme of religious struggle that had appeared in his preface to Philby's book to defend his disloyalty. Philby was a spy of the worst kind, he had caused innumerable deaths of men whom he either knew or who were fighting in causes that he pretended to believe in. How could anyone find merit in such disloyalty? Greene had been a friend of Philby's during the war and everyone knew E. M. Forster's dictum that, faced with the choice of betraying his country or his friend, he hoped he would have the courage to betray his country. But surely Greene was going so far the other way that it might be better for him to make his exile from Britain absolutely permanent by going the final mile and joining Philby in Moscow – or so a very large body of critics said.

Greene's attack on Shakespeare came from an entirely unexpected angle. It was a renewal of the high-level literary assault on traditional English values which Evelyn Waugh had launched in his biography *Edmund Campion*. Greene focuses on the martyr poet Southwell, having quoted Shakespeare's praise of England – 'This blessed plot . . .':

> These complacent lines were published in 1597. Two years before, Shakespeare's fellow poet Southwell had died on the scaffold after three years of torture. If only Shakespeare had shared his disloyalty, we could have loved him better as a man.[13]

He then drew an adroit parallel between Southwell and the German pastor Dietrich Bonhoeffer in Nazi Germany, who, he said, had chosen to be executed just as Southwell had done. Both men Greene preferred to Shakespeare, seeing in them an example to all authors, who had a duty to make the work of the state more difficult. Greene was careful not to appear partisan. He listed Soviet writers who had suffered persecution as well as those in the West – he did not name himself but obviously he was sure he fell into this category – including even the Paraguayan writer Roa Bastos. He had first discovered Bastos in his search for the roots of his own view of the world, of capitalist colonial wars in South America, and already he had incorporated him into his own personal mythology.

The speech was a brilliant summing up of his own position as he had conceived it in adult life after university, through the influence of Jarrett and the Mathew brothers, and of course Waugh himself. But it left out his own personal loyalties that began as a young boy with his reading of Stevenson, and the personal experiences which formed him. Greene saw the role of the state in psychological terms, its interest, he said in his speech, being 'to poison the psychological wells ... it makes government easier when the people shout Galilean, Papist, Fascist, Communist'. And the defect of this 'psychoanalytic' view is seen immediately when he says that it is the writer's vocation to be a Protestant in a Catholic society, and vice versa. This is a direct contradiction of his own beliefs, and the beliefs which made him look at Southwell's life in the first place. Greene would not have been disloyal to Southwell, and he ends his lecture, having said that Shakespeare was the greatest of all poets, by decrying him for exchanging beliefs and virtue for a coat of arms, a large house and the backing of the state.

A Sort of Life was published in 1971 and gave the public its first real insight into the world that had created Greene. It is obvious to us now that it represented only the beginning of a process of self-analysis, a process which he never really finished. The passing reference to J. D. Beresford's *Revolution* and the influence it had on him at the time was no more than that, a passing reference. Had his mind not been clouded by the metaphysics of the psychoanalyst's couch he might perhaps have re-read the book and looked at the way his literary life had developed since those days. For his public it would have been an invaluable exercise, but perhaps he felt that the task was too great. Even a literary critic who set out to examine the situation of a forgotten author such as Beresford would have had a difficult task; for Greene it would have meant changing course entirely and becoming an academic writer. In fact he was a novelist living in the present, proceeding along a path which, he hints, had been found by Beresford.

The private world which Greene protected so carefully, and the private lives of those close to him meant so much to him that he could go no further in describing his personal life with any honesty later than his mid-twenties. Even then what could he say about Zoe Richmond, who was still alive and very much of sound mind, still with her beliefs in spiritualism, which she held until she died?

Perhaps the closest Greene gets to a clear understanding of his position as it was determined in those early days is in his account of his father's enthusiasm for Browning. He revealed that he still had the copy of Browning's poems that his father gave him at his confirmation. He quotes the lines from 'Bishop Blougram's Apology' which he wanted to stand as an epigraph for all his novels, 'The Dangerous Edge of Things', but then describes the world he found in Browning as a boy which would have shocked his father:

> With Robert Browning I lived in a region of adulteries, of assignations at dark street corners, of lascivious priests and hasty dagger thrusts, and of sexual passion far more heady than romantic love. Did my father, under that potent spell, not even notice the meaning of the lines he read us?[14]

Whatever effect writing *A Sort of Life*, and its publication, may have had soon evaporated. 'Chile: The Dangerous Edge', his *Observer* article, plunged him back into the present in the most graphic manner imaginable. Read in *Reflections*, the invaluable collection of his writings published in 1990 shortly before he died, the essay is forcefully argued. Seen in the *Observer* it is as pungent and powerful a piece of political writing as anything he ever wrote. The cover for the issue devoted to Greene's analysis of affairs in Chile showed a photograph of that country's leader at the microphone addressing a rally, with the caption: 'Marxist President Allende rallies his supporters'. And Greene was obviously one of them.

The origin of Greene's interest in South America appears again, for those who knew of it. He refers directly to the Chaco Wars, though without naming them directly, when discussing whether Allende should fear a war of revenge financed by the CIA and America's allies on the continent:

> the possibility can never be quite discounted. British industrialists, for the sake of the copper and the nitrate, fabricated that costly and terrible war in the desert, where men fought and died for water-holes ... Is it impossible that another imperial Power might follow the British example, tempted by the greatest copper mine in the world, the former Anaconda mine, in full production?[15]

Since he does not identify which desert he was referring to, readers without the historical background Greene possessed might for a moment wonder whether he was talking of the desert war Greene had recently experienced in Israel. Those who knew would feel the vicious attack against American business aims and the military–industrial complex.

The core of the article is a sustained attack on the United States, with gloating over its defeat in Vietnam and a detailed analysis of the CIA activity in South America. Greene's old colleagues in MI6 must have sighed with relief that he was no longer with them, even as a conscious source acting independently. Had the article appeared a decade or more before, they would have been acutely anxious that the CIA might think Greene was acting as a covert agent for Britain in the oldest colonial war in Latin America. As it was, Greene had gone, was labelled 'Red' and was obviously attacking Britain's past as much as America's.

Greene's view of the situation in Chile of course took in the Catholic Church. Even in this short article he is careful to deny the usual stereotypical view of the Church which still dominated thinking in academic left-wing circles in Britain and America, going back to the days of the Spanish Civil War. He describes with great amusement the National Day held in Chile on 18 September at which the highlight of the celebrations was an ecumenical 'Te Deum' attended by Allende and representatives of all the communist states. Even China was present, he commented, implying perhaps a celebration of the victory in Vietnam.

The role of the Catholic Church was so strong in Chile that Greene focused on a dispute between the Church and the Government over whether the television channel run by the Catholic University in Santiago could transmit all over the country. This should not be seen as a real dispute between Church and state, of the kind seen in Poland: 'The Catholic Church in Chile is progressive. Eighty priests, nearly all of whom are working in the slums, have signed a declaration in support of socialism ...'[16] As Greene approached his seventies he had discovered liberation theology at work on the ground. It was the fulfilment of all he had originally hoped for in the Church and he was to espouse the cause vigorously, to the wry embarrassment of Father Durán, who was his constant companion and disputant over these years.

CHAPTER FIFTEEN

Father Oscar Maturet and *The Honorary Consul*

In 1980 in his volume of autobiography called *Ways of Escape* Greene said that he preferred his novel *The Honorary Consul*, published in 1973 when he was sixty-nine, to all his others. He described how he had come upon the setting for the book, the small town of Corrientes in Argentina on the border with Paraguay, almost by chance. He passed it in a boat on his way somewhere else and found himself drawn back, as an old local saying said always happened. He talked also of an incident involving a Third World movement priest but without naming him – perhaps it was too much of a risk writing so soon after the events.

As always when Greene spoke in vague terms as if there was not much at stake, this is a sure sign that anyone on the quest for Greene will find something worthwhile with a little digging and panning. The Greene files in Texas soon provided answers to many questions Greene left open in his cryptic comments in 1980. A good starting point was a cutting he kept, sent to him by Durrants press-clipping agency. Since 1880 Durrants has been a byword for tracing obscure references in the world's press, often ignored by conventional historians. Greene subscribed to its service for that reason; the clipping it provided about Corrientes was from the *Irish Times* for 6 April 1970, when Greene had just started writing *The Honorary Consul*.

Under the headline 'Rebel Priests' Work Praised by Novelist', the paper gave a graphic account of the Third World movement of young Catholic priests and quoted Greene in Corrientes as praising the good work they were doing. The local Archbishop, the Most Reverend Dr Vincentii, had excommunicated one of the most active Third World priests, Father Oscar Maturet. Four churches had been closed as a result of police action taken when their congregations refused to go to churches where replacements for the Third World priests had been installed by the Archbishop. The seriousness of these developments was emphasised by the report that the Archbishop had taken the extreme step of approaching the local army commanders of the Seventh Infantry Brigade, who had given him their backing.

Greene mentions these events in passing, and plays them down as something which just happened to occur on his second day in Corrientes. The origin of the book, he claimed, was in the cave of his subconscious – a dream that developed to involve the two leading characters: a doctor with an English father and Paraguayan mother, Doctor Plarr, and the Honorary Consul himself, Charley Fortnum, whose physical appearance Greene modelled on the author Ford Madox Ford. But the leading character in the book is a Third World priest called Father León Rivas. The inspiration for him, and the main theme of the book, came from Greene's close involvement with the struggle of these young priests against the right-wing dictatorships in Paraguay and elsewhere in South America.

Father Rivas is a late twentieth-century development of the whisky priest Greene created in his novel set in Mexico, *The Power and the Glory*. But though he also has a wife and is therefore outlawed from the Church, Father Rivas has taken up a rifle and the revolutionary struggle rather than whisky. He has been given the task of kidnapping an American consul by the revolutionary leader called 'El Tigre', whom we never see. In a classic piece of bungling the revolutionaries kidnap the Honorary British Consul by mistake and the book follows his fate from the moment of his kidnap to the expiry of the deadline the kidnappers have set with the Argentinian authorities.

Father Rivas is the central focus of the book and Greene uses the novel as a platform from which to propagate the ideas of the third world movement for his readers in England and America. The character of Rivas is not of course based on Father Maturet directly in any way.

The conversations between Doctor Plarr and Father Rivas, with whom he went to school – a typical Greene detail – contains the best description of how Greene thought the Third World movement saw the Church. Plarr says:

'It's a long time since I listened to a priest. I thought you taught that the church was infallible like Christ.'

'Christ was a man,' Father Rivas said, 'even if some of us believe that he was a God as well. It was not the God the Romans killed, but a man. A carpenter from Nazareth. Some of the rules He laid down were only the rules of a good man. A man who lived in his own province, in his own particular day. He had no idea of the kind of world we would be living in now. Render unto Caesar, but when *our* Caesar uses napalm and fragmentation bombs ... The Church lives in time too. Only sometimes, for a short while, for some people – I am not one of them – I am not a man of vision – I think perhaps – but how can I explain to you when I believe so little myself? – I think sometimes the memory of that man that carpenter, can lift people out of the temporary Church of these terrible years, when the Archbishop sits down with the General, into the great Church beyond our time and place, and then ... those lucky ones ... they have no words to describe the beauty of our Church.'[1]

Later in their conversation, when Doctor Plarr has asked Father Rivas how God will view his killing of the hostage, the Honorary Consul, and how that squares with the belief that God is Love, Father Rivas replies:

'Was it love which sent six million Jews to the gas ovens? You are a doctor, you must have often seen intolerable pain – a child dying of meningitis. Is that love?...'
'I have never heard a priest blame God for things like that before.'[2]
'I don't blame Him. I pity Him,' Father Rivas said...

The question of God and medicine is defined more closely later when Father Rivas says that he believes in the old legend that God made us in His image, and that he therefore believes in His evil as well as His goodness. To persuade Doctor Plarr he draws a parallel from medicine:

Eduardo, you know well how many truths in medicine lay in old legends. It was not a modern laboratory that first discovered the use of snake's venom. And old women used the mould on overripe oranges long before penicillin. So I too believe in an old legend which is almost forgotten. He made us in His image...'[3]

The detail here about penicillin and overripe oranges is unexplained in the book and has not been noticed by any of Greene's critics. The explanation was simply that the mould on the oranges was penicillin and that this was known long before formal medicine realised what it was. However, the files in Texas once again provide an insight into what lay behind Greene's discussion of medicine here, his employment of obscure facts such as the function of orange mould, and beyond that his continual use of doctors and medicine in his books.

When Greene obtained proof copies of *The Honorary Consul* he sent one to his brother Dr Raymond Greene. It was Raymond who provided the medical detail about the mould on oranges for him, in a letter sent to him in November 1972, now in Texas. In it he comments on the medical matters in the book, such as the drug given to Charley Fortnum when he is kidnapped, and he also corrects the penicillin references, which Greene had got wrong. The earlier allusions to children suffering from meningitis, taken with the mention of penicillin, takes us back immediately to *The Third Man*, where children suffering from meningitis have their suffering multiplied by the adulterated penicillin supplied by the corrupt doctor Harry Lime. It is obvious that Greene's discussions with Raymond are at the heart of his interest in medical themes. Greene's obtaining introductions from Raymond before going to the leper hospital in the Congo have already pointed to this, but here is a rare direct link in one of the novels. The character of Doctor Plarr does have some hint of the private family background which Greene put into so many of his novels. His father was an Englishman who has been imprisoned in Paraguay for opposing Stroessner's regime. Plarr talks of his father's literary interests and describes him reading Stevenson and Conan Doyle, his favourite authors. He talks of him reading aloud: 'In his childhood his father had read him stories of heroism, of wounded men rescued under fire, of Captain Oates walking out into the snow ...'[4] And the idea that this origin in Greene's life is a far-fetched allusion, and a confusion of fact with fiction, is refuted in this case by Raymond's letter to Greene also lighting on this detail, and pointing out that Oates was not a doctor, as Greene had originally described him, but a captain, a correction Greene immediately made in his proof.

In one of his notebooks in which he developed his ideas for *The Honorary Consul* Greene at first suggested that what he called the 'I' character, Plarr, would be a political journalist; he decided instead to make him a doctor. The difficulty was that Greene found that he had to draw a sharp distinction between the work he was doing as a political journalist himself, and his other writing as a novelist. Making the 'I' character a political journalist would have presented him with many difficulties. But he did not reject the idea of having a character who was a writer, and to that extent an *alter ego* for himself. He chose to make him an Argentinian author, Jorge Julio Saavedra, or Doctor Saavedra as everyone calls him. He has many of Greene's habits, writing a careful 500 words a day, not a word more, not a word less – Greene's practice over a lifetime. But Greene goes on to use the character to explain the remarkable shift *The Honorary Consul* represents back to the ideas he had in Chipping Camden before the war; the rebel priest is even named after Trotsky. One of his followers during the kidnapping, a revolutionary poet Aquino Ribera, refers to Trotsky, to his belief in democracy within the party, and also more pointedly in the circumstances – he is talking to Fortnum – to what Trotsky said when shown his home in Mexico, that it reminded him of his first prison.

In a technical device which only his most devoted readers would follow, Greene refers directly to *It's a Battlefield*. Doctor Saavedra lives in a modern apartment block, alongside several others. Greene describes them as being like the block in a prison: 'One expected them to be lettered A, B and C and to be reserved for different categories of prisoner.'[5] This is precisely the description of prison blocks in *It's a Battlefield*, written in 1934. And Saavedra echoes Greene's own account of that book, when speaking of the novel he is intending to write next. 'For the first time,' he says, 'I am proposing to write a political novel.' Clearly it is Greene who has decided to write a political novel, and a further clue to the reason for his setting it on the Argentinian border with Paraguay can be found in the first sentence in the book: 'Doctor Eduardo Plarr stood in the small port on the Paraná, among the rails and yellow cranes, watching where a horizontal plume of smoke stretched over the Chaco.'[6] The Chaco and Britain's part in the Chaco Wars are the unspoken background to the whole book. Those days of direct British intervention are long gone; Britain has been replaced by America and there are allusions to the most brutal torture by agents of the CIA.

In another reference to his own viewpoint, expressed through the character of Doctor Saavedra, Greene develops a point which he first made in his introduction to Philby's book *My Silent War* and later elaborated in his defence of disloyalty:

> A poet – the true novelist must always be in his way a poet – a poet deals in absolutes. Shakespeare avoided the politics of his time, the minutiae of politics. He wasn't concerned with Philip of Spain, with pirates like Drake. He used the history of the past to express what I call the abstraction of politics. A novelist today who wants to represent tyranny should not describe the activities of General Stroessner in Paraguay – that is journalism not literature. Tiberius is a better example for a poet.[7]

Though Greene is here, of course, creating literature with a frontal attack on Stroessner.

There is one area where Greene's character Saavedra does not share his own views, and that is the detective story. He proclaims that he will never write one, comparing them to jigsaws. This seemingly bizarre intrusion in the book – if Saavedra is not interested in detective stories, why introduce them at all? – is explained by the most personal theme to be found in *The Honorary Consul*. While he was writing the book in Antibes, late in November 1971, he received a telephone call from his secretary in London. Dorothy Glover had died. He flew to England immediately and attended her funeral. His diary entry for that day, 30 November, said simply, 'D's funeral. The horror.'

This sad end to his long friendship, with all its memories of the Blitz and the struggle to survive, affected Greene deeply. This is surely the explanation for his discussion of the place of detective fiction in modern literature in *The Honorary Consul*. The discussion does not take place with Saavedra; he is dismissed as a literary author who is not even capable, when pressed to write a letter to try and save the Honorary Consul's life, of adding a few words to the letter without thinking about style. Instead Greene has the rebel priest defend the role of the detective story. Towards the end of the novel Father Rivas is found reading a book. It is not his breviary but a detective story – an English detective story. He explains after referring to the comfort he found in a story with a certain end:

> There were no detective stories in the age of faith – an interesting point when you think of it. God used to be the only detective when people believed in him. He was law. He was order. He was good. Like your Sherlock Holmes. It was he who pursued the wicked man for punishment and discovered all. But now people like the General make law and order. Electric shocks on the genitals. Aquino's fingers [cut off by CIA-funded agents in the novel]. Keep the poor ill-fed and they do not have the energy to revolt. I prefer the detective. I prefer God.[8]

Greene suggests that the detective story of the nineteenth century in England is a halfway house between the age of faith and the modern godless society where terror rules. He had first become aware of South American publication of Spanish translations of detective fiction and thrillers when he had his own books translated. *The Honorary Consul* is dedicated to his publisher in South America, Victoria Ocampo. The significant factor for any unorthodox Catholic author was that publication in Spanish in South America avoided Franco's censorship in Spain. This meant that there was always a political dimension to being published in South America, as long as censorship lasted in Spain itself. But in going one stage further and raising detective fiction to a theological plane he might even have startled Dorothy, who had shared his passion for twenty years.

The book ends with the faintest hint of the ending of a detective story. Doctor Plarr and the priest Father Rivas are both killed, while the Honorary Consul, Charley Fortnum, survives. After the funeral the British Ambassador sends a man to see Fortnum who mentions that Plarr had been shot by Father Rivas, who in turn had been shot by the police. Fortnum is indignant and immediately proves that this cannot have been the case from the evidence of his own senses. Doctor Plarr was shot by the soldiers, and Father Rivas had gone out to attend to him, as a priest would. He is shot in his turn.

Not only does Charley Fortnum survive, like Wormald in *Our Man in Havana* he is awarded an OBE on his retirement. For the rest of his active life Greene behaved as though he was a travelling Honorary Consul. However, at the time he created Fortnum he was still preoccupied with his own exile, as he saw it. There are frequent references in *The Honorary Consul* to exile and exiles. South America is called the continent of exiles, 'of Italians, of Poles, of Czechs, of Welsh, of English'. The possibility that Greene was thinking of joining these people is suggested not just by these references but by his writing such a book at all – is it the first English novel set in Argentina, and written on such themes? But the attractions of South America were counterbalanced by his happy life in Antibes, and by the continuing development of his friendship with the Spanish priest Father Durán, whom he was now seeing every year in long journeys around Spain visiting monasteries and discussing theological matters which still interested him.

For a decade after the publication of *The Honorary Consul* Greene pursued South American affairs, chiefly in Panama. He became very close to the head of state General Omar Torrijos, and when he was killed in a plane crash Greene decided to write of their friendship in his book *Getting to Know the General*, published in 1984. As this book follows directly from the interests first made known through his adventure on the Argentinian/Paraguay border it is discussed here rather than in the final chapter dealing with the last decade of Greene's life. The geographical separation of the old world and the new automatically creates a divide between different parts of his life which overrides the natural chronology to a great extent. Greene made four visits to Panama, just as in his earlier life he had made four annual visits to Indo-China – a coincidence of course, like two cars side by side with the same number. The first was in 1976, and he was packing his bag for his fifth and final visit when he heard that Torrijos had been killed. He decided to write his book then and there, as death so often decided him. He had given the longest interview in his life to Marie-Françoise Allain, the daughter of an old friend after he had been killed in equally mysterious circumstances.

Greene never explains how it came about that Torrijos sent him a first-class return ticket to Panama with an open invitation to stay as his guest. There are few clues, apart from Greene's reputation as an author who had written a book set in South America which dealt with the highly unusual subject, for an Englishman, of the Third World priests. It was known also that he was sympathetic to the left and had visited Castro. One possible explanation stems from the links between Israel and Panama. In his first visit in 1976 Greene records a singular conversation with Torrijos, about his wife, who was the daughter of a Jewish businessman living in New York. He had been married for twenty-five years but on the day of his marriage his father-in-law had sworn never to speak to his daughter again. This had been the cause of increasing unhappiness, so Torrijos decided to take some action:

A few days ago I asked General Dayan to intercede for me in New York. My father-in-law wouldn't even listen to Dayan. Panama had voted at the United Nations in support of Israel over the Entebbe affair. We were the only state in Latin America to do so, and afterwards the Israelis were grateful and they offered me all sorts of help. I told them that I had asked Dayan for only one thing I needed and he couldn't help me. Then suddenly, yesterday, my father-in-law telephoned from New York and asked to speak to my wife.[9]

The links between Israel and Panama were not well understood at the time, but according to a very old friend of Greene's he was aware of them and had discussed Panama with contacts in Israel after he had expressed his interest in Nazi war criminals who might be hiding in South America. These connections of Greene's are amongst the most obscure in his life and go back to the early days with Alexander Korda and his espionage activities. They will almost certainly never be revealed, but they form part of the link Greene had with Panama – it is very unlikely that Torrijos would have spoken to Greene about such questions in detail unless he had known that Greene was capable of appreciating them.

After recounting this conversation Greene made a remark about Torrijos which went a long way towards explaining the attraction he felt for the man saying that 'he was a man who had a deep loyalty to the past and was faithful above all to friendship though he was not the type of man to be faithful to one woman.[10]'

And this was very close to Greene's own system of ethics on personal questions, when he was a younger man. On other matters *Getting to Know the General* revealed to a shocked general public in England that Greene was not merely an armchair socialist when it came to the struggles in Nicaragua against the Somoza regime. He describes sitting in his flat in Antibes when he received a visit from someone raising money to buy anti-aircraft guns for the Sandinista guerrillas:

> He gave me the name and number of an account in Panama City in case I knew of any rich sympathisers. There was no problem he said about small arms. They could capture enough of these from Somoza's National Guard. It was anti-aircraft guns which were needed. Alas! I was of little use to them. I could only send off a small cheque of my own to Panama in the hope that it would buy a few bullets, one of which might put paid to Somoza.[11]

To those versed in espionage, this passage arouses uneasy feelings. Greene must have been trusted greatly to have been given this information about a very sensitive bank account in Panama. Sending a small cheque into an account is a classic way first of verifying that the account is real, and then of finding out how it clears its funds – for Greene's cheque would eventually be presented to his bank for payment. Greene would be able to have his bank trace the cheque back to find where it was paid in. It was a technique used to trace laundered money and terrorist accounts.

The question raised is a blunt one: was Greene once again working for MI6 or any other organisation? There is a pointer elsewhere in the book, when he comments on American annoyance at his public support of the Sandinistas and other rebel groups in Latin America:

> There were many in the United States, I was sure, who would consider that I was being 'used', but that thought didn't worry me in the least.

They could say that I had been 'used' too in Cuba in 1958 when I had carried warm clothes to Santiago for Castro's men in the Sierra Mastra, and, through an Irish MP, a friend of mine, I had been able to question the Conservative Government in the House of Commons on the sale of old jet planes to Batista, but I regretted nothing then and I regretted nothing now. I have never hesitated to be 'used' in a cause I believed in, even if my choice might be only for a lesser evil. We can never foresee the future with any accuracy.[12]

The sentiments seem clear. But all is not quite what it appears to be. The Irish Member of Parliament who placed questions in Parliament has already been identified here as Hugh Delargy. However, while this book was being written it was realised from the Cabinet Office briefing that Greene had mentioned Delargy in one of his letters to Poland in the 1950s. It was logical for Greene to have thought that Delargy's contacts behind the Iron Curtain were known from that moment on. In 'planting' these questions in the House of Commons through Delargy, was Greene simply establishing his *bona fides* as an active sympathiser with the Castro regime disguising his links with MI6? If this were the case, Greene's apologia to those in the United States who thought he was being 'used' was in reality directing them to other examples which they would have realised proved exactly the reverse of what they seemed to be proving. Greene was speaking up for the Sandinistas because that was what he believed; but at the same time he was happy to feed this information back to his contacts, whoever they might be. He was being both spy and political activist and on this dangerous edge only he knew, finally, what the truth was.

The highlight of Greene's connection with Torrijos was his appointment to the delegation to Washington at the time of the signing of the Panama Treaty in 1977. He travelled on a Panamanian passport and was greatly amused at the reception after the ceremony when the Paraguayan delegation was obliged to cut him on realising who they were talking to.

Some American critics have gone a stage further in attacking Greene and his role in Panama, saying that he was a close friend of its ruler General Noriega and that he was fully aware of the drug dealing the General was later imprisoned for after the United States was obliged to invade Panama. The point was made forcibly to me in a telephone call from America which came out of the blue from an author who had seen details of my research on a global information service. In fact Greene was profoundly suspicious of Torrijos' death and felt that Noriega may have known something of how it happened. After *Getting to Know the General* was published Greene, as so often, was in two minds about it. He wrote to his old friend Tom Burns in February 1985: remarking that he was in two minds about *Getting to Know the General*. He could see its faults and was not overly enamoured of it.[13] Greene had earlier spoken warmly to Burns of Torrijos at the time of his death. He was glad of Burn's sympathy and was not shy of saying, at over eighty, that he would miss him the most of his many friends. Though Panama was a small country Torrijos he thought a great man, but unspoilt by his position as its ruler. Greene was often thought a dour person, lacking in humour, yet he valued Torrijos for his laughter, and the laughter they shared.[14] But Greene's book was surely not so bad, for it conveyed in great detail exactly those sympathies.

Greene's involvement in political action in Panama did not lessen his interest in religious questions. He continued to take the closest interest in the real-life equivalents to Father Rivas in his novel *The Honorary Consul*, even if they did not go as far as taking up arms and kidnapping politicians. In 1983 he visited Nicaragua and recorded his being welcomed when he got off the plane at Managua airport by Father Cardenal, the Minister of Culture; but it was in his later tour around the country that the roots of his loyalty are to be found:

I drove on to a town renamed Ciudad Sandino to visit two American nuns who belonged, like Father D'Escoto [the Foreign Minister in the government], to the Mary Knoll order. The town consisted of about 60,000 very poor inhabitants. The nuns lived in the same conditions as the poor – a tin-roofed hut and a standing pipe for water in the yard. One of the two, quite a young woman, particularly impressed me. She had lived for ten years in the town so that she had experienced the dictatorship of Somoza and the whole civil war.[15]

231

Greene went on to report that the medical conditions had improved since the days of Somoza, that the single doctor of those days had been replaced by three clinics and that the children's health had improved immeasurably. Immediately we recall the image of nuns caring for sick children in the film of *The Third Man*.

CHAPTER SIXTEEN

Ieuan Thomas and *The Human Factor*

The Honorary Consul was a novel about exiles set in a continent of exiles. Hovering over Greene's next novel was the fate of the most notorious example of self-imposed exile from Britain, Kim Philby, still living in Moscow. Greene had started his book shortly after Philby defected in 1963 and had finally abandoned it, as we have seen, after writing a preface for Philby's own book *My Silent War*. But still he described the book as hanging like 'a dead albatross around my neck', with his imagination as dead as the bird, blocking all work. Writing *The Honorary Consul* had removed the block, which was surely caused by Greene's own exile as a result of the Roe débâcle. He was now able to give the book a title, *The Human Factor*, and overcome the earlier obstacles to finishing it, paramount amongst them the impossibility of writing anything about MI6, his original idea, which would not seem like a *roman-à-clef* based on Philby's case.

When *The Honorary Consul* was published in 1973 Philby's defection was already old news, but this did not lessen the interest of MI6 in what he was doing. It has even been suggested that Philby was still acting for MI6 and that his defection had been a ruse. This was not true, but it must have been extremely uncomfortable for the government, let alone the hierarchy at MI6, to know that Philby was where he was. At the most basic level he represented a political reality – many in England who were sympathetic to the Soviet cause regarded him as the ultimate hero, who had sacrificed his career for his beliefs. If anyone was to get in touch with him Greene might seem the most likely candidate. He eventually succeeded, though it was to be a long road. The writing of *The Human Factor* was a stage along the way. It enabled general discussion about the reality of the position of a double agent whose conduct might seem to have nothing to be said for it at all.

Greene's last trip to Moscow, and his only visit after Philby's defection, before his extensive visits in the 1980s, was in 1971. Greene made no mention of meeting Philby then, but he did establish a completely neutral contact through an unlikely channel in 1974. The contact was very much at arm's length. Greene had appointed his official biographer Professor Norman Sherry and it was he who wrote to Philby asking him for any memories he had of Greene during the war when they had worked together in MI6. Sherry received his first reply on 9 April 1974. There was no political or espionage context; it was almost, to someone reading the extracts Sherry published in the first volume of his biography, as if Greene were already dead.

The last letter cited by Professor Sherry was received on 8 April 1978, by which time *The Human Factor* was finished and Greene had sent Philby an advance proof asking him for comments. Philby's letter suggested alterations in a few trivial areas, and Greene mentioned this provocatively in his autobiography – for it revealed that he was in touch with Philby. But the message to Philby could not have been clearer: we have entered the endgame, all these events are in the past, material for biographers and memoirs and well on the way to becoming history. As will be seen in the last chapter it was not long after this that Philby wrote independently to Greene setting the stage for the final act.

There was another problem with writing the book in the late 1960s. Few books existed about MI6. It was assumed that there was a lifelong duty of confidentiality, and when people rumoured to have had a connection with MI6 such as John Le Carré wrote espionage thrillers there was no possible political motive, nor any possibility of deliberate betrayal of secrets. The secrets of the service were still very much secrets; the Blunt affair – the discovery of his guilt and its suppression by MI5 – was still unknown. The mania for spy books culminating in *Spycatcher* by Peter Wright – an MI5 man – was some way in the future. Even the discoveries of Harry Chapman Pincher concerning the great mole-hunt within MI5 when Sir Roger Hollis was thought to have been a Soviet spy were inconceivable in the late 1960s. One book had appeared giving an insider's idea of MI6 life, *British Agent*, published in 1966 by 'John Whitwell', pseudonym of Leslie Nicholson, who had worked with Greene, Muggeridge and Philby. Significantly the introduction to this book was written by Malcolm Muggeridge, whom Greene was to lampoon without mercy in *The Human Factor*. In the early days of exile Greene had been visited by Muggeridge, as we have seen, shortly before *British Agent* was published. Whether they discussed the book is not known. Certainly over the next few years Greene developed a very low opinion of Muggeridge. His own position in MI6 was defined precisely by Muggeridge: 'It is interesting that Greene was also in Whitwell's *apparat*, both of us being equipped with one-time pads, secret ink, ball-pointed pen and other espionage props, and posted to Africa, he to Freetown and I to Lourençço Marques.'[1]

By the time Greene came to write *The Human Factor*, the heat created by Whitwell's book and by the defection of Philby had died down. There was talk of banning *The Human Factor*, just as there had been talk of stopping *Our Man in Havana*, but it came to nothing. Instead there was quite good evidence that Greene had mended his bridges with MI6, for those who knew where to look. Greene's choice of Maurice for the Christian name of the double agent in MI6 was a little too obvious as a joke at the expense of the then head of MI6 Maurice Oldfield.

The decision to set Castle's early career as a field agent in South Africa might have seemed an obvious development from Greene's and Muggeridge's wartime experiences, moved slightly to give the post some contemporary reference, but Greene makes it clear in his autobiography that he wished to make a political statement, as he had against Papa Doc Duvalier in Haiti:

Perhaps the hypocrisy of our relations with South Africa nagged me on to work too. It was so obvious that, however much opposed the governments of the Western Alliance might pretend to be to apartheid, however much our leaders talked of its immorality, they simply could not let South Africa succumb to Black Power and Communism.[2]

But nowhere did Greene refer to his fellow member of the Communist Party all those years ago who had made his life in exile in

South Africa, Ieuan Thomas. While Thomas was at the forefront in the struggle against apartheid, nobody in South Africa knew of his communist past. Had they done so the government would have exposed it ruthlessly and the career he had built up over forty years might have been destroyed. Greene visited South Africa once, meeting several anti-apartheid leaders. There is reference in his files at Boston to an Afrikaaner friend of Greene's, the novelist Etienne Leroux, but no other indication of whether Leroux knew Thomas or whether Greene himself met Thomas on his visit. Greene sent Leroux an advance proof of *The Human Factor*, as he had to Philby. It is difficult now to recreate the fear that the Apartheid regime generated, especially in the form of BOSS, the South African government Bureau of State Security. Greene would have known that anyone who met him when he was writing the book would be in great danger after its publication. However, the knowledge we have of Thomas' existence in Greene's past and his role in the struggle gives us the broader framework of Greene's novel for the first time.

The Human Factor can now be seen as effectively two books. The first, the original 22,000 words of text, written in 1967, aches with an exile's nostalgia. Maurice Castle, an MI6 officer who has been working in the same office for thirty years, commutes daily from Berkhamsted. Greene describes the streets of the town, every detail pulled from his lifetime of memories of the place. Colonel Daintry, his chief at MI6, lives in a flat in St James's Street, exactly as Greene had done next door to Catherine Walston's flat, before the Walstons, with Greene following, went over to Albany. Even the cheese shop off St James's Street, still there, forms part of the topography of the novel, which seems to have been constructed to cover every aspect of what England meant to Greene. In his interview with Marie-Françoise Allain in 1979 Greene said that he did not feel an exile in any way; that was not the case when he began writing *The Human Factor*, even if his own exile did become by slow degrees more like the normal retirement to the South of France that improved travel and long years of peace were making possible.

Arthur Davis, Castle's assistant, the character based on Malcolm Muggeridge, is also developed in the first part of the book written in 1967. In the original text the portrait of Davis has some additional features that were suppressed in the published version; perhaps the idea of a character based on Muggeridge being a life member of the striptease club Raymond's Revuebar in London's Soho was thought a little too revealing; it would have been a shock to the majority of Muggeridge's followers, not to mention Muggeridge himself. Greene had not been able to resist putting pen-portraits in his books since the days of his attack on Priestley in *Stamboul Train*. The only sign of his growing years was that he edited out these references himself before the book went to press. It was enough that he and his editors had seen the lines.

The fate Greene reserved for Davis was harsh. Davis had long wanted to go to Lourenço Marques, and Castle manages to arrange that he should go there, just as Greene arranged the same posting for Muggeridge. However, the counter-espionage officer in MI6 has been alerted to a security leak. It is in fact Castle, but he manages to throw suspicion on Davis. It is decided that the best way out of the situation would be for Davis to be killed. MI6's doctor is called in and he soon finds a poison that will be impossible to detect in someone who drinks quite heavily – Davis is never happier than when drinking vintage port. The plan is successfully carried out and Davis dies from the poison aflatoxin. As before, the detail in his plot came from Greene's brother Raymond. Aflatoxin is derived from a mould on peanuts; unlike the mould on oranges this substance is lethal. Greene makes one uncomfortable addition to the idea that his brother proposed: when the MI6 doctor Percival comes to administer the drug, he mistakenly gives too much. Did Raymond, when he read this, remember Bede Jarrett's death before the war?

As Special Branch go through Davis' flat looking for any clues to his espionage activities they find a book of Browning's poems, a present to Davis from his father on his graduation day. The only sense that they can make of the poetry is as a possible key to some book-based code. Castle has to point out that the passages they have found marked with a small 'c' are love poems which Davis has marked as reminding him of the secretary in their office with whom he is in love. The initial 'c' stands for her christian name. Greene's affection for Browning was not confined to 'Bishop Blougram's Apology', and the contrast between the feelings in his poems, the sanity of the nineteenth century, and the world in 1978, when the poems are read without comprehension by men standing over the body of someone they have murdered, brilliantly illustrates this.

The idea that MI6 might actually murder someone in this way shocked even Philby, who wrote to Greene that he thought this was more the line of the CIA. In Greene's mind it was simply one stage along from leaving the Honorary Consul to die at the hands of his kidnappers without anyone troubling to do much about it. Although this was Greene's fiction, the development of similar feelings in his characters across several novels makes it clear that he did think such things were possible. Another example relates to the kind of society which uses napalm. Greene felt strongly about this and put a severe condemnation of it in the mouth of the revolutionary priest Father Rivas in *The Honorary Consul*. In *The Human Factor* Castle is visiting Halliday, a Soho bookseller who is his KGB contact. Castle is talking with Halliday about Tolstoy's *War and Peace*, a book that has been chosen as Castle's next book-code source. They are talking of Napoleon's retreat from Moscow, and Halliday says:

'It's a terrible story.'

'It seems a lot less terrible to us today, doesn't it? After all, the French were soldiers – and snow isn't as bad as napalm, you fall asleep, so they say – you don't burn alive.'

'Yes, when I think of all those poor children in Vietnam ... I wanted to join some of the marches they used to have here but my son would never let me. He's nervous of the police in that shop of his, though what harm he does with a naughty book or two I cannot see. As I always say – the men that buy them – well, you can't very well do much harm to them can you?'

'No, they are not clean young Americans doing their duty like the napalm bombers were,' Castle said. Sometimes he found it impossible not to show one splinter of the submerged iceberg life he led.[3]

The characters are different, in different novels, but Greene's feelings about napalm are clear.

The second part of the book, written in the mid-1970s, comes alive. The depressive nostalgia for England is replaced by an acute interest in the day-to-day politics in South Africa. Castle is married to an African woman who was one of his spies when he was an MI6 agent in the field. She had been in danger, but the selfless heroism of a freedom fighter called Carson saved her. Castle married her when they returned to England and they have a son. Castle's position has always been dangerous, but he is finally exposed in a complex and carefully worked out plot that is set in motion by the arrival in London of a BOSS agent with whom Castle has to co-operate in an MI6 briefing. Because the BOSS agent is away from home Castle invites him back to his house, knowing that he is the agent who tried to capture his wife.

The BOSS man, Cornelius Muller, is co-ordinating an operation with the code name Remus, which involves America and South Africa in some kind of joint nuclear exercise. Castle feels he has to get this information to Moscow, although he knows, with Davis dead, it will be obvious that he is the source of the leak. He decides to go ahead, accepting that it will mean he has to break cover and escape from the country. For once Greene has to devise a way of escape for one of his own characters – it was a phrase first used by Douglas Goldring as the title of his first book of travels, and one which Greene himself used often, finally choosing it for his second volume of autobiography. The details of the escape are worthy of anything in Buchan or Le Queux, and Castle gets away, but he is forced to leave his wife and child behind. The most poignant moment in the escape comes when Castle realises that he will have to shoot the family dog if it is not to raise the alarm.

A stark contrast to this act, which has been forced on him, is a scene where Castle talks to his wife about her escape:

> When people talk about Prague and Budapest and how you can't find a human face in Communism I stay silent. Because I have seen – once – the human face. I say to myself if it hadn't have been for Carson Sam [his son] would have been born in prison and probably have died in one. One kind of Communism – or Communist – saved you and Sam. I don't have any trust in Marx or Lenin, any more than I have in St. Paul, but haven't I the right to feel grateful?[4]

Castle's belief in the human face of communism is focused on the escape of his family, and that is the single factor that makes his escape from England to Moscow conceivable. But he is betrayed in his belief. He finds himself allocated a cheerless Moscow flat, with uncomfortable furniture; for friends, he has other defectors who have escaped in similar circumstances. He asks repeatedly when his family are going to join him and is put off. Finally he insists at least in being allowed to telephone them. When at last he talks to his wife it has become obvious that there are going to be difficulties in getting her out of England. They seem reasonable – their son's name does not appear on her passport, there would be difficulty at the borders because a black woman and her black son would stand out – but the truth was that the human face of communism which Castle had thought he had found in South Africa did not fit in Europe. What was possible in South Africa was impossible in Moscow. Castle's last conversation with his wife ends when the line goes and she is left speaking into a dead telephone.

This harrowing ending was a final answer to any thought that Philby or his masters in the KGB might have had that Greene could be persuaded to defect to Russia and join him. When Philby replied to Greene's letter, sent with the proof copy of *The Human Factor*, his one pertinent comment was that Greene's description of the kind of flat awaiting anyone who defected as cheerless and unwelcoming was wrong. When he arrived, Philby had been provided with everything, including a shoe-horn, which he had never possessed before. A shoe-horn seems a poor substitute for a human face. In choosing South Africa for his background Greene had picked on the one place in the world where he could agree that communism had a human face; and surely the face was that of Ieuan Thomas.

Some critics have suggested that the book showed too much sympathy for Philby, and that it caused annoyance in MI6 because of what it revealed and because of the severity of its implied criticism. In reality the idea that the novel was written without the knowledge of MI6 is naive. Although they were not as sophisticated as they later became in obtaining advance copies of texts likely to cause embarrassment, there was no problem with Greene's book. It is more than likely that he allowed MI6 a set of advance proofs – galley proofs indeed, before page proofs, since there are changes in these which suggest some informed editing. To take an early example in the novel, the published text reads:

> The fate of the world, Davis used to declare, would never be decided on their continent [Africa] however many embassies China or Russia might open from Addis Ababa to Conakry or however many Cubans landed.[5]

The original text, as Greene wrote it and as it appeared in the galley proof, was:

> The fate of the world, Davis used to declare, would never be decided on their continent however many embassies China might open from Addis Ababa to Conakry or however many Cubans landed in Angola.[6]

The details of how to obtain a false passport have been deleted, and one of Greene's jokes – he refers to the famous Russian MI6 agent-in-place Penkovsky as Pestovsky – also goes. The reference to Malcolm Muggeridge's life membership of the Raymond Revuebar was also perhaps deleted out of respect for a distinguished former colleague. Were these alterations suggested by MI6, or were they merely Greene's own careful review of the implications of what he had written? Since Greene was routinely copying over his letters to and from Philby, including the letter with Philby's comments on the final proof, it seems more than likely that the blue pencil applied to the galley proofs was MI6's though this cannot be inferred from any command in the Cabinet Office briefing. A final telling point was that the titles given to all government departments in the novel had been corrected with the greatest care.

In 1979 Greene was awarded an honorary degree at Oxford. He was seen during the ceremony talking to Sir Maurice Oldfield and this caused wide comment, even though Greene was now seventy-five, an age perhaps at which bygones might be thought bygones. Oldfield was asked about this by a friend and he replied enigmatically that there was no point in bearing grudges, a comment which was then widely circulated to show the magnanimity of MI6's old boss. But to whom was this comment meant to apply? The obvious implication is that MI6 was no longer angry with Greene after the Philby preface.

It is equally possible that Oldfield meant it the other way around – that Greene no longer bore a grudge against MI6. Greene was still the principal in everything that happened, both in his writings and in the journeys he took. At the time Oldfield spoke, he knew perfectly well that Greene had unique access to the leading political figures in one of the most difficult areas in the world. He himself, on the other hand, was a retired civil servant. By the same token Greene's book was his own, even if he had allowed MI6 an advance view and permission to say a few words about it.

The Philby affair was to carry on for some years yet, until the final endgame culminating in his death. The final chapter here examines in detail the nuances of the game played out between Greene and Philby in Moscow, an encounter only made possible by the longevity of the participants.

Greene's imagination, revived by his success with *The Human Factor* unexpectedly sprang to life once again in 1978, as he was having Christmas lunch with his daughter's family in Switzerland. The idea that came to him developed into *Doctor Fischer of Geneva or the Bomb Party*, published in 1980. It was to be the last of his novels apart from revivals of past projects, *The Tenth Man* and *The Captain and the Enemy*, and the novel written almost in counterpoint with the development of his friendship with Father Durán, *Monsignor Quixote*.

As a very late work Greene's novel might be thought necessarily weak, but it stands as a work in its own right, even if Greene's themes are constant and some of the detail is recognisable from his earlier works. When the narrator Jones begins to talk of his days in the Blitz in London it is only the detail of his having lost an arm that prevents us wondering for a moment whether a character from *The Comedians* has not wandered by mistake on to the wrong set. Jones is a junior clerk at a chocolate manufacturers in Vevey – well known as the home of Nestlé – and is clearly related to the hero of *Loser Takes All*. In this case, rather than win a large sum at roulette, Jones meets the only daughter of a millionaire, Doctor Fischer, whose fortune comes from a toothpaste business.

Greene describes how Doctor Fischer corrupts the wealthy people whom he regularly has to his house, watching them with amusement as he uses their greed to drive them to almost any indignity. All Doctor Fischer's games are strictly within the confines of polite society, at a series of dinner parties each held on a different theme. The party which gives the book its name is one in which each guest is asked to choose a cracker from a tub which contains the same number of crackers as there are guests. However, while most of the crackers contain cheques for millions of Swiss francs one contains a small bomb with enough force to kill the person pulling it. As each guest takes a cracker the odds against survival dwindle. Greene has gone to his old game of Russian roulette for his plot, and he later said that he certainly would never have had the idea had he not once played the game. But the inspiration for Doctor Fischer also owes much to Tom Roe. And Greene had fallen in with just such party games, along with Charlie Chaplin, Noël Coward and the others drawn into Roe's net.

As the number of crackers left in the tub gets lower the tension mounts, but Doctor Fischer has been playing a game on them and there is no bomb in any of the crackers; shortly after the guests leave he kills himself; the winner loses all.

One typical Greene hallmark appears in the novel, a reference to the classics of English literature. The device by which they are introduced is similar to the way he introduced poems of Browning into *The Human Factor*, through a book one of the characters owns. This time it is an anthology of poems compiled by Greene's friend Herbert Read called *The Knapsack*. Jones describes passing the time between air raids by dipping into the book. Greene has Jones reading brief extracts from Keats's 'Ode to a Grecian Urn', just as in the previous novel he reads poems of Browning into his text. But then Greene has Jones stop his reading to go off into action, inviting the reader to go on and finish the poem in the anthology – the ode appears there on page 328. But he carries this game further, for when Greene has Jones read Ezra Pound's 'Seafarer' he is adding to the anthology a favourite poem of his own; 'Seafarer' does not appear in the index of Read's book. Greene's very late contribution to the anthology had taken his memory back to the days when he first discovered Pound's poems as he wandered around the bookshops during his stay at the Richmonds'.

CHAPTER SEVENTEEN

Reflections from the Dangerous Edge

One gift that Greene was sure he did not possess was that of longevity. He had dismissed thoughts of suicide just before his marriage and they did not return, but he still believed his would be a short life. In 1961 doctors thought he might have cancer of the lung, but these fears were groundless. Then in 1979 it was found that he did have intestinal cancer; the operation which followed was completely successful and there was no return. Greene later remarked that 1979 was a difficult year: '1979 has not been a year of serenity: I was ill and given my age people assumed that *The Human Factor* was to be my last book, so they gave me no peace – it was a nightmare.'[1]

For years Greene himself had assumed he was writing his last book. Sometimes this was because he thought he was in his last decade, as he put it, but at other times it was sheer exhaustion from the concentrated intellectual effort of his writing – *The Burnt-Out Case* is a classic example of this. But in 1979 many of those closest to him were beginning to die. Dorothy Glover had died first; she was older so that was to be expected, but it was a shock. The few mute words noted in his diary expressed his distress eloquently. Catherine Walston was a different matter. She died in 1978 at the early age of sixty-two. Zoe Richmond was still alive and it seemed as though she might even outlive him; after all Dorothy's mother had outlived her, an extraordinary crossing of the generations. Zoe finally died in 1986 at the age of ninety-eight. His wife Vivien lives today, still with her lucid intelligence and an authority on doll's houses, the owner of a museum of them which she has curated for over forty years. Yvonne Cloetta, Greene's companion for the last thirty years of his life, still lives in his final home in Switzerland.

Greene's brother Raymond died in 1982; more unexpected perhaps was the death in 1987 of his youngest brother Hugh, whose public career – and an author's career is always to some extent private – was far more successful than his own. Hugh had become Director-General of the BBC, one of the highest establishment posts in Britain in those days, but on his retirement had pursued an interest which would have been equally congenial to Greene had he lived in England. He set up a bookshop specialising in first editions and modern literature generally and would often serve in the shop himself, watching the world passing by along London's Gloucester Road. Hugh had accompanied Greene on his book-hunts and they had jointly edited *The Spy's Bedside Book* published in 1957 by Rupert Hart-Davis, Greene's friend from his Chipping Camden days. An anthology of espionage tales, the book was dedicated 'To the Immortal Memory of William Le Queux and John Buchan', a dedication that would stand for much of Greene's life as well.

Partly as a result of the pressure on him in 1979 Greene began to gather together collections of his own work which would answer some of the requests for further information about him and his personal life – despite his interviews with Marie-Françoise Allain he was still regarded as the most secretive and least known of British authors. He began with what was published as the second volume of his autobiography, *Ways of Escape*, but was really a collection of the prefaces he had written for various novels prepared for the edition of his works published jointly by the Bodley Head and Heinemann, a final resolution of the struggles of his conflicting loyalties to the two houses. There was a fresh introduction and linking material and additional *rapportage*, but he was never happy with the result. Greene knew that Professor Sherry was working steadily and travelling extensively and would have far more to say than he ever could.

Greene was engagingly frank about his own weak memory, even of his own work. He would not re-read his books except when forced to for a new edition. He thought that every author had a subconscious spring of creative ideas and that this would be damaged by too close scrutiny. One of the most revealing passages in his interviews with Marie-Françoise Allain concerned the possible existence of a pattern in his works, the pattern in the carpet which Henry James referred to in his story. Greene was sure there was a pattern in his work, but he did not want to know what it was:

> When a critic discovers certain keynotes, that's fine and maybe of interest, but I don't want to be steeped in his discoveries. I want to remain unaware of them. Otherwise I think my imagination would dry up ... I've not the slightest wish to have my nose rubbed into 'the pattern in the carpet'.[2]

But, for all that, he did subsequently identify what he thought the pattern in the carpet was from his own point of view, as we shall see shortly.

An astonishing example of Greene's very weak memory of his own work occurred in 1985 when the discovery of a lost novel of his, *The Tenth Man*, was broken to the world. Michael Shelden in his unauthorised biography suggests that this discovery was no more than a publicity exercise to launch the book and that Greene had known of it all along. Greene's papers at Boston College demonstrate beyond doubt that this was untrue. When he was approached for comment by the press with news of the discovery he was completely mystified. Eventually it was discovered that he had written one of his typical outlines for a film which had never been made. Having identified the project, he still had no memory of having written a publishable text or that he had assigned the publication rights. When he learned that he had and that his treatment was eminently publishable he gave it the go-ahead and contributed a brief intro- duction which contained a truthful account of what had happened. He describes writing the book as part of a 'slave contract' in 1944 for MGM; interestingly that is exactly the phrase he used to describe the contract he signed with Tom Roe in 1960.

The only other novel of Greene's to appear in the 1980s besides *Monsignor Quixote* was *The Captain and the Enemy* in 1988 when he was eighty-four. Greene had referred to this book in his Allain interview, but no reason has ever been offered for why he did not complete and publish it before. From the contents, and their seeming parallel with his early life, the delay was almost certainly because Zoe Richmond was still alive. After she died in 1986, publication became possible. However, so much time had passed that, even if the book has more of a resemblance to a *roman-à-clef* than many of his other novels, it is difficult to be precise about what was intended. The book begins with a young boy being taken away from his school in Berkhamsted by a man who seems respectable but turns out to be an engaging rogue. The boy goes to live in a house which has clear resemblances to the Richmonds' house behind Paddington station, and in particular to life in the basement there. The boy is portrayed as an innocent in an adult world and the book is certainly deeply felt. It is possible to embark on a fresh quest for Greene's life through this one book – the basement features in his early short story made into a film with Carol Reed and Alexander Korda, *The Fallen Idol*, and in his novel *The Confidential Agent*, where a murder is committed in a basement – but it would be a fruitless one. We know only that those scenes from his early youth meant a great deal to Greene.

This record of the death of people close to him, and the running down of his published work gives a completely misleading portrayal of Greene's later years. There was never any question of Greene fading away into decent obscurity, despite his age. Perhaps the most startling appearance on the public stage was in 1982 in connection with the influence of organised crime in Nice. After writing letters to the press, Greene published *J'Accuse*, which was described as an exposé of organised crime and its influence over even the police and judiciary, but was actually an attack on one man. Yvonne Cloetta's daughter had unknowingly married a man with an organised-crime background, and the man and the problems he caused those near to him were the focus of Greene's attack.

Many saw this campaign as a symptom of his great age and thought it wrong that what seemed to be a private feud with one man should be elevated to the point where Greene thought his subject worthy of bearing the title of one of the great political pamphlets, Emile Zola's defence of Dreyfus, *J'Accuse*. There was some justice in this view, but Greene's reasons were quite genuine, and the evil he saw was also real. If age was beginning to affect him, it was not in his dealing with the subject, but in his not having the energy to pursue it further and expose more of what he had come across by complete chance.

Since the days of Tom Roe, Greene had made few allusions to the

Mafia in his work; he refers once in *The Honorary Consul* to a young Mafia man who had acted without the authority of his seniors. His old friend James Hadley Chase had written several thrillers attacking organised crime, some reflecting the world in which Tom Roe had caught them up as innocent victims, but they were not taken seriously as literary works, nor did they accurately represent the underlying reality they dealt with. But the world of *J'Accuse* is the same world of organised crime that Roe dealt with; one of the companies Greene mentions was directly connected to the same Mafia groups that had caused such trouble for him not twenty years before. In this context Greene's anger becomes understandable. His age and inability to do anything directly were only part of the difficulty. Omar Torrijos knew a lot about organised crime, particularly the cocaine trade. He learned of Greene's problem and offered to have something done about it; Greene immediately declined, not that he necessarily believed the proposal. Instead he decided to write his protest to the best of his ability.

Without question the highlight of Greene's final decade was the playing out of the endgame in his relationship with Kim Philby. Greene must surely have been the oldest agent in the world's second oldest profession, but his journeys to Moscow in 1986 and 1987, and the letters he exchanged with Philby before that, were serious matters and can help explain the changing climate in Russia immediately prior to the collapse of the Soviet bloc.

In January 1979 Greene received a postcard of the Floridita Bar in Havana, where the daiquiri was invented. It was a typical tourist card with a brief message: 'New Year Greetings from your fan in Havana – Muchos Daiquiris en la Floridita. K.P.'[3] The card was postmarked 8 January 1979. It was so innocuous that Philby later wondered whether Greene had understood who it was from. Greene had understood and the card and the letters that followed were all copied to MI6 through another retired officer who acted as Greene's contact. It was assumed that Philby would know this. As one memorandum commented: '[Kim Philby] probably assumes that his letters to Graham are passed on. After all no-one in his senses would maintain a correspondence with such a hot-potato as Kim without letting it be known.'[4] The real question, of course, was whether Philby's side of the correspondence was being written under the guidance of the KGB. His sending such an anonymous card suggested that perhaps it might not be, at least at the start.

The letters the two old colleagues exchanged covered a wide range of topics, but the difficulties that Russia was having in Iran and shortly afterwards in Afghanistan were early subjects which they covered extensively. During the war Britain and the Soviet Union had had a common frontier in Iran, with common censorship arrangements. Philby harked back to those times in response to a suggestion of Greene's relating to the hostages then being held in Iran:

> There seem to be two problems: the hostages and the future of Iran. On the hostages, I think we are all agreed, if only because Allah alone knows whose Embassy is next on the list for sacking, looting, burning or occupation. But how best to free them? By action or inaction? I have no insight into the mind of the A[yatollah] or of the holiday-making students so I just don't know. On the bigger question, your idea of joint action, culminating perhaps in spheres of influence, may look attractive (I have passed it on to the competent authorities). But surely such an operation in such an area as Iran presupposes mutual trust and good will – commodities in distressingly short supply these days, and getting shorter (it seems to me) by the hour.[5]

Greene's former MI6 colleagues now retired noted with intense interest that Philby had passed Greene's suggestion on to the authorities. From this moment on Philby's views on Afghanistan and the NATO threat, as perceived by the USSR, were taken as strong evidence of the internal moves taking place within the Soviet Union. Philby's comments on Afghanistan were surprising:

> And now this infernal Afghan business. I need hardly tell you that I am very unhappy about it; what may surprise you is that I have met no one here who is happy about it. It was apparently very necessary to get rid of Hafizullah Amin who was literally making a bloody mess of things, calling himself the Stalin of Afghanistan and acting as if to prove it. But was it essential to take up the military option as it is called nowadays? Wouldn't a quiet kinjal from behind an arras have done

just as well? These, of course, are simple gut-reactions. I don't know the facts behind the decision to intervene.[6]

Here was Philby, at least, expressing doubt and thinking the unthinkable and, indeed, detecting the embryo of all that was to follow, in this letter of his pounded out on his typewriter in his Moscow flat in January 1980.

During the war Greene and Philby had had a common skeleton in their closets, as we have seen, that both had members of their family detained under Emergency Powers Regulation 18B. In Philby's case his father H. St John Philby had finally reached prison after a long journey from Saudi Arabia via India, where he was arrested and brought back to Britain. He was well known as an expert in Islamic affairs and one of Philby's letters mentions this, and indirectly his and Greene's shared past:

> I don't think that being my father's son qualifies me to speak of the Ayatullah. I have never had any religious experience, and probably find it more difficult than most to understand irrational behaviour, even when it is my own. I tend to the view that the Ayatullah is a hateful old fraud and that his precious Islamic republic is meaningless. But the point is that he stands for a very powerful negative – revulsion against great power domination – which is not confined to Muslim peoples.[7]

It was quite clear from comments of this type that Philby was shifting very rapidly from the 'hard-line' position which the public and the media normally attributed to Russia, particularly after the invasion of Afghanistan itself. But the question was: was he speaking for himself, or for the KGB? A memorandum to a very senior figure in MI6 raised these questions succinctly:

> I have felt, for some time, that the KGB were probably doves rather than hawks and this [letter] seems to bear this out. Is it, do you think, a tentative feeler for the initiation of a dialogue between the KGB and SIS [MI6]? No doubt you possess a canteen of long spoons. The fact that Kim, in one of his recent letters asked Graham [Greene] to send his regards to [—] may be more significant than I thought at the time. Old spies never die...[8]

Until the Foreign Office files are opened in thirty years' time we will not know whether this approach was real, and, if it was, whether it came to anything and what role the exchange of letters between Greene and Philby played in the emergence of the regime which created Gorbachev, and in its turn the collapse of the Soviet system. There may have been files within MI6 that relate to this area, but they are not amongst those that the Cabinet Office briefing covered. It is to be hoped that eventually some partial release can be made, for it will help give a further insight into Greene's extraordinary ability in these fields, which remained unimpaired almost to the last. The letters here mentioned show if nothing else that his involvement in the strange affair which prompted *J'Accuse* was not a sign of a failing of his powers.

Despite the exchange of letters between Philby and Greene, there still appeared to be barriers to prevent the two old friends from actually meeting. Then in 1986 Genrikh Borovik, a Russian author, was appointed Secretary for Foreign Affairs of the Writers' Union of the USSR. He had always been friendly with Greene and undertook to do what he could to make a meeting possible. Borovik's efforts succeeded, and finally Greene, with Yvonne Cloetta, visited Philby and his wife in their Moscow apartment late in 1986.

Genrikh Borovik published an account of the meeting in his book *The Philby Files*, edited with an introduction by Phillip Knightley and published in 1994. He records scraps of their conversation – Philby saying that he thought *The Quiet American* Greene's best work (which would have come as no surprise to Greene), but picking a single phrase in the book describing Pyle, the quiet American: 'He is absolutely convinced of his righteousness and absolutely indifferent.' He then turned the point against Greene by saying, 'Any conviction should leave a chink for doubts, for the possibility of thinking that you're wrong. Otherwise a conviction can turn into a fanatical inquisition.' And there in the final word was the thrust against Greene's belief in Catholicism. Or so it seemed, for there was a game being played even at this stage, one belief against another, with both men trading move for move. Philby had said he had no religious interest, but he still *believed*.

Despite the obvious goodwill surrounding Greene's visits, to be seen plainly in the photographs taken in Philby's flat, there were still mysteries that the two men kept from those around them. It is doubtful whether Borovik knew of the letters Greene and Philby had recently exchanged or of their earlier letters that we have seen here. Although his book was said to rely on direct access to Philby's personal KGB files, it appears that he was shown only a heavily vetted selection of the KGB papers on Philby. There is the clearest evidence of this, and proof that Greene's visit was stage managed, in Borovik's own book. When he describes Greene's reason for wanting to come to Russia, apart from wanting to see Philby, he says: 'As for Greene I saw that he was dying to visit our country which he had never visited, and he asked only one question: was the editor of a popular Moscow newspaper, which had published an insulting article about him fifteen years earlier, retired now?'[9] Astonishingly Greene managed to conceal from Borovik that he had visited Moscow on many occasions, in the 1950s and 1960s, and as recently as 1971, the year the offending review had been published. Philby never disabused Borovik either and it seems that the only person who might have let the cat out of the bag apart from Philby was the newspaper editor, whom presumably the KGB had not been able to reach. Why this pretence should have been necessary is indeed a mystery worthy of John Buchan or William Le Queux. Borovik was dealing directly with the KGB, which must have decided on this line. It was perhaps its way of putting the past behind it as it turned to face the Gorbachev-inspired dawn.

A few months later, in February 1987, Greene addressed a cultural congress in Moscow, with Gorbachev himself presiding. Greene began by saying that he had been criticised for making his journey – he did not say by whom – and for agreeing to address the congress. His answer was to restate the position he had worked out for himself many years before:

There is no division in our thoughts between Catholics – Roman Catholics – and Communists. In the Sandinista Government my friend Tomás Borge, the Marxist Minister of the Interior, works in close friendship with Father Cardenal, the Minister of Culture, the Jesuit Father Cardenal, who is in charge of health and education; with Father

D'Escoto, who is Minister for Foreign Affairs. There is no longer a barrier between Roman Catholics and Communism.[10]

Greene knew of course that his views about Father Cardenal and Father D'Escoto were not shared by the Pope or by the Curia in Rome. But his belief that he was talking from a Catholic standpoint was completely genuine. He was, however, fully conscious that he was taking a stand.

Initially he had warmly greeted the election of Pope John Paul II because of the new pontiff's background in Poland, where he had been a worker before becoming a priest. Greene knew the reality of the struggles of the Church in Poland from his visits there and his dealings with PAX. However, he turned away from John Paul II when it became obvious that he was going to adhere firmly to the Church's teachings in controversial areas. Greene agreed with a celibate clergy, and deeply regretted the passing of the Latin Mass, arguably the greatest serious mistake in the history of the Church. But at all other points he found himself in violent disagreement, and most of all in any area where the Church became involved in politics. Greene had taken the Third World movement in South America to his heart; it meant more to him than any other aspect of contemporary Catholicism because it resolved his own personal political and religious quandary. In a letter he wrote to Tom Burns in 1989 he explained his feeling on the subject of infallibility he did not believe that the Pope was any more infallible than the rest of the body of the Church, which he took to include Burns and himself. Infallibility was not to be found this side of the grave.[11]

In his letters to Philby he had been equally candid about John Paul's political views. Philby had drawn him out on the subject with some irreverent views on the Pope:

I know very little about Central America but I have a feeling that the next few years [he was writing in 1985] will see much nastiness and I doubt whether John Paul II's visit to Hispaniola will do much for the descuperados. I don't like the shobiz [sic], kissing the tarmac etc. and his views on sexual matters seem to be unimaginative and unkind. As for politics he is involved willy-nilly and must know it.[12]

Greene was equally dismissive, and threw in some candid opinions of President Reagan in turn whom he referred to strangely as a man in Washington – probably worried in case the letter was intercepted. Greene revealed that he had attended a seminar at Georgetown University and had hoped to be asked questions about Reagan or even the Pope whom he thought more highly politicised than his predecessors. One question from the audience had enabled Greene to give his views on Central America and Nicaragua. He did not share these with Philby but the assumption of mutual agreement was plain. Greene also referred to Reagan habitually as an actor in B-films and speculated about a meeting between Reagan and Gorbachev. He did not go further and speculate on the Pope being present at such meetings.[13] What either man would have made of that same Pope, who outlived them both and saw the fall of the Soviet system, shaking hands with Fidel Castro in the Vatican and agreeing to return his visit can only be imagined. Greene certainly would have been profoundly moved; seeing it as a fulfilment of the logic he had spelt out in his address in Moscow nine years before that extraordinary meeting.

Greene's comments about President Reagan were not an attempt to mislead Philby. He had said very similar things to Father Durán during one of his many visits to Spain. Indeed he had been even more outspoken. Father Durán described in his biography of Greene *Graham Greene: Friend and Brother* how Greene had once looked him in the eye and said that if Reagan were elected for a second term of four years he would become a communist. He was emphatic and bound Father Durán to make the statement public:

> Tomorrow I am leaving by plane for Antibes. One never knows whether a plane will crash. Should that happen, I entrust your conscience, in all seriousness, with these words which I would like you to make known: Should Regan continue as President for a further four years, Graham would probably have become a Communist.[14]

Greene did not become a communist, although his making the speech in Moscow came close, as far as many Americans were concerned. However, when Greene gave that speech it was obvious that the religious element was the predominant one in his mind. The fact that he made his statement to a priest shows this clearly, and Father Durán was able to reveal such statements and others in his book because he was, as he says, his friend and brother, not his father-confessor.

But what sort of Catholic had Greene become? Where were the roots of this seemingly unfathomable contradiction in his view of the world? One brief section in the speech in Moscow gives a vital clue: 'For over a hundred years there has been a certain suspicion, an enmity even, between the Roman Catholic Church and Communism. This is not true Marxism, for Marx condemned Henry VIII for closing the monasteries.'[15] This comment on Marx and Henry VIII is an obvious allusion to the ideas of medieval socialism and his early friendship with Bede Jarrett during his second stay in Oxford in the 1930s. Beyond that was the feeling of fighting in a common cause with people who were the underdogs, often living in poverty, as he had seen them in occupied Germany and Ireland; and beyond that again was Father Damien, as seen through the eyes of his cousin Robert Louis Stevenson. In one of his interviews with Marie-Françoise Allain, despite saying that if there was a 'pattern in the carpet' in his works he did not wish to see it, he contradicted himself in his last interview with her. He had had time to think and when she raised the question of religious themes in his books Greene said: 'There does exist a pattern in my carpet constituted by Catholicism, but one has to stand back in order to make it out.'[16]

Greene's final book *A World of my Own*, although a posthumous publication, in 1992, is definitely his work and not merely a compilation of unpublished fragments of this kind frequently produced when a great author dies. Greene made the selection from his dream diary, and this must have represented an exhausting exercise in his last few months, for there were over 800 pages written across a quarter of a century. Father Durán described how Greene always had with him some very strong sleeping pills which his brother Raymond had prescribed for him. He had been a bad sleeper all his life and, even with the pills, used to wake in the night to write down a note of one of his dreams.

The obvious reason for Greene's keeping of a dream diary is

Kenneth Richmond's suggestion that he do so in 1921. Greene did mention this as a possible origin of his interest in dreams on several occasions, but in *A World of my Own* he points to an earlier explanation. He quotes an interview given by Robert Louis Stevenson on the origin of his most famous story, *Strange Case of Dr Jekyll and Mr Hyde*:

On one occasion I was very hard up for money and I felt I had to do something. I thought and thought, and tried hard to find a subject to write about. At night I dreamt the story, it practically came to me as a gift, and what makes it appear more odd is that I was quite in the habit of dreaming stories.[17]

Greene does not say when he found this account or who the interviewer was, but it shows once again in the origin of much of his ambition, and his ideas, in Victorian literature and in Robert Louis Stevenson in particular.

Even in the brief selection of his dreams that Greene made for *A World of my Own* it is possible to resume the search for the origins and background of Greene's work as if the book were simply another novel. Perhaps the most interesting is a dream he had which tied together both his religious life and the troubles he had over Tom Roe. Greene dreamed that he had been appointed Archbishop of Westminster and happened to bump into his predecessor, Cardinal Heenan. Naturally Heenan had been surprised by the choice of his successor and had decided to do some checking: 'The Cardinal had interviewed the Inland Revenue, who claimed that I had cheated on my income tax by transferring money abroad. This did make me uneasy. Might they intend to reopen the case?'[18]

Greene's last days were spent in Switzerland. He had fallen in his flat in Antibes and had rung up his wife Vivien, out of the blue, to explain what had happened. He was glad when the family suggested a move to Switzerland, where his daughter lived. Chaplin had died in Switzerland, and Greene's old friend René Raymond – James Hadley Chase – had died in the same village where he now decided to make his final home, Corseaux-sur-Vevey. Greene was to die in exile, one of those good people who, for peculiar undefinable reasons in the middle and later years of the twentieth century, Britain chose to force into exile.

In his last days he became so weak that everyone by him, including his daughter and Yvonne Cloetta, realised the end was near. Father Durán, friend, brother and priest for over quarter of a century, was summoned from Spain to be at his bedside in his last moments. The mysteries of the great Church which had fascinated him all his life found their last solution here in a few moments. Like the countless Catholic refugees who had died in exile in their turn, fleeing the Reformation, he died in the arms of the Church.

Sources

Preface

1. Cabinet Office Briefing.
2. Ibid.
3. Norman Sherry, *The Life of Graham Greene*, Volume Two: *1939–1955* (1994) (hereafter NS2), p. 234.

Chapter one: Psychoanalysis and the Birth of an Author

1. Christopher Burstall, 'Graham Greene Takes the Orient Express', in Henry J. Donaghy (ed.), *Conversations with Graham Greene* (1992), p. 53.
2. Graham Greene, *A Sort of Life* (1971) (hereafter SL), p. 55.
3. May Quinlan, *Damien of Molokai* (1909), p. 158.
4. Ibid., p. 167.
5. Marie-Françoise Allain, *The Other Man: Conversations with Graham Greene* (1983), p. 115.
6. SL, p. 117.
7. Ibid., p. 100.
8. Ibid., p. 103.
9. Ibid., p. 104.
10. Paragraph drawing on facts in a letter, Greene Collection Boston College, Boston, Massachusetts (herefter BC).
11. Norman Sherry interview with Ben Greene cited in *The Life of Graham Greene*, Volume One: *1904–1939* (hereafter NS1), p. 109.

Chapter two: An Oxford Political Odyssey

1. Letter to Evelyn Waugh cited in NS1, p. 101.
2. Peter Quennell, *The Marble Foot* (1976), p. 113.

3. Graham Greene, *Reflections* (1990), p. 3.
4. Ruth Fry, *A Quaker Adventure: The Story of Nine Years' Relief and Reconstruction* (1926), p. 169.
5. Letter, Famine Relief Files, Friends House, London.
6. Geoffrey Moss, *I Face the Stars* (1933), p. 12.
7. Graham Greene, *The Name of Action* (1930), p. 167.
8. Ibid., p. 169.
9. Ibid.
10. Ibid., p. 219.
11. Ibid., p. 212.
12. Ieuan Glyn Thomas, *Address to the Council and Senate of Witwatersrand University* (1974), p. 7.
13. Ibid., p. 8.
14. Letter cited in NS1, p. 221.

Chapter three: Journalism with a Little Help from his Friends

1. Letter cited in NS1, p. 253.
2. SL, pp. 191–2.
3. Graham Greene, *A Quick Look Behind Footnotes to an Autobiography*, Limited Edition, Los Angeles (1983).
4. Letter cited in NS1, p. 368.
5. Ibid.
6. Marie-Françoise Allain, op. cit., pp. 45–6.
7. SL, p. 206.
8. Ibid.
9. Based on facts in a diary, Harry Ransom Humanities Research Center, The University of Texas at Austin (hereafter HRHRC), entry for 28 July 1932.
10. Ibid., entry for 2 August 1932.
11. Graham Greene, *Stamboul Train* (library edition 1959), p. 66.

Chapter four: Politics and Religion: The ILP and Father Bede Jarrett

1. Graham Greene, *Ways of Escape* (1980) (hereafter WE), p. 36.
2. Based on facts in a diary, HRHRC.
3. Graham Greene, *It's a Battlefield* (Library Edition 1959), p. 194.
4. Ibid.
5. Based on facts in a diary, HRHRC.

6. Letter cited in Michael Tracey, *A Variety of Lives: A Biography of Sir Hugh Greene* (1983), p. 33.

7. Graham Greene: *England Made Me* (Collected Edition 1970), p. 161.

8. WE, p. 73.

9. Ibid., p. 24.

10. Based on facts in a diary, HRHRC.

11. Public Record Office, Kew.

12. Ibid.

13. Ibid.

Chapter five: The Chaco Wars: Arms and the Guilty Men

1. *The Times*, 19 February 1935.

2. WE, p. 72.

3. *The Times*, 2 May 1935.

4. WE, p. 73.

5. Ibid., p. 72.

6. *Spectator*, 12 January 1940, as published in David Parkinson (ed.), *Mornings in the Dark* (1993), p. 363.

7. WE, p. 66.

8. Ibid., p. 67.

9. Christopher Burstall, op. cit., p. 57.

10. Michael Shelden, *Graham Greene: The Man Within* (1994), pp. 146–7.

11. Based on facts in a letter, Greene papers, BC.

12. Graham Greene, *Brighton Rock* (Collected Edition 1971), p. 243.

13. Graham Greene, *The Lawless Roads* (Penguin edition 1947), p. 93.

14. Ibid., p. 105.

15. Ibid., p. 102.

16. Graham Greene, *The Great Jowett*, in *Collected Plays* (1985), p. 349.

17. W. S. Hiscock (ed.), *The Balliol Rhymes* (1955), p. 1.

18. Graham Greene, *The Great Jowett*, ed. cit., p. 349.

19. Ibid. BBC typescript with ms additions in private collection.

20. Ibid.

Chapter six: Benzedrine and the Blitz

1. Graham Greene, *The Confidential Agent* (Library Edition, 1960), p. 66.

2. Ibid., p. 137.

3. Ibid., p. 87.

Chapter seven: The Ministry of Fear and Philby's Empire

1. Graham Greene, *The Ministry of Fear* (Collected Edition 1974), p. 122.
2. Ibid., pp. 24–5.
3. O. F. Snelling, *Rare Books and Rarer People* (1982), p. 42.
4. Graham Greene, *The Ministry of Fear*, ed. cit., p. 121.
5. Ibid., p. 28.
6. Ibid., p. 65.
7. Ibid., p. 188.
8. Ibid., p. 133.
9. SL, p. 117.
10. Graham Greene, *The Ministry of Fear*, ed. cit., pp. 88–9.
11. Ibid., p. 89.
12. Ibid., p. 163.
13. Ibid., p. 203.
14. Letter from Kim Philby to Graham Greene, 2 January 1980, BC.
15. Memorandum, 22 January 1980, BC.
16. Based on facts in a diary, 'The Second Siege of London', HRHRC.
17. Ibid.

Chapter eight: A Publishing Affair

1. Anthony Powell, *Faces in my Time* (1980), p. 199.
2. Dust-jacket blurb on Edgar Lustgarten, *A Case to Answer* (1947).
3. James Hadley Chase, *More Deadly Than the Male* (Guild Books edition 1953), p. 16 (originally published as the work of 'Ambrose Grant', a pseudonym used only once by René Raymond).
4. Graham Greene, *Brighton Rock*, ed. cit., p. 7.
5. Ibid.
6. Malcolm Muggeridge, *Chronicles of Wasted Time*, Vol. 2 (1973), p. 236.
7. Douglas Jerrold, *The Necessity of Freedom* (1938), p. 99.
8. Anthony Powell, op. cit., p. 201.
9. Inscribed filmscript of *Brighton Rock*, HRHRC.

Chapter nine: Doctor Harry Lime and James Hadley Chase

1. Graham Greene, *The Third Man and The Fallen Idol* (Pan Books edition 1955), p. 81.
2. Ibid., p. 109.

3. Ibid., pp. 109–10.
4. Ibid., p. 107.
5. WE, p. 132.
6. Graham Greene, *The Third Man*, ed. cit., p. 57.
7. NS2, p. 438.

Chapter ten: Faith-Healing and The End of the Affair

1. Graham Greene, *The End of the Affair* (1951), p. 109.
2. Ibid., p. 233.
3. Ibid., p. 234.
4. Ibid., p. 237.
5. Ibid., p. 132.
6. Ibid., p. 133.
7. Letter cited in NS1, p. 109.
8. Basil Dean, *Mind's Eye, an autobiography* (1973), p. 306.
9. Letter to *The Times*, 21 June 1949, as published in Graham Greene, *Yours Etc.: Letters to the Press 1945–89*, ed. Christopher Hawtree (1989), p. 14.
10. Letter to *The Times*, ibid., p. 15.
11. Basil Dean, op. cit., p. 306.
12. Graham Greene, *The Heart of the Matter* (Heinemann–Octopus edition 1977), p. 21.
13. Ibid., p. 22.
14. Kenneth Tynan, *Persona Grata* (1953), p. 55.
15. Artur Lundkvist, *Morgen-Tidningen*, 4 November 1952, cited in NS2, p. 453.
16. Graham Greene, *The Living Room* (1953), p. 24.
17. Ibid., p. 25.
18. Ibid., p. 63.
19. Ibid., p. 64.
20. Graham Greene, *The Complaisant Lover*, in *Collected Plays* (1985), p. 154.
21. Ibid., p. 161.
22. Ibid., pp. 179–80.

Chapter eleven: Poland, Indo-China and The Quiet American

1. Public Record Office, Kew: LC2862/2349/452 1948.
2. Cabinet Office briefing.
3. Ibid., based on a letter, 2 March 1956.
4. WE, p. 169.
5. William Colby, *Honorable Men: My Life in the CIA* (1978), p. 144.
6. Graham Greene, *The Quiet American* (Heinemann–Octopus edition 1977), p. 577.
7. Ibid., 577.
8. Ibid., p. 554.
9. WE, p. 171.
10. Graham Greene, *The Quiet American*, ed. cit., p. 554.
11. Cabinet Office briefing.
12. Letter, 26 January 1956, BC.
13. Cabinet Office briefing based on a report by Graham Greene to MI6, 26 June 1957.
14. Graham Greene, letter to *Daily Telegraph*, 4 June 1957.
15. Graham Greene, *Our Man in Havana* (Collected Edition 1971), p. 71.
16. Ibid., p. 177.
17. Ibid., p. 35.
18. Ibid., pp. 216–17.
19. Hansard, Vol. 59, 15 December 1958.

Chapter twelve: The Business of A Burnt-Out Case

1. WE, p. 209.
2. Graham Greene, *A Burnt-Out Case* (1961), p. 20.
3. Ibid.
4. Ibid., p. 25.
5. Ibid., p. 149.
6. Ibid., p. 248.
7. Ibid., p. 221.
8. Brian Aherne, *A Dreadful Man* (1979), p. 96.
9. Eric Ambler, interview with author, 1996.
10. Charles Chaplin, *My Autobiography* (1964), p. 417.
11. Graham Greene, *The Comedians* (Penguin edition 1967), p. 246.
12. Ibid., p. 139.

13. Ibid., p. 60.
14. Ibid., p. 276.
15. Ibid., p. 286.

Chapter thirteen: Blues for Uncle Charlie

1. Andrew Lycett, *Ian Fleming* (1995), p. 332.
2. *Victorian Detective Fiction: A Catalogue of the Collection Made by Dorothy Glover and Graham Greene* (1966), p. viii.
3. WE, p. 296.
4. Ibid., p. 297.
5. Quentin Falk, *Travels in Greeneland: The Cinema of Graham Greene* (revised edition 1990), p. 155.
6. WE, p. 285.
7. Ibid.
8. Letter to *The Times*, 4 September 1967, as published in *Yours Etc.*, ed. cit., p. 135.
9. Ibid., p. 136.
10. Philby letter quoted in Henry J. Donaghey (ed.), *Conversations with Graham Greene* (1992), p. 133.
11. *Spectator*, 22 September 1967.
12. *Times Literary Supplement*, 26 September 1968.
13. Graham Greene, introduction to Kim Philby, *My Silent War* (Panther edition 1969), p. 7.

Chapter fourteen: A New Life in Exile

1. Christopher Burstall, op. cit., p. 51.
2. Ibid., p. 47.
3. Ibid., p. 48.
4. Graham Greene, *May We Borrow your Husband?* (1967), p. 33.
5. WE, p. 285.
6. Graham Greene, *Travels with my Aunt* (1969), p. 17.
7. Ibid., p. 81.
8. Ibid., p. 301.
9. Ibid., p. 159.
10. WE, p. 292.
11. Graham Greene, *Reflections* (1990), p. 259.
12. Ibid., p. 319.

13. Ibid., p. 268.
14. SL, p. 118.
15. Graham Greene, *Reflections* (1990), p. 279.
16. Ibid., p. 278.

Chapter fifteen: Father Oscar Maturet and The Honorary Consul

1. Graham Greene, *The Honorary Consul* (1973), p. 261.
2. Ibid., p. 262.
3. Ibid., p. 269.
4. Ibid., p. 278.
5. Ibid., p. 194.
6. Ibid., p. 15.
7. Ibid., p. 71.
8. Ibid., p. 247.
9. Graham Greene, *Getting to Know the General* (1984), p. 56.
10. Ibid., p. 56.
11. Ibid., p. 111.
12. Ibid., pp. 170–1.
13. Based on facts in a letter to Tom Burns, 15 February 1985, HRHRC.
14. Based on facts in a letter to Tom Burns, 17 August 1981, HRHRC.
15. Graham Greene, *Getting to Know the General* (1984), p. 174.

Chapter sixteen: Ieuen Thomas and The Human Factor

1. John Whitwell [pseudonym of Leslie Nicholson], *British Agent* (1966), Introduction by Malcolm Muggeridge.
2. WE, p. 309.
3. Graham Greene, *The Human Factor* (1978), p. 116.
4. Ibid., p. 132.
5. Ibid., p. 9.
6. Graham Greene, *The Human Factor*, undated galley proof, private collection.

Chapter seventeen: Reflections from the Dangerous Edge

1. Marie-Françoise Allain, op. cit., p. 24.
2. Ibid., p. 22.
3. Postcard from Kim Philby to Graham Greene, 8 January 1979, BC.
4. Memorandum, 22 January 1980, BC.

5. Letter from Kim Philby to Graham Greene, 2 January 1980, BC.
6. Ibid.
7. Ibid.
8. Memorandum, 22 January 1980.
9. Genrikh Borovik, *The Philby Files* (1994), p. 370.
10. Graham Greene, *Reflections* (1990), p. 317.
11. Based on facts in a letter to Tom Burns, 25 October 1989, HRHRC.
12. Letter from Kim Philby to Graham Greene, 13 October 1985, BC.
13. Based on facts in a letter to Kim Philby, 24 October 1985, BC.
14. Leopoldo Durán, *Graham Greene: Friend and Brother* (1994), p. 91.
15. Graham Greene, *Reflections* (1990), p. 316.
16. Marie-Françoise Allain, op. cit., p. 159.
17. Graham Greene, *A World of my Own* (1992),
18. Ibid., p. 61.

Bibliography

Aherne, Brian, *A Dreadful Man*, 1979.

All About Eve, film, 1950.

Allain, Marie-Françoise, *The Other Man: Conversations with Graham Greene*, 1983.

Ambler, Eric, *The Ability to Kill*, 1963.

Aquinas, St. Thomas, *Summa Theologica*, ed. Thomas Gilby.

The Architectural Review

Augustine, St., *The City of God*

Beresford, Elizabeth, *The Wombles*, television series.

Beresford, J. D., *The Camberwell Miracle*, 1933. *The Case for Faith Healing*, 1934. *The Hampdenshire Wonder*, 1911. *Nineteen Impressions*, 1918. *Revolution*, 1921.

Beresford, J. D. and Kenneth Richmond, *W. E. Ford: a Biography*, 1917.

Birmingham Gazette

Blackfriars

The Bookseller

Borovik, Genrikh, *The Philby Files*, 1994.

Boyle, Andrew, *The Climate of Treason*, 1979.

Brandel, Marc (pseudonym of Marcus Beresford), *The Ides of Summer*

The British Gazette

Brockway, Fenner, *The Bloody Traffic*, 1933.

Browning, Robert, 'Bishop Blougram's Apology'

Buchan, John, *The Thirty-Nine Steps*, 1915.

Chaplin, Charles, *My Autobiography*, 1964.

Chase, James Hadley, *Blonde's Requiem*, 1945. *Miss Callaghan Comes to Grief*, 1941. *More Deadly than the Male!*, 1946. *No Orchids for Miss Blandish*, 1939.

Chase, James Hadley (as René Raymond), *Slipstream*, 1946.

Colby, William, *Honorable Men: My Life in the CIA*, 1978.

Daily Chronicle

Daily Telegraph

Daily Worker

Dane, Clemence (pseudonym of Winifred Ashton), *St Martin's Lane*, unpublished film script, 1938.

Dane, Clemence, *A Bill of Divorcement*, 1921. *Regiment of Women*, 1917. *Will Shakespeare*, 1921.

Death of a Scoundrel, film, 1956.

de la Mare, Walter, *The Veil*, 1921.

Donaghy, Henry J. (ed.), *Conversations with Graham Greene*, 1992.

Dostoevsky, Fyodor, *The Brothers Karamazov*, 1912.

Durán, Father Leopoldo, *Graham Greene, Friend and Brother*, 1994.

Falk, Quentin, *Travels in Greeneland*, 1990 edition.

Faulkner, William, *Sanctuary*, 1931.

Farber, Stephen and Marc Green, *Hollywood on the Couch*, 1993.

The First Freedom, television series by Christopher Burstall, 1967.

Frank, Leonhard, *Brother and Sister*, 1930.

Fry, Ruth, *A Quaker Adventure: The Story of Nine Years Relief and Reconstruction*, 1926.

Galsworthy, John, *The First and the Last*, 1918.

Gheerbrant, Alain, *The Rebel Church in Latin America*, 1974.

Gide, André, *Voyage au Congo*, 1927.

Goldring, Douglas, *Ways of Escape*, 1911.

Gray, Frank, *Confessions of a Candidate*, 1925.

Green, Marc, see Stephen Farber

Greene, Graham, *Anthony Saint*, unpublished novel. *Babbling April*, 1925. *Brighton Rock*, 1938. *A Burnt-Out Case*, 1961. *The Captain and the Enemy*, 1988. *The Comedians*, 1966. *The Complaisant Lover*, 1961. *The Confidential Agent*, 1939. *Doctor Fischer of Geneva or the Bomb Party*, 1980. *The End of the Affair*, 1951. *England Made Me*, 1935. *Getting to Know the General*, 1985. *The Great Jowett*, 1939 radio play, printed 1981. *The Green Cockatoo*, film script, 1937. *A Gun for Sale*, 1936. *The Heart of the Matter*, 1948. *The Honorary Consul*, 1973. *The Human Factor*, 1978. *In Search of a Character*, 1961. *It's a Battlefield*, 1934. *J'Accuse*, 1982. *Journey Without Maps*, 1936. *The Lawless Roads*, 1939. *The Little Fire Engine*, 1950. *The Little Train*,

1946. *The Living Room*, 1953. *Loser Takes All*, 1955. *Lord Rochester's Monkey*, 1974. *The Man Within*, 1929. *May We Borrow Your Husband?*, 1967. *The Ministry of Fear*, 1943. *Monsignor Quixote*, 1982. *The Name of Action*, 1930. *Nineteen Stories*, 1947. *Our Man in Havana*, 1958. *The Power and the Glory*, 1940. *The Quiet American*, 1955. *Reflections*, 1990. *Rumour at Nightfall*, 1931. *The Second Siege of London*, unpublished diary, 1944. *A Sort of Life*, 1971. *Stamboul Train*, 1932. *The Tenth Man*, 1985. *The Third Man*, 1950. *Travels with my Aunt*, 1970. *The Virtue of Disloyalty*, speech on receiving the Shakespeare Prize, Hamburg, June 1969. *Ways of Escape*, 1980. *A World of my Own*, 1992. *The Worm Inside the Lotus Blossom*, article in the *Daily Telegraph*, 3 January 1969.

Greene, Graham (ed.), *An Impossible Woman*, 1975.

Greene, Graham, *Mornings in the Dark*, edited by David Parkinson, 1993. *Reflections*, edited by Judith Adamson, 1990. *Yours Etc.: Letters to the Press 1945–89*, edited by Christopher Hawtree, 1989.

Greene, Graham and Hugh Carleton Greene, *The Spy's Bedside Book*, 1957.

Greene, Graham and David Lowe, *Dear David, Dear Graham: a Bibliographic Correspondence*, 1989.

Greene, Graham and Sir Hugh Carleton Greene, See Graham Greene

Haggard, H. Rider, *King Solomon's Mines*, 1885.

Harrison, H. D., *Industrial Psychology and the Production of Wealth*, 1925.

Heine, Kurt, *Inner Journey*

Hisock, W. S. (ed.), *The Balliol Rhymes*, 1955.

The Hunted Man, television programme in the 'Omnibus' series by Christopher Burstall, 1968.

The Irish Times

Izvestia

James, Henry, *The Figure in the Carpet*, 1896.

Jarrett, Bede, *Medieval Socialism*, 1912, reissued in 1935. *Social Theories in the Middle Ages*, 1926.

Jerrold, Douglas, *The Necessity of Freedom: Notes on Christianity and Politics*, 1938.

Kipling, Rudyard, *Wee Willie Winkie*, film script, 1937.

Knight, Maxwell, *The Comintern is Not Dead*, unpublished MI5 report.

Kuhnelt-Leddihn, *The Gates of Hell*, 1933.

Lehmann, John, *New Writing and Europe*, 1940.

Le Queux, William, *The Invasion of 1910 with a full account of the Siege of London*, 1906.

Le Queux, William, *Things I know about Kings, Celebrities and Crooks*, 1923.

Lowe, David, see Graham Greene

Lycett, Andrew, *Ian Fleming*, 1995.

Lustgarten, Edgar, *A Case to Answer*, 1947.

Mallock, W. H., *The New Republic*, 1877.

Mockler, Anthony, *Graham Greene: Three Lives*, 1994.

Morton, H. V., *I James Blunt*, 1942.

Merrick, Leonard, *The Position of Peggy Harper*, 1911.

Moss, Geoffrey, *Defeat*, 1924. *I Face the Stars*, 1933. *The Epic of the Alcazar*, 1937.

New English Review

The New Leader

The New Yorker

Night and Day

Nottingham Journal

The Observer

Orwell, George, *Nineteen Eighty-Four*, 1949.

Oxford Outlook

Palgrave, Francis Turner, *The Golden Treasury of the Best Songs and Lyrical Poems in the English Language*, 1861.

de Paravicini, Baroness, *Do We Remember? A Story of Oxford Under the Tudors*, 1928.

Peake, Mervyn, *Titus Groan*, 1946.

The Phantom Executioner, film script

Philby, Kim, *My Silent War*, 1968.

Powell, Anthony, *Faces in my Time*, 1980. *John Aubrey and his Friends*, 1948.

Pravda

Quennell, Peter, *The Marble Foot*, 1976.

Quinlan, May, *Damien of Molokai*, 1909.

Rattigan, Terence, *Separate Tables*, 1954.

Read, Herbert (ed.), *The Knapsack*, 1939.

Reade, Charles, *Hard Cash: A Matter of Fact Romance*, 1863.

Rhythm

Richmond, Kenneth, see J. D. Beresford.

Richmond, Nigel, *Christ's Drama: The Nature of Spiritual Growth*, 1961.

Bibliography

Roberts, Cecil, *Havana Bound*, 1930.

Sanders, George, *Memoirs of a Professional Cad*, 1960.

Sartre, Jean Paul, *The Flies*, 1943.

Sharrock, Roger, *Saints, Sinners and Comedians*, 1984.

Shelden, Michael, *Graham Greene*, 1994.

Sherry, Norman, *The Life of Graham Greene, Volume One 1904–1939*, 1989. *The Life of Graham Greene, Volume Two 1939–1955*, 1994.

Snelling, O. F., *Rare Books and Rarer People*, 1982.

Sparrow, John, *After the Assassination: A Positive Appraisal of the Warren Report*, 1967.

The Spectator

The Star

Stevenson, Robert Louis, *Strange Case of Dr. Jekyll and Mr. Hyde*, 1886.

The Sunday Times

The Sydney Presbyterian

Symons, A. J. A., *The Quest for Corvo*, 1934

The Tablet

Taxi Driver, film, 1976.

Thomas, Ieuan Glyn, *Address to the Council and Senate of Witwatersrand University*, 1974.

Time

The Times

Tolstoy, Leo, *What I Believe, War and Peace*, 1889.

Torres, Camilo, *Revolutionary Priest*, 1971.

Trevelyan, Sir George O., *Life and Letters of Lord Macaulay*, 1876.

Trotsky, Lev, *History of the Russian Revolution*, 1919.

Verne, Jules, *Around the World in Eighty Days*, 1874.

Victorian Detective Fiction: A Catalogue of the Collection Made by Dorothy Glover and Graham Greene, 1966.

Wasserman, Carl Jacob, *Christopher Colombus, Don Quixote of the Seas*, 1930.

Wasserman, Carl Jacob, *H. M. Stanley-Explorer*, 1932. *My Life as German and Jew*, 1934.

Waugh, Evelyn, *Black Mischief*, 1932. *Brideshead Revisited*, 1945. *Edmund Campion*, 1935.

The Weekly Westminster Gazette

Westminster Gazette

Whistler, Theresa, *Imagination of the Heart: The Life of Walter de la Mare*, 1993.

Whitwell, John (pseudonym of Leslie Nicholson), *British Agent*, 1966.

Wickham-Crowley, Timothy P., *Guerillas and Revolution in Latin America*, 1992.

Wilson, Edmund, *Devil Take the Hindmost*, 1932.

Wright, Peter, *Spycatcher*, 1987.

Index

Works by Graham Greene appear directly under title; works by others appear under authors' names

Index

Index

Index

All Orion/Phoenix titles are available at your local bookshop or from the following address:

Littlehampton Book Services
Cash Sales Department L
14 Eldon Way, Lineside Industrial Estate
Littlehampton
West Sussex BN17 7HE
telephone 01903 721596, *facsimile* 01903 730914

Payment can either be made by credit card (Visa and Mastercard accepted) or by sending a cheque or postal order made payable to *Littlehampton Book Services*.

DO NOT SEND CASH OR CURRENCY.

Please add the following to cover postage and packing

UK and BFPO:
£1.50 for the first book, and 50P for each additional book to a maximum of £3.50

Overseas and Eire:
£2.50 for the first book plus £1.00 for the second book and 50p for each additional book ordered

---

BLOCK CAPITALS PLEASE

name of cardholder ....

delivery address
(if different from cardholder)
....

address of cardholder ....
....
....
....

....
....
....

postcode ....

postcode ....

☐ I enclose my remittance for £...............................

☐ please debit my Mastercard/Visa (delete as appropriate)

card number [ ][ ][ ][ ][ ][ ][ ][ ][ ][ ][ ][ ][ ][ ][ ][ ]

expiry date [ ][ ][ ][ ]

signature ....

prices and availability are subject to change without notice